Cooler Than Fiction

Cooler Than Fiction

A Planning Guide for Teen Nonfiction Booktalks

JILL S. JARRELL *and*
TARA C. CANNON

BIBLIOTHEQUES
u Ottawa
LIBRARIES

McFarland & Company, Inc., Publishers
Jefferson, North Carolina, and London

LIBRARY OF CONGRESS CATALOGUING-IN-PUBLICATION DATA

Jarrell, Jill S., 1979–
Cooler than fiction : a planning guide for teen nonfiction booktalks /
Jill S. Jarrell and Tara C. Cannon.
p.   cm.
Includes bibliographical references and index.

ISBN 978-0-7864-4886-9
softcover : 50# alkaline paper ∞

1. Young adults' libraries—Activity programs—United States.   2. Book
talks—United States.   3. Teenagers—Books and reading—United
States.   I. Cannon, Tara C., 1983–   II. Title.
Z718.5.J37   2011   027.62'60973—dc22   2010040710

British Library cataloguing data are available

Cover image © 2011 Shutterstock

Manufactured in the United States of America

*McFarland & Company, Inc., Publishers
Box 611, Jefferson, North Carolina 28640
www.mcfarlandpub.com*

To our supportive husbands,
Mark and Seth,
for encouraging us to write what we know.
And to the Pikes Peak Library District,
for letting us be a part
of the best booktalking program in the nation.

Table of Contents

Acknowledgments   ix

Introduction   1

  1. Funny, Gross, and Disturbing   5

  2. History   17

  3. Biographies and Memoirs   29

  4. Crimes   40

  5. Food and Crafts   50

  6. Art   61

  7. Short Stories and Poetry   70

  8. Graphic Novels   82

  9. Science   92

10. Animals   104

11. Nature   114

12. Knowing Your World   125

13. Life Skills   136

14. Pairing   148

15. Interactives   159

Booktalking Resources   173

Index   183

Acknowledgments

Many people helped prepare us to write this book, primarily the Teen Services Team at Pikes Peak Library District in Colorado Springs, Colorado. Through their creativity, idea sharing, and booktalking with us, we were able to refine and share our favorite books with you. Thanks specifically to Jessica Friesema for her book suggestions. The librarians and teachers at the Colorado Teen Literature Conference inspired us to write this book — proving that there was a need for nonfiction in our public libraries and classrooms. To Janice Mcpherson whose unwavering support and encouragement provided the solid foundation for our booktalking program, thank you.

Also, thanks to Danny Walter for setting up the shots and taking all of the photos. Thanks to Susi Bonato for helping us organize all of the necessary permissions and for all of her proofing efforts. Thanks again to Pikes Peak Library District for allowing us the use of their video studio and amazing teen center to take our photos. And to the teens who volunteered to be part of our photographs (Jonathan Luna, Joshua Luna, Jennifer Eltgringham and Wes Walters), thank you.

Introduction

How many of us spent our teen years with our eyes and hearts glued to books? Did you spend your Saturday nights curled up on the sofa or in your room reading Madeleine L'Engle? Did you ravage the teen section of your public library in less than a year? Were you one of those teens who asked the librarian for something new to read and with every suggestion she made, you told her that you had already read it? Did you wish you were Elizabeth Bennet from *Pride and Prejudice*? Or did you imagine yourself on Prince Edward Island with Anne (with an "E") of Green Gables? Being librarians and teachers, we have grown up with a desire to share our literature addiction with today's youth. We want to inspire our students with the love of reading that we developed as young adults. We desperately want our students to discover the pleasure of getting lost inside books the way we did. We want to see our teens engrossed in *To Kill a Mockingbird* while walking down the hallways at school, standing in line at the checkout desk, or eating lunch. And what teacher wouldn't be secretly thrilled to call out a student for reading *1984* in class rather than calling him out for texting?

Unfortunately, many students are not like us. We became librarians and teachers for a reason: we already love these books! While there are students who are addicted to reading and already know the pleasure that can come with reading a riveting novel, there are also students who are not going to voluntarily pick up a book. Too many students must be coerced and cajoled into reading, but there are ways to show teens that reading can be enjoyable. Just as our tastes for food grows and matures as we become adults, our reading tastes grow and change as well. For some students we may need to start with the flashy, fast-paced, and shocking books before we can prove to these teens that our beloved classics have value.

While working with schools on Colorado's Front Range, we have found booktalking to be one of the surest methods to garner teen interest in reading. Each fall and spring 8–10 library staff from the Pikes Peak Library District visit over 4,000 students at area middle and high schools to convince students that leisure reading is possible if they can just find the right book. We would go in pairs loaded with wheeled suitcases full of mystery, romance, horror, science fiction, fantasy and realistic fiction as well as a large amount of teen nonfiction. We alternated presenting various books in whatever manner would catch teens' interest. We would act, rap, quiz the students, tell a story — anything to entice the teens to read. Our goal: convince these students to read one or

The authors, Tara Cannon (left) and Jill Jarrell, present nonfiction book ideas to Colorado teachers and librarians at the Colorado Teen Literature Conference.

more of these books for their own enjoyment. (For more information please see the section "Booktalking Resources" at the back of this book.)

While it seems the common trend is to booktalk novels, we have discovered that nonfiction books are some of the best tools for teaching teens that reading can be addictive and enjoyable. Many authors of teen nonfiction know how to make everyday life seem outlandish and almost too odd to be true. These authors take normal, common truths that we often take for granted and paint them in a new light. Booktalking titles such as *The Beast of Chicago* by Rick Geary, *Things to Do Before You're Old and Boring* by Richard Horne or *Freaks of the Storm* by Randall Cerveny will get every teens' attention. Who can resist knowing more about the 6-million pound mountain of cow poop (*Chew on This*) or discovering the world's deadliest poison (*For Boys Only: The Biggest, Baddest Book Ever*)? Graphic novels and manga are not the only option for enticing low-interest readers. Nonfiction is just as bewitching! We have often found that teens we talk to perk up and participate in our booktalks in earnest when we talk about nonfiction books. We have discovered that because nonfiction is true, teens are more spellbound than they are with fiction. They are seduced by the gross facts and hideous truths. We often get responses like "Is that really true?" or "Did that REALLY happen?" Students will continue to ask questions about the booktalk, and we love being able to tell the students that they will have to read the book for more details.

This book presents nonfiction in a whole new light and we hope it will help you get started booktalking nonfiction to your students. We present options for discussion questions and project ideas for your classes and your library. There are hundreds of great nonfiction books perfect for supplementing your booktalks, lesson plans, discussion groups, and library programs.

To tackle the versatility of nonfiction, we have arranged the chapters to include:

- **book ideas** to get you in touch with your inner nonfiction booktalker and become familiar with nonfiction booktalking styles and methods;
- a set of **discussion questions** with each sample booktalk for those of you who want to incorporate nonfiction into your book groups, use as discussion prompts in your class, or as homework;
- **project ideas** that can be expanded into lesson plans or class assignments, developed into activities to stimulate your book discussion groups, or even broadened into full-fledged library programs;
- **classroom integration** tips are included in a few of the sections to meld the various topics into your classroom environment; and
- a list of **suggested nonfiction books** to booktalk to your students, incorporate into your curriculum, supplement your lesson plans, and use in your book discussion groups.

Each chapter is organized by subject or genre with clearly designated sections so you may choose to read through this book in its entirety or use the book to get lesson plan ideas, grab a quick booktalk when you need one in a hurry, or get some book ideas for your library, classroom or your next round of booktalks. We hope that once you are comfortable using nonfiction books, you may discover that these books are actually some of the most exciting in your repertoire.

1

Funny, Gross, and Disturbing

Starting off with the eye-catching, attention-grabbing books will set a humorous, attentive tone to your booktalking session.

While talking to a group of 8th graders about the possibility of people disappearing into portable toilets (from an article from *Bat Boy Lives!: The WEEKLY WORLD NEWS Guide to Politics, Culture, Celebrities, Alien Abductions, and the Mutant Freaks that Shape Our World* by David Perel), the students, especially the boys, were laughing when the teacher pipes up in the back of the room. She claims she does not read that kind of potty humor (no pun intended, we're sure) and doesn't understand why anyone would want to even think about it. She may have missed the point but her students most certainly did not. They eagerly responded to questions, guessed out loud, groaned in delighted disgust, and laughed in horrific amazement. And many of them ran to grab the book and read for themselves after the booktalking session.

We booktalk to encourage students to read *anything*. They have a lifetime to spend reading the classics; too many of our students resist picking up a book for sheer enjoyment. They see school, learning and the world around them to be boring, lukewarm, and not worth their attention. Funny, gross, disturbing or just plain weird books are wonderful tools to get teenagers tuned in to just how interesting nonfiction and life can be. Young and old, we are all enthralled by the bizarre, twisted, and wicked. We stop what we are doing and listen in morbid fascination to the story as it is laid out in front of us, and we are even more disgusted when we learn that the legend is real and that these nightmares are truly out there. Who would believe that the skipper caterpillar, which is only an inch and a half long, can shoot its poop six feet (*The Truth About Poop*)? Truth really is stranger than fiction.

Book Ideas with Booktalks, Discussion Questions, and Project Ideas

The Stupid Crook Book
by Leland Gregory

*The Stupid Crook Book is a funny little book full of paragraph-length stories of

---

*Words in italics are instructions for the booktalker while words not italicized are meant to be spoken as part of the booktalk.

not-so-bright, would-be criminals. While teens may be easily embarrassed when they do something brainless, they love to hear about others' stupidity. Plus, the brevity of these stories is ideal for reluctant readers. For this booktalk, we just read a few of the stories and let the book speak for itself. For example, the very first of Leland's stories combines stupidity and the gross-factor.

"People arrived on the scene at a recreational vehicle park to discover a very sick man vomiting and complaining of stomach cramps. The man admitted he had attempted to siphon gas from a motor home but had inadvertently put the siphon tube into the wrong tank. Instead of gasoline the man had sucked out the contents of the sewage holding tank."

For this first story, we don't hesitate to ask the students if they know what siphoning is, especially if they are middle school students. The more the students know what is actually happening in the story the funnier it is, and students love to show off their knowledge. We also make sure to say that students should never, ever try this at home or anywhere for that matter!

Other interactive tidbits we like to include:

"A man robbed a liquor store in the Roswell area of New Mexico. Although he wore a bag over his head, the police got an excellent description of the perpetrator." *And here we always ask,* "Does anyone know why?" *We often get the response,* "Because he's an alien?" *due to the Roswell detail of the story, but inevitably a sharp-witted student will retort,* "Because it was a clear bag!"

"A burglar who was watching his four-year-old daughter broke into a Newark, New Jersey, home, stole several items, and successfully got away, leaving only one small clue." *And then, we ask,* "Can anybody guess?" *We're always met with a rousing chorus of* "His daughter!"

DISCUSSION QUESTIONS

1. A lot of information can be gleaned from just a few sentences. In the tidbit, on page 166, the crook has a 4-year-old daughter for whom he is responsible. Why would he bring her along? What does the fact that he brings her say about this crook?
2. Why do you think the crook with the 4-year-old daughter is willing to break the laws?
3. Why do you think he left his daughter? What do you think was happening inside his brain?
4. Why would anyone use a clear plastic bag to cover his face when robbing a store or bank? Why would this seem like a good idea?
5. It seems like some of these crimes are pretty desperate acts. Why do you think the crooks are so desperate?
6. In the case of the clear plastic bag criminal, the author throws in the detail "In the Roswell area of New Mexico...." However, this detail seems to have no significance. Why do you think this detail is included?
7. This book highlights a rather large number of criminals who messed up and were caught. What does this tell you about the importance of proper planning, the impor-

tance of being able to think clearly in tense situations and the importance of considering all possible outcomes, including getting caught?

8. What do you think about the idea that without laws there would be chaos? What keeps you from harming or stealing from others? Do you think it is the current laws or your own sense of right and wrong? Where do you think your sense of right and wrong comes from?

PROJECT: PROJECT PLANNING WITH CRIME

This project will take quite a bit of planning but the outcome will teach students the process of planning any project (not just crime!) and at the same time will provide your students a glimpse of just how difficult it is to get away with breaking the law.

Supplies you'll need include: simplified blueprints of an imaginary building, details of the heist objective, lots of paper, pencils and sticky notes. Divide your students into teams (the size of the teams is your choice).

For the first half of the project, have the teams plan a heist. Ideally, you would provide students with a simplified blueprint of an imaginary building and give them an objective (i.e., successfully steal the diamond from the secure casing). Be sure to provide details such as building hours, security measures in place, where the building is located (in the center of a large city, a rural small town, middle of the desert, center of Alaska), and other details that will affect how they plan the heist.

Students will need to figure out how and when to enter the building, get past any security measures, meet the objective, leave the building and successfully get 100 miles away from the building undetected. All of these plans will need to be written down. Students will also need to make a list of everything they will need for the heist, assign tasks for each member of the team and estimate how long each segment of the heist will take, again being sure to write everything down. It may be a good idea to make a worksheet for the teams to fill in.

Once the teams have completed their heist planning, they will give their heist plan to another team. Each team will now become the Teen Bureau of Investigation (TBI) and will pour over the plans looking for any glitches that could mess up the criminals and get them caught. The TBI will be sure to point out every flaw in the plan. These flaws should also be written down. Once all of the flaws are analyzed and considered, the TBIs should then report to the class whether or not the criminals were able to escape, or if they were caught mid–heist or before they were able to make it past the 100 mile radius of the crime zone.

After the TBI presentations, finish up with a group discussion on the effort that planning any project takes and how difficult it is to get away with criminal acts. You may also want to discuss how the teens felt about planning a criminal act. Did they experience a sense of excitement, concern about getting caught, or dislike for planning something illegal?

Weird U.S.
by Mark Moran and Mark Sceurman

If you're looking for a book that is as creepy as it is funny, Weird U.S. *is definitely it. Filled with urban legends and true tales of "weirdness" from across the United States, teens will be fascinated. Typically we begin the booktalk by asking where they have vacationed in the United States. After a smattering of answers, we encourage them to investigate the strange, obscure, and gross facts about the various places they plan to vacation.*

To provide a few examples we read some of the examples word for word while for others we simply provide a synopsis, but we always show pictures. The examples we use are: "The Strange, Ax-wielding, Child-killing Bunny Man" (page 19); "Hornet Spook Light" (page 100); "The Ghost of Ethyl Work" (page 253); and "Casket Cascade" (page 308). While these are wonderfully disturbing, spooky, and gross examples, we encourage you to choose the tales to fit your location and your own personal experiences in order to make the stories more realistic for your students.

And of course, you've got to leave them wanting more. This book is filled with information about the Frog People, Booger Beast, Lizard Man, lawn of 2093 Milk Jugs, and, if you're interested, how to take a trip down Route 666.

Discussion Questions

1. Where are some "weird" places you have lived? Visited?
2. What are urban legends?
3. Where do you think stories, such as "The Strange, Ax-wielding, Child-killing Bunny Man" come from?
4. What steps should someone take to determine if a story is true?
5. What is the difference between a primary and secondary resource? Which is more reliable? Why?
6. Do you think science can explain all phenomena or do you think some things, like the "Hornet Spook Light," may be supernatural?
7. What supernatural, or seemingly supernatural, experiences have you had?

Project: Your Weird Town

By interviewing people in your town and doing research on your town, have students find their own "weird" stories and facts about your town. Each student should bring in an article they wrote about the odd happening and a photo or picture. (If their story is about a ghost or a past event, obviously, they can't take a photo, but they could take a picture of a gravesite or draw a picture of how they imagine it. If they get discouraged with this part, use the book as an example of how seemingly normal pictures, paired with a story, can be seen in a new light.) Compile these articles and pictures into a homemade bound book and create your own "Your Weird Town."

The Alien Invasion Survival Handbook
by W. H. Mumfrey

Are you prepared for an alien invasion? First thing you should consider is how to recognize the warning signs of an abduction. Raise your hand if any of these applies to you: You thought you took a glass out of the cabinet to get something to drink but when you went to pour your drink, the glass was gone. You know you put the remote on the coffee table but after some searching it turns up under a sofa pillow. You thought you felt someone watching you but when you turned around no one was there. You're sure you saw something move out of the corner of the eye when you're home alone. Your dog (or fish or cat) has started acting really strange — animals sense things like earthquakes and storms. Don't think they don't sense an alien watching you to plan the perfect abduction.

Let's say you do, in fact, have a run-in with an alien, you should know the areas on his body that are most sensitive. *Show the picture titled "Alien Target Zones" in the "Attack" chapter.* If you are in a combat situation with an alien, you must keep your mp3 player safe because some music can protect you from alien electroparalysis. *Turn to the "How to Keep Your MP3 Player Safe During Combat Conditions" section in the "Defense" chapter and read the four suggestions and explanations.*

Discussion Questions

1. What is alien electroparalysis and how can you protect yourself from it?
2. What types of traps should you use on aliens?
3. What are different ways you can escape from an alien abduction?
4. What are some of the myths about aliens?
5. Why does the author think aliens want to invade Earth? Do you have any other theories?

Project: Practice Creative Writing — The Alien Edition

In Appendix C in the back of the handbook is a section called, "Alien Encounter Logbook." Have your students create their own logbook with at least three different instances. Then instruct students to fill in each section, even the drawings and diagrams, with their own creative ideas. Encourage them to use scenes from alien movies or other books to spur on their creativity.

Can You Drill a Hole Through Your Head and Survive?
by Simon Rogers

Tell the class to choose one of the three questions for you to answer:

- Is it safe to eat mud?
- Can you die from heartbreak?
- How can you interrogate someone using the theme from *Sesame Street*?

They seem to always choose the last question. Locate the question in the book and either read the answer or summarize.

This book answers other questions such as... (*Read as quickly as possible! If you're not a fast reader, find another way to make it interesting such as, read it in an animated voice or use different voices for each questions.*)

- How long can you survive in a freezer?
- Why do the Japanese live so long?
- What is hot tub lung?
- Are cloned animals safe to eat?
- Is eating live insects a bad idea?
- Are BBQs seriously bad for your health?
- How do I become a synchronized diver?
- How does an elephant give birth?
- Do cats and dogs need sunscreen?
- What should you do if you meet a tiger in the street?
- Are chow-chows the most stupid dogs in the world?
- Will a meteorite land in my living room?
- How can I intercept other people's text messages?
- Can iPods make you hallucinate?
- Can too much sleep kill you?

(These questions were taken from the back of the book. Feel free to choose your own list to read from the Table of Contents.)

DISCUSSION QUESTIONS

1. What was the most interesting thing you learned?
2. Were there any questions you had always wondered about in the book? What were they?
3. Are there any questions you've always wondered about but never asked because you are afraid they're too stupid? What are they? How do we find answers to those questions?
4. Are there certain things it's not acceptable to question? Why or why not?
5. Why are questions so important?
6. Have you ever gotten in trouble for asking too many questions?
7. Has there been a time in your life when you should've asked questions but were too afraid?
8. Why are people afraid to ask questions?

PROJECT: QUESTIONING THE NORM

The world is full of peculiarities and there seems to come a time when we stop questioning — whether it's because we've simply grown accustomed to our surroundings or because we've annoyed one too many people with our infinite queries. After going through this book, encourage students to spend the next day questioning the world around them, and when they return to class, have them write down the question they want the answer to most! Go around the room and share the different questions people have. Now instruct them to spend the next day finding the answer to their question — whether through interviews, books, the Internet, etc. Encourage them that some questions don't have straightforward answers, only speculation. If their question falls into that category, they simply need to return with the theories. When you meet again, go around the room and have each student read their question and the answer. This is a great project to encourage to students to not only question everything but find the answers.

10 Sure Signs a Movie Character Is Doomed and Other Surprising Movie Lists
by Richard Roeper

If you're a movie buff, here is a book for you. *10 Sure Signs a Movie Character is Doomed and Other Surprising Movie Lists* by Richard Roeper contains a lot of lists about movies, movie characters, actors and predictable movie situations. For example, there's the list of movies in which Ben Affleck cries like a big fat baby, or the list of movies that are NEVER played on an airplane (*Final Destination* anyone?) or the 10 highly stupid habits of movie characters for example, when you find yourself screaming at the screen, "Don't go in there!" or "Don't open that door!" We know it, most everyone knows it, but somehow the movie characters just don't get it. And then, of course, there's the 10 movie characters who just don't stand a chance. Ready?

- If a characters gets a phone call in the middle of the night from someone claiming, "I know who did it. Meet me alone." Dead.
- The spunky little kid or wizened old soul in the hospital who befriends the main character. At some point in the movie we're going to see a nurse stripping the hospital bed because nothing says "dead" like stripping hospital beds.
- The solider who talks endlessly about his girlfriend, shows her picture to everyone and constantly says, "We're having a baby!" Dead.
- The pregnant young wife who exclaims, "I've never been happier in my entire life!"
- Any anonymous henchman who attempts to fight the hero one-on-one
- All lusty teenagers in the '80s horror movies
- The veteran police officer who is a week away from retirement
- The one black guy on the team who isn't played by an actor as famous as everyone else
- Any and all wise old timers
- Whenever the hero and the bad guy are locked in a wrestling match to the death and the gun goes off and the hero has this shocked look on his face — when they fall away from each other, who is dead?

DISCUSSION QUESTIONS

1. What makes these lists funny? What is it about the language that is humorous? What is it about the lists themselves that is funny?
2. Making lists means making connections. For each list there is one unifying thread (i.e., movie characters that are going to die, Ben Affleck crying, names of movie characters that Meg Ryan has played are all the same or similar). What is it about these connections that we love so much?

3. For lists that you did not find humorous, what barriers were in the way? Why didn't you find these lists funny?
4. Were there any lists that you thought were not meant to be humorous?
5. What is the point of this book? Why was it written?
6. If you were going to make a humorous list, what would you write about? Why would you write about this topic?

PROJECT: THE COMEDY SHTICK

This book is a good example of using lists as comedy and a great opportunity to give your students some experience with humorous creative writing. (*The Book of Lists for Teens* is another good example of this type of writing.) The end goal for this project is to have teens create their own humorous lists using some basic comedic rules as well as some humorous writing techniques. For more information on humorous writing techniques, try *Comedy Writing Secrets* by Melvin Helitzer and Mark Shats, *Damn! That's Funny!* by Gene Perret, or *Comedy Writing* by Jenny Roche.

According to Roche there are 3 golden rules to comedy writing: (1) Keep it short. Wordiness and long-windedness will lose your audience. (2) The punchline must be self-explanatory. If you find yourself giving a ton of background or explaining the joke, it isn't funny. Look for facts that are mainstream or common knowledge. (3) Make it funny. There is no hard and fast rule to how or what is funny, but if your audience doesn't laugh, it isn't funny.

Personal anecdote: In high school, a sweetheart couple in Jill's Latin class decided to write a humorous list on the various types of number 2s a person might experience (yes, think potty humor) rather than paying attention to the teacher. This topic hit all of the golden rules. (1) The individual list points were very short, not even a sentence long. (2) Everyone could associate with the various types, even if we were embarrassed to admit it. (3) It was potty humor — we were in high school, need we say more?

Start with a discussion on why these lists are funny (feel free to use the discussion questions listed with this book idea to help you get started on this discussion). Discuss which topics your students would like to turn into lists. Have your students write a humorous list with at least 10 items in the list. As an additional task, have your teens read their lists out loud to the group.

How to Survive a Robot Uprising
by Daniel H. Wilson

Do you know how to spot a hostile robot? What are the warning signs? Do you know how to survive a car chase with an unmanned ground vehicle? What about those pesky robot insect swarms? Let's say that your family just purchased a new home. It's a smart house. It knows when to turn on the lights for you or start your shower in the morning, takes messages while you're away, cooks dinner for you and even turns down your bed for you at night. Beware, this house is watching your every move. It knows your behavioral patterns. What if it doesn't like you? How do you escape when the house decides you are no longer worthy to live? Too many robots today look exactly like humans. Can you tell the difference between real humans and robots mimicking humans? If your life depended on it, could you mimic a robot? Do you know how to stop a giant walking robot? Learn how to survive the coming robot uprising with Daniel Wilson's manual *How to Survive a Robot Uprising.*

Discussion Questions

1. Wilson begins the "Briefing" section with the statement, "If popular culture has taught us anything…." What is popular culture?
2. According to Wilson, what is a robot's greatest weakness? What are humans' greatest strength? What will save us when the robot uprising comes?
3. What is a robot? Why do humans build them? What is their purpose?
4. Where do you think Wilson gets most of his information for this book?
5. What types of robots are there? Which one do you think is the most dangerous?
6. Do you think the science of robotics will ever evolve to the point where civilization uses intelligent robots on a daily basis?
7. How does the author use humor in his book? What makes this book funny rather than scary or ominous?

Project: Potential Robots Become Art

Don't give those unused robots a chance to rebel! Does your school or library have unused and outdated computers sitting in a storage room? What about keyboards and mice that no longer work? Those guys are sitting in a locked closet somewhere getting angry and disgruntled with their lack of use. Destroy them before they act! Ask your IT department for any unused equipment they may have designated to recycle. Let them know that any equipment they hand over to you will be dismantled and destroyed never to return. Other supplies you'll need are safety goggles, working gloves and some general dismantling tools such as hammers, pliers and scissors. Let your teens rip apart all of the equipment you acquired. Your teens will thoroughly enjoy breaking everything, digging into the heart of the computers, prying off keys and ripping out cords. You may want to reserve one whole session just for the destruction of the electrical equipment.

For the second session, however, let your teens create works of art using the left over bits and pieces. Rings, necklaces and earrings can be made from keyboard keys. Electrical cords and wires can be transformed into belts and bracelets. Use all of the itsy-bitsy pieces to create a mosaic or a 3 dimensional representation of a landscape. The possibilities are endless! You'll want some constructive supplies for this part such as scissors, hot glue, glitter, sequins, poster board, cardboard, paint, yarn and anything else you can think of to transform those old ugly computers into shining works of art.

R.I.P.
by Susan K. Hom

Raise your hand if you've ever been to a cemetery. Well, then you probably know that most of the tombstones look the same — they have the person's name, birth date,

Students tear apart leftover technology before it has the opportunity to rebel. They use the dismantled equipment to create original art.

and date of death and sometimes they'll have something like "Mom" or "Grandmama." However, sometimes you'll find the unique ones—they're typically pretty old and have poems or sayings. Some are morbid, some are funny, and they're all pretty interesting. *Before the class starts, be sure you have whittled your way through the book and found your favorites.*

DISCUSSION QUESTIONS

1. What was your favorite entry?
2. Were there any that didn't make sense to you?
3. If you had to create your own epitaph, what would it say?
4. According to the section "Beloved Animals," it is appropriate to create epitaphs for your animals. What epitaph would you give your pet?
5. Why do you think humans make fun of death?

PROJECT: TOMBSTONE OBSERVATION AND CREATIVE WRITING

Field trip time! Take the students to the largest cemetery in your area. Instruct the students to read the different tombstones and to each find one that appeals to them — it could be because of the epitaph, the shape, or even simply the age of the deceased. Each student needs to photograph or draw the stone they have chosen. When you return to the classroom, each student will need to write a fictional background story for the deceased.

Classroom Integration

The best funny, gross, and disturbing nonfiction books we find are often about science, history, social studies, geography and other scholastic subjects. For example, *Weird U.S.* is a great way to start talking about United States history and geography, *Weird and Wonderful Words* makes the discovery of new words and their etymology more interesting, *Bat Boy Lives!* provides a unique method to discuss English and writing in mass communications, and *Be Afraid, Be Very Afraid* is a creepy beginning to a section about mythology.

More Great Books

The Alien Invasion Survival Handbook: A Defense Manual for the Coming Extraterrestrial Apocalypse by W. H. Mumfrey

Backyard Ballistics by William Gurstelk

Bat Boy Lives! The WEEKLY WORLD NEWS Guide to Politics, Culture, Celebrities, Alien Abductions, and the Mutant Freaks that Shape Our World by the editors of *Weekly World News* and David Perell

Be Afraid, Be Very Afraid: The Book of Scary Urban Legends by Jan Harold Brunvand

The Book of General Ignorance by John Mitchinson and John Lloyd

The Book of Lists for Teens by Sandra Choron and Harry Choron

Can You Drill a Hole Through Your Head and Survive? 180 Fascinating Questions and Amazing Answers About Science, Health, and Nature by Simon Rogers, ed.

Encyclopedia Horrifica: The Terrifying Truth About Vampires, Ghosts, Monsters, and More by Joshua Gee

Exploding Ants: Amazing Facts About How Animals Adapt by Joanne Settel

For Boys Only: The Biggest, Baddest Book Ever by Marc Aronson and HP Newquist

Grossology by Sylvia Branzei and Jack Keely

Gross-Out Cakes: The Kitty Litter Cake and Other Classics by Kathleen Barlow and Britney Schetselaar

How to Hold a Crocodile by Diagram Group

How to Survive a Robot Uprising: Tips on Defending Yourself Against the Coming Rebellion by Daniel H. Wilson

Mini Weapons of Mass Destruction: Build Implements of Spitball Warfare by John Austin

Monster Hunt: The Guide to Cryptozoology by Rory Storm

Oh Yikes! History's Grossest Moments by Joy Masoff and Terry Sirrell

The Other Book of Perfectly Useless Information by Mitchell Symons

Outbreak: Plagues That Changed History by Bryn Barnard

Rats: Observations on the History and Habitat of the City's Most Unwanted Inhabitants by Robert Sullivan

R.I.P.: Here Lie the Last Words, Morbid Musings, Epitaphs and Fond Farewells of the Famous and Not-So-Famous by Susan K. Hom

Ripley's Believe It or Not! by Ripley Entertainment, Inc.

The Stunning Science of Everything: Science with the Squishy Bits Left In! by Nick Arnold and Tony De Saulles

The Stupid Crook Book by Leland Gregory

10 Sure Signs a Movie Character Is Doomed and Other Surprising Movie Lists by Richard Roeper

That Book of Perfectly Useless Information by Mitchell Symons

Toilets, Bathtubs, Sinks, and Sewers: A History of the Bathroom by Penny Colman

The Truth About Poop by Susan E. Goodman

Wearing of This Garment Does Not Enable You to Fly: 101 Real Dumb Warning Labels by Jeff Koon, Andy Powell, and Tim Carroll

Weird and Wonderful Words by Erin McKean, Roz Chast, and Simon Winchester

Weird U.S. by Mark Moran and Mark Sceurman

The Zombie Survival Guide: Complete Protection from the Living Dead by Max Brooks

2

History

Did you know that Ethan Allen was a revolutionary war hero who tried to take over Montreal single-handedly and was carted off to England in chains? Or that aunts in ancient India had two fingers cut off when their nieces and nephews were born? History books often contain fascinating facts like these.

Jill's history teachers spent day in and day out lecturing about American presidents, causes of World War I and the wives of Henry VIII, but all of these facts have gone foggy over the years. Jill does remember one history lesson, the one about the little blue naked men invading Rome. This story has stayed with her not because of a fascination with naked blue men but because her history teacher stepped away from his lectern and simply told a story. He didn't require that his students take notes or exercise critical listening skills for the pop quiz later. He just told a very funny and incredible story. Naked blue men ransacking Rome? Awesome! History comprises the entire story of the human race with all of our magnificent advances and horrid deeds. Everything we've ever done is history and everything we will ever do will become history. History doesn't have to be dry. It doesn't have to be all dates, lists or politics. Make history a story and suddenly it becomes real.

Book Ideas with Booktalks, Discussion Questions, and Project Ideas

The Wicked History of the World
by Terry Deary and Martin Brown

For this booktalk we give the students selections from the "Superstitions and Quaint Customs" quiz. Our favorite questions are:

- In Jericho (7500s BC) people would cut off the heads of their dead granddads, stick them on the floor and worship them. True or False? (True. They filled the old geezer's head with clay, painted the skull to look like flesh and stuck shells in the eye holes to look like eyes. Then they put it on the floor in the living room.)

- In France (4000 BC) a witch doctor would cure a headache by beating a patient over the head to scare out the demons in the skull. True or False? (False. It was much worse. The doctor used a sharp flint to drill a hole into the skull and let the evil spirits out.)
- In India (middle ages) when a child was born, the mother would have 2 of her fingers cut off. True or False? (False. The child's oldest aunt would have 2 fingers cut off. It was the last 2 fingers on the right hand, which a carpenter would take off with a chisel.)
- On the Sanghi Island of the Pacific Ocean (during the middle ages) a child would be tortured to death to stop an erupting volcano. True or False? (True. The village priest killed a kid cruelly every year to keep the god of volcanoes happy. First he cut off the child's fingers, then the nose and ears and other body bits before finishing it off with a dagger in the chest. The village then had a party for a week.)

DISCUSSION QUESTIONS

1. The *Wicked History* authors assert that prehistoric people survived and made it to the top of the animal kingdom by "being more horrible than anything the world had ever seen." Do you think this is true? Why or why not?
2. The *Wicked History* describes cities throughout history as dirty, smelly and dangerous, but people still lived in them. Why do you think people still live in towns and cities if they are so dirty and dangerous?
3. Do you think Hammurabi's code and the Bible's punishments described in *Wicked History* are fair?
4. Which tales about Huang Di do you think are true and which are false? Do you think there could be explanations for the ones you think are false? Why would ancient people have believed these stories?
5. Read through the "Rotten Rulers" section. Why would people allow rulers to be so cruel? Why did rulers get away with so much nastiness?
6. Read through the "Rotten Rome" section. What reason do you think made Rome great? What reason do you think is the most important?
7. What is the point of the Geneva Convention rules if no one follows them? Do you think the United States follows these rules?
8. Read Olaudah's story. Why do you think an ex-slave would keep his own slaves after gaining his freedom?
9. According to George Hegel, we learn nothing from history but according to the *Wicked History* authors, "We learn an awful lot from horrible history." What do you think they mean? Why does it take horrible history for humans to learn from their mistakes?

PROJECT: FIRST PERSON WITNESS LETTERS

The authors of *Wicked History of the World* provide several easy projects to compliment the stories in their book. Your teens could present their version of the "Goose

Magic" play, take the "Quaint Customs" quiz, try their wits at the "Cutter Whey Castle" puzzle, take the "Spell-ing Test" or play the "Slum Street" boardgame. All of these projects are included in the *Wicked History of the World*. However, *Wicked History* also presents history through creative letters, putting their stories into the words of fictional (or not so fictional) characters of the appropriate time period. For a more robust project, ask your teens to research a story discussed in *Wicked History* and then write their own letter that describes the historical event. Be sure to ask each student to pick a historical event from the book, a character who is writing the letter and a person to whom they are writing the letter. All characters should be appropriate for the time period of the historical event.

Written in Bone
by Sally M. Walker

One of the earliest European settlements in North America was Jamestown, founded in 1607; but by the 1630s the original fort, James Fort, had vanished and Jamestown settled into dust — all except the crumbling brick tower of a church. All we knew of Jamestown came from rare records and hand-me-down stories. What was Jamestown really like? Who really lived there? Where was the fort? How large was it? How many died there? How many lived there? In the mid–1990s archeologists made an amazing discovery — James Fort. They began digging up the area to rediscover its long lost secrets. And what they found was more than just old wooden posts, clay pots and abandoned belongings. They found graves. The archeologists were meeting the very first settlers of Jamestown, like JR1225B, a teenager with a broken neck and an arrowhead still embedded in his leg bone; a long dead captain whose grave was so quickly forgotten that it soon became a trash pit; or another teenager, an indentured servant who died from blunt trauma and then was hastily buried in a cellar. Was it a cover-up for murder? Probably. If you love the details of detective work and if you love discovering the secrets of the past and investigating bones, skulls and grave pits, then *Written in Bone* is for you.

DISCUSSION QUESTIONS

1. Why is discovering James Fort so important?
2. Do you think the excruciating detail that goes into uncovering the identity of these settlers is worth the effort? What do we get out of it?
3. How do the archeologists figure out the age, gender and cultural background of the people buried at James Fort and surrounding areas?
4. How do the archeologists determine how these people died?
5. What is the significance of being buried in a coffin versus being buried without a coffin?
6. What is an indentured servant? How do the archeologists determine if the remains of a colonists belonged to an indentured servant?

PROJECT: ONLINE INTERACTIVES

To help your teens discover Jamestown and James Fort for themselves, there are a few interactive resources online.

- Teens choose where to settle, what to plant and hunt and how to communicate with the Native Americans in the game at historyglobe.com/jamestown.
- Reproductions of the fort as well as videos and other multimedia resources can be found at ngm.nationalgeographic.com/2007/05/jamestown/jamestown-standalone.
- Interactive maps of John Smith's voyages and settlement patterns over time, as well as moving panoramas are provided at virtualjamestown.org/interactive.html.

The Wall
by Peter Sis

Imagine that you lived in a country where your every action is monitored. You had to behave exactly as the government told you to or you would be sent to prison. You had to learn another language. You were forced to join a club supporting the government. You were encouraged to tell on your parents if they spoke against the government. You were forced to collect scrap metal, help in the fields to harvest the crops, and march in parades celebrating the government. How would you feel if your telephone was bugged, your letters and mail were read, the radio only played government-approved stations and you were only allowed to paint official art sanctioned by, you guessed it, the government. Rock and Roll? Banned. Police would stop you in the street and cut your hair if it is too long. The government of another country (the invading, ruling country) sends in tanks and soldiers to depose your leader because they do not approve of the election results. You're afraid to draw your dreams and hopes because you'll get into trouble. You're afraid to paint what you want because it's not allowed. This is life for Peter Sis, artist and film maker. He grew up in Czechoslovakia — behind the Iron Curtain — ruled by the Soviet Union and Communists. All he ever wanted was to be free — free to draw his dreams and listen to rock and roll. *The Wall* is a history of the Iron Curtain told through the drawings of Peter Sis.

DISCUSSION QUESTIONS

1. Peter Sis lists compulsory rules, rules that had to be followed: taking Russian language classes, joining the Young Pioneers Movement, collecting scrap metal, participating in the Workers of the World Parade and showing public displays of loyalty. Why would the Communist government demand that their citizens do these things?
2. Why was it called the Cold War?
3. Why couldn't Peter Sis paint whatever he wanted?
4. Why did the government monitor its people so closely by reading their mail and listening to their phone calls?
5. Read the entry from Sis' journals on February 1957. He says that when he got off the train there were 2 extra pairs of skis and 2 people were missing. What do you think happened to the missing people?
6. Why does Peter Sis only use color on certain parts of his drawings? What does color signify?
7. What about the color red? What does this color signify?

PROJECT OPTION 1: BERLIN WALL ART

Research images of Berlin Wall art (very prevalent on the Internet) as well as the images recreated in *The Wall*. What do these works of art depict? What is their focus? Why would so many people draw on the Berlin Wall?

For this project you will need enough white or gray bulletin board paper to cover at least one wall of your classroom, teen area or art gallery area, paint supplies, and paintbrushes. Find a place to put up the long section of bulletin board paper and let your teens recreate their own version of Berlin Wall art. When you are finished with this lesson or need your wall space back, let your teens tear the paper down, ripping it into large pieces. You can then hang the smaller ripped pieces around your classroom or library to celebrate the freedom now enjoyed by those who suffered behind the Iron Curtain for so long.

PROJECT OPTION 2: VISIT THE BERLIN WALL

There are numerous locations around the world that house pieces of the Berlin Wall; in fact, there are at least 38 different places in the United States. Take your students to the closest locale and allow them the opportunity to see history up close.

Phineas Gage
by John Fleischman

Before beginning this book, take time to mark pictures to show throughout the booktalk such as the picture of the tamping iron in the "Putting Phineas Together Again" chapter, the picture of the path of the tamping iron in "Horrible Accident in Vermont," and the skull photo in "Following Phineas Gage."

Before we get started, who can describe a tamping iron? *If no one responds, ask if anyone has any guesses.* A tamping iron has been confused with a crow bar for good reason. It is an iron rod that weighs about 13½ lbs., about the size of a medium turkey. It comes to a point on one end, used for poking holes in gunpowder to set a fuse, and the other end is fat and round, used for packing down (or tamping down) the loose powder. *Show the picture in "Putting Phineas Together Again."*

Imagine that you are a 26-year-old, normal-sized man. You work on the railroad, long before bulldozers, and you are in pretty good shape. It's nearly 4:30 in the afternoon in September 1848. Performing a routine job of blasting a solid rock into small pieces, you and your assistant begin setting up. At this point, the story gets fuzzy but the bottom line is this: the tamping rod you're holding slips out of your hands and down into the gunpowder filled hole, striking the granite and exploding.

This is precisely what happened to Phineas Gage, and at this point in the story you may want to stop imagining it's you. What happens next is a baffling medical wonder. The explosion sends the tamping rod into the air and up through Gage's left cheek, behind his left eye, and out through his forehead. *Show picture in "Horrible Accident in Vermont."* And Phineas Gage lives.

DISCUSSION QUESTIONS

1. Why does the author call the event that happened to Phineas Gage both lucky and unlucky?
2. What are animalcules?
3. What were Gage's lasting results of the tamping iron injury?
4. In your own words, discuss one interesting fact you learned about the brain.
5. How does Phineas Gage die?
6. What side effects do people with frontal lobe damage suffer? How was this apparent in Gage's life?
7. Do you think Phineas Gage was lucky or unlucky?

PROJECT: DISCOVERING THE TEEN BRAIN

There is so much going on inside our skulls that we do not notice! This is an excellent opportunity to discuss the teen brain. Divide your students into 5 groups and provide them each a large piece of poster board or butcher paper. Assign each group one of these ages: 9, 13, 15, 17, and 21 and instruct them to present how the brain is evolving at the group's respective age. After completion, have each group (beginning with group age 9 and ending with group age 21) present their findings to the class.

Web site suggestions include:

- "3-D Brain Anatomy" from PBS: www.pbs.org/wnet/brain/3d
- an interactive brain detailing the differences in the brain during childhood development: www.nytimes.com/interactive/2008/09/15/health/20080915-brain-development.html

"Discovering the Teen Brain" Discussion Questions

1. Give specific examples of issues that each age group is not mentally prepared to handle, according to their brain development.
2. After discussing how different parts of the brain develop at different times, are there any areas science says you're ill equipped based on your brain development?
3. How should you deal with issues that are beyond your brain development?

Red Scared!
by Michael Barson and Steven Heller

Who do you think is the greatest enemy of the United States, past or present? *Allow a handful of students to answer with their opinions and brief explanations.*

If you had been asked that question in 1920, you probably would have responded, "Communists." The United States was overrun with the fear that Communists were trying to take over and the press exploited that fear. Can anyone explain what propaganda means? *Allow various students to answer until an accurate definition is found. You could also have a dictionary up near the front of the room with propaganda already located—*

simply select a student to come up and read it and ask them to summarize the definition in their own words.

Stalin, the leader of the USSR, was called the ally of Hitler and a man for the people all within the same decade. There were novels, movies, and more magazine articles than you could count — including one titled "How to Identify an American Communist." *Red Scared!* is full of the real history of the Cold War, as well as the way the entertainment industry and the press handled it. It's full of romance, bombs, bad government, good government, and just about everything else.

DISCUSSION QUESTIONS

1. What is communism? When did the scare begin in the United States?
2. What happened on June 22, 1941, that made the United States change its perception of the Soviet Union? What were some ways the press described Stalin that changed?
3. How did the entertainment industry respond to the Cold War? How do you think this affected the perceptions of communism with American citizens?
4. What was the HUAC and what was its function?
5. How did the propaganda reach children?
6. What was the Space Race?
7. Describe bomb shelters.

PROJECT: PROPAGANDA

Split your class into groups of 2–4 and assign each group an American war. Providing access to history books and the Internet, each group must come up with the following information based on their respective wars: three ways propaganda was used in America, three visual examples of propaganda (if they can't find original reproductions, encourage them to reproduce them on their own), and theories why it was used in those situations. After the information is assembled, it must be compiled into a 3–5 minute speech and presented to the class.

2000 Questions and Answers About the Civil War
by Webb Garrison

Before doing this booktalk, choose a couple questions from the book to ask the class. Write them on notecards and as soon as the first few students trickle in, secretly give them the notecard. Encourage them to try to memorize the notecard and throw it away. When you ask the question in class, they are to answer the question.

Who can tell me what the American Civil War was about? *Field questions. Be sure to know the major reasons the war was fought before asking this question.*

What was the southern states' label after they seceded from the United States? *Be sure they answer the Confederate States of America or the Confederacy.*

At this point ask the questions you passed out at the beginning of class. Call on the students you selected and, after a few obscure questions are answered perfectly, at least a portion

*of the class will be impressed. Then ask the students you previously selected to reveal how
they knew the answers.*

Wouldn't it be amazing to know random and obscure trivia in situations like this?
This book is not like many others, it's simply filled with questions and answers. No need
to shuffle through paragraphs and wade through chapters; it's already broken down into
easy to read, easy to remember trivia.

DISCUSSION QUESTIONS

1. What was the purpose of the American Civil War?
2. In what ways do you think the North was right? Wrong?
3. In what ways do you think the South was right? Wrong?
4. What was the most obscure thing you read?
5. For the rest of the discussion questions, simply refer to the book's questions.

PROJECT: AMERICAN CIVIL WAR QUIZ SHOW

While the students are reading the book, encourage them to memorize as many facts
as possible. After the class or group has completed the book, split your students into
groups of three and put on a quiz show. If you have more than six students, simply structure it in the style of a tournament —first rotating groups and then winners must compete
against winners.

To make it fun, set up the room in the style of a quiz show with the groups facing
each other with you, the host, in the middle. Based on your supplies, decide how students
must respond that they know the answer — either taking turns or with buzzers. If you
have time, build up the anticipation by allowing students time to meet together in their
groups and practice questions.

Island of Hope
by Martin W. Sandler

Imagine you are moving to another country. To get there you have to travel by foot
hundreds of miles to reach the seaport where you find a ship that will take you across the
ocean. Before you are allowed onto the ship, you have to be vaccinated and disinfected.
You are asked hundreds of questions. Then you spend months on board an overcrowded
ship in a dark room with vomit and human waste that is never cleaned. You finally reach
your new country but you don't get to enter right away. Instead, you are herded onto an
island where you are separated from your father. You are asked more questions but you
don't speak the language. You are given a new medical exam. You are forced to take
mental tests like "What is 1 plus 2"? or "Do you wash the stairs from top to bottom or
bottom to top?" You are then asked legal questions. "Why are you coming to our country?" "Are you an enemy of the government?" "Do you already have a job waiting for
you?" If you answered yes to this question, you were put back on your ship and sent back
to your former country. Finally! You are finished with all of the tests and questions. But
you don't get to leave the island yet. Instead you are given a detention note because your

Tara (left) and Jill (right) pitch history facts to a group of teens at the Pikes Peak Library District.

relatives have not arrived to pick you up. You are stuck in a room with hundreds of other immigrants who cannot yet set foot in their new country. This was the journey for immigrants to America who had to go through Ellis Island. And yet millions of people made this journey and now their descendants (most of you) call the United States home.

DISCUSSION QUESTIONS

1. Why did so many people immigrate to America between 1892 and 1954?
2. What was the voyage to America like for most immigrants?
3. What was the Ellis Island experience? How did immigrants feel when they entered Ellis Island? Why did they feel this way?
4. Why were immigrants forced to go through physical, mental and legal examinations?
5. With thousands of immigrants moving through Ellis Island every day, one inspector said, "We were swamped by that human tide." What did he mean? How did that affect his daily work at the island?
6. Why were some people detained on the island? What was life like for them?
7. What was life like for families after they finally arrived in New York?
8. Why did so many immigrants travel beyond New York to the American West?

PROJECT: GENEALOGY!

This book is a great segue into a genealogy project. If you are in a public library, be sure to show your teens how to use your genealogy databases, and if you are in a school library, you may want to check with your local history librarian to schedule a genealogy workshop to help get your students started with this project. This is a lengthy project that will take your teens several weeks to complete. Don't expect all of your teens to be able to find their ancestors and do expect some of your teens to already have family trees completed by other family members. This project will have a varied difficulty level for each of your students but finding a new ancestor can be very rewarding.

History's Greatest Lies
by William Weir

It's easy to sit in class and believe everything someone standing at the front of the room (like me) is saying. But maybe I'm wrong — maybe Jesse James wasn't a wild west Robin Hood; maybe Paul Revere wasn't the only guy shouting "The British are coming!"; and maybe, just maybe, the reason Galileo went on trial wasn't only because his work conflicted with the accepted religious beliefs of the time. Some people would say it's disrespectful to doubt what a teacher is telling you, but I say, when you leave school, check everything that is said with other resources — because you never know if history is lying.

DISCUSSION QUESTIONS

1. What was the most surprising chapter?
2. Who were the Goths and how were they misunderstood?
3. How has the story of Galileo been skewed?
4. What is the myth surrounding the Bastille?
5. The Earp brothers have commonly been considered heroes. Is this an incorrect view-point? Explain your answer.
6. Why do you think history is relayed incorrectly? Use stories from the book to support your answer.

PROJECT: A CREATIVELY ALTERED HISTORY

This is an individual project. Have students to choose a favorite true story in history and do plenty of research to ensure they have their facts correct. Then, instruct them to write a five or more paragraph alteration of their historical event. It must have the same ending so as not to change history in a drastic way — for example, the Union has to win the American Civil War but the method is the part students are free to creatively alter.

Once the stories are written, have students stand up one-by-one and read their papers to the class. The class must guess the facts that have been altered in each student's new rendition of their historical event.

Classroom Integration

The foremost reason we love to share nonfiction books with teens is to bring reality to life. The real world is by far more interesting than any work of fiction, and history is a perfect subject with which to use nonfiction books to liven up the facts. No matter what historic era your students are studying, there are great nonfiction books to include in your lessons. Read aloud to your students from *The Wicked History of the World* to give your students a few facts that are not only true but fascinating. Read aloud *Red Scared!* or *The Wall* to provide your students with another point of view of the Cold War. Let your teens read books like *Island of Hope* to provide them with a more personal perspective on immigration. Use *History's Greatest Lies* to teach your teens to question what they are told and to seek out the truth for themselves. Integrating nonfiction books into your history curriculum can be as simple as assigning nonfiction books from the library for reading homework and will show your students that history thrives outside of their textbook.

More Great Books

Always Faithful: A Memoir of the Marine Dogs of WORLD WAR II by William Putney
Amazing Leonardo da Vinci Inventions You Can Build Yourself by Maxine Anderson
Ask the Bones: Scary Stories from Around the World by Arielle North Olson and Howard Schwartz
The Beast of Chicago: An Account of the Life and Crimes of Herman W. Mudgett by Rick Geary
Black Potatoes: The Story of the Great Irish Famine by Susan Campbell Bartoletti
Bury the Dead: Tombs, Corpses, Mummies, Skeletons & Rituals by Christopher Sloan
Che: A Graphic Biography by Spain Rodriguez
The Children We Remember by Chana Byers Abells
The Duel: The Parallel Lives of Alexander Hamilton & Aaron Burr by Judith St. George
First Kids: The True Stories of All the Presidents' Children by Noah McCullough
Getting Away with Murder: The True Story of the Emmett Till Case by Chris Crowe
Hidden on the Mountain: Stories of Children Sheltered from the Nazis in Le Chambon by Deborah Durland DeSaiz and Karen Gray Ruelle
History's Greatest Lies by William Weir
Immigrant Kids by Russell Freedman
I Never Saw Another Butterfly by Hana Volavkova, ed.
Island of Hope: The Story of Ellis Island and the Journey to America by Martin W. Sandler
Jack the Ripper by Rick Geary
J. Edgar Hoover: A Graphic Biography by Rick Geary
Kids on Strike! by Susan Campbell Bartoletti
Maus: A Survivor's Tale by Art Spiegelman
More Bones: Scary Stories from Around the World by Arielle North Olson and Howard Schwartz
The Murder of Abraham Lincoln by Rick Geary
Mysteries Unwrapped: Secrets of Alcatraz by Susan Sloate
Nat Turner by Kyle Baker
101 Things You Wish You'd Invented and Some You Wish No One Had by Richard Horne and Tracey Turner
Outbreak: Plagues That Changed History by Bryn Barnard
People's History: Locked-Up: A History of the U.S. Prison System by Laura B. Edge
A People's History of the American Empire by Howard Zinn
The Perilous Journey of the Donner Party by Marian Calabro
Phineas Gage: A Gruesome but True Story About Brain Science by John Fleischman

Pyongyang: A Journey in North Korea by Guy Delisle

Red Scared! The Commie Menace in Propaganda and Popular Culture by Michael Barson and Steven Heller

The Saga of the Bloody Benders by Rick Geary

Spies: The Undercover World of Secrets, Gadgets and Lies by David Owen

Sweet! The Delicious Story of Candy by Ann Love and Jane Drake

Thieves! Ten Stories of Surprising Heists, Comical Capers and Daring Escapades by Andreas Schroeder

Toilets, Bathtubs, Sinks, and Sewers: A History of the Bathroom by Penny Colman

Triangle Fire by Leon Stein

2000 Questions and Answers About the Civil War: Unusual And Unique Facts About the War Between States by Webb Garrison

The United States Constitution: a Graphic Adaptation by Jonathan Hennessey

The Wall: Growing Up Behind the Iron Curtain by Peter Sis

The Wicked History of the World: History with the Nasty Bits Left In! by Terry Deary and Martin Brown

Written in Bone by Sally M. Walker

You Want Women to Vote, Lizzie Stanton? by Jean Fritz

3

Biographies and Memoirs

Libraries are filled with biographies about athletes and famous historic figures, but if you look closely enough you'll also find biographies about ordinary people doing extraordinary feats. You'll find biographies of teenagers becoming heroes, heroes surviving against all odds, and genuinely fascinating people whose stories are actually worth telling.

We understand biographies are important to curricula because when we worked with the Pikes Peak Library District, we would get glum teens in our library every year looking for a biography to read. Sometimes these students would have no requirements other than that the biography be longer than 200 pages. These teens were so overwhelmed with the endless possibilities from which to choose that they couldn't pick anyone to read about. Us: "So, do you know who you want to read about?" Teen: "No." Us: "Any ideas at all?" Teen: "Nope." From there we would begin asking teens about their interests, hobbies or extracurricular activities. "Oh, you play basketball? Would you like to read a biography about Michael Jordan?" Teen: "Who?" Eventually the teen would leave the library with a biography or two in hand. Sometimes they found someone they were remotely interested in reading about while other times the teens left as glum as they came into the library. But, honestly, there are plenty of interesting biographies out there — biographies that tell the stories of genuinely interesting people, biographies that have the potential to spark the imagination of our teens and keep them reading, not for the grade but to satisfy their curiosity. Because, really, people are fascinating. Their lives are worth telling and they have a lot to teach us. We just have to find the right biography.

Book Ideas with Booktalks, Discussion Questions, and Project Ideas

A Long Way Gone
by Ishmael Beah

"When I was twelve, I left my village with my older brother, Junior, and our friend Talloi. We were going to rap in a talent show. We never saw our families again. Rebels attacked. And they attacked the next village and the next village, killing everyone. Families running, bullets flyings, blood spattering, mothers crying, children dying. We saw the rebels and we ran. We ran across rivers, through forests, past dying villages. Everyone was dying. We ran for months. We met other boys running. Some died. I lost my brother running. When I was 13, I found a village where the army was camped. I was safe for a bit but then I was handed an AK-47 and learned to shoot the rebels. I learned to slit their throats without mercy, to chase them down and slice them open. I was given cocaine and caffeine pills. I had no memories of my family. My fellow soldiers were my family. But then my lieutenant gave me away to a group of sissy city men with a truck and I became a child again. I have been a child twice and have grown up twice. Do you think it is possible to be a child again after committing these horrors? At least when the rebels and the army attacked the city together, I wasn't as frightened as these sissy city people."

These are the memoirs of Ishmael Beah who, at the age of 17, after being rescued from his life as a boy soldier, traveled to New York City to speak to the U.N. on behalf of the children in his country of Sierra Leone, and who, by age 18, was once again running for his life. But this time he knew where to run to— the United States. Today, Beah works with the Human Rights Watch in the Children's Rights division advisory committee doing his part to end the use of child soldiers throughout the world.

Discussion Questions

1. Read the page just before chapter 1 called "New York City, 1998." Why do people think war is "cool" if it isn't happening to them?
2. Why would adult soldiers keep the boys hopped-up on cocaine and caffeine?
3. In the rehabilitation center, Ishmael encounters a group of boys who fought for the RUF, the rebels. One boy says, "We fought for freedom, and the army killed my family and destroyed my village." Both the army and the rebels are responsible for many deaths. What do you think is the real reason these teens would support one side or the other?
4. Why did the staff at the rehabilitation center keep saying, "It's not your fault"? Do you believe that? Why didn't Ishmael and the other boys want to believe it?
5. Why do the boys hate civilians so much? Why do they get angry when civilians insist that they are in charge of the boys?
6. Read the story of the hunter and the monkey at the end of the book. Which choice would you make? What do you think of Ishmael's answer? Why do you think the storytellers told this story every year?

Project Option 1: Debate

Juniata College faculty, Sarah May Clarkson and Mary Murray, have provided a Web site of resources on this memoir. One group activity is a debate between your teens. You can find a list of statements to debate at their Web site http://staff.juniata.edu/murraym/beah/teaching.html listed under the link "Group Activity—the Spectrograph Game."

Project Option 2: Red Hand Day

You may also check the Web site redhandday.org. On February 12, 2009, 250,000 red hands were delivered to the UN General Secretary by children and teens from around the world. These hands were delivered as a plea to the UN to stop the use of child soldiers in countries like Sierra Leone. Check here to see if Red Hand Day continues or how to host a Red Hand Day in your school or library in order to boost community awareness.

Project Option 3: Read Aloud

A third project option is to simply read this memoir aloud to your class or discussion group. Search for "Ishmael Beah" on Youtube in order to listen to a 5 minute segment of Beah reading from his memoir.

The Diary of Ma Yan
by Ma Yan

We have found that sometimes it is better to do your booktalk by reading excerpts directly from the book, making it appear more legitimate to the students. This booktalk is primarily made up of excerpts from the book, as well as a small explanation.
Read September 12 (part 1).
Read September 20 (part 1).
Ma Yan is a young girl who grew up in one of the poorest areas of China. She walks four hours to school on Mondays and four hours home on Fridays and for most meals she eats bread rolls, or rice, with vegetables occasionally. Her parents have to work very labor-intensive jobs just to send her and her brothers to school.
Read November 5 (part 1).
Her diary includes many things your diary might — disappointments, people gossiping, and her dreams. Also, her diary outlines her persistence to stay in school, hope for college, and a better future for her and her family.
Read November 15 (part 2).

Discussion Questions

1. Describe Ma Yan's home.
2. Would you fight, like Ma Yan, to stay in school?
3. In what ways are families in China the same as they are in the USA? How are they different?
4. Do you think pressures in school are different in China than they are in America? Explain.
5. When Ma Yan's mother yells at her for failing, why do you think Ma Yan does not yell back? How would you respond?
6. Ma Yan writes about how you have to look out for yourself, even with family (especially referring to her cousin). Have you experienced this? Explain.

PROJECT: THE JOURNAL EXPERIMENT

For one week have the students spend 10–15 minutes writing in independent journals. Encourage them to write about good and bad things that happen and their hopes. Reassure them that no one (including the teacher) will ever read these journals, thus grammar, spelling, and sentence structure are not issues.

After the week, take their journals and put them in a safe place for one month. After one month, return the journals and allow the students to read their entries. Instruct them to take out a sheet of paper and answer two questions:

- What has changed? What problems have been solved or simply went away?
- What issues still exist? What do I need to do to fix them or find closure?

This is an excellent opportunity to teach students to be reflective and instill critical thinking skills.

The Burn Journals
by Brent Runyon

Brent Runyon's autobiography is a stark journey through the year of a teenager after he sets himself on fire in an attempted suicide. We keep this booktalk rather short as the book's dark subject does most of the work for us. We begin by reading a small portion of the attempted suicide description and then we end with a short description of the rest of the biography.

"I take off all my clothes and put on the pair of red boxers with glow-in-the-dark lips. I bring my bathrobe into the shower and I pour the gasoline all over it. The gas can is only about a quarter full, but it seems like enough. I step into the bathtub and I put the bathrobe over my shoulders. It's wet and heavy, but there's something kind of comforting about the smell. I hold the box of matches out in front of me in my left hand. I take out a strike-anywhere match and hold it against the box. Should I do it? Yes. Do it."

When Brent Runyon was 14 years old he lit himself on fire in an attempted suicide. What follows is a year in his own mind as he deals with the torture of intense rehabilitation, the torture of his family's pain, the torture of dealing with the pain that brought him to that pivotal point and the torture of struggling back toward normalcy.

DISCUSSION QUESTIONS

1. Do you like Brent? Are you sympathetic to him? Does your attitude toward him change as the story progresses?
2. Why does Brent set the gym locker on fire?
3. Why does Brent set himself on fire?
4. Why is Craig angry?
5. Brent's story after the burning "accident" begins very haltingly with only a few phrases per page. Why does he write this way? What is he feeling and thinking at this point?
6. Why won't Brent talk to his parents about his suicide attempts?

7. Describe Brent's friends' reactions to the "accident."
8. During his recovery, Brent gets to meet a few famous people. Why is this? How do you feel about Brent's opportunities to meet these people?
9. Why is Brent afraid to go back to school?
10. How is Brent at the end of the story different from the Brent at the beginning of the story?

PROJECT: STATUS UPDATE

We didn't have online social networks like Facebook or MyYearbook back in 1991, but what if we did? What would Brent's online mood have been during his year of recovery? What would his status messages have said?

First, create a visual timeline of Brent's recovery year with 15–25 significant dates. These dates can be specific dates mentioned in the book or they can be representative dates of general days when he was going through specific rehabilitation. Begin with the days before his "accident" and conclude with his first day back to public high school. Each date should be listed and should also include a one to two sentence description of the significance of this date. What was Brent doing that day?

Next, what was Brent's mood? Create a one word descriptor to describe Brent's mood on each of those days. Was he angry, scared, curious, depressed, sleepy, calm, happy? Be sure to create an emoticon to represent this mood as well.

Third, what was Brent's status message? Does he say what he's thinking about doing? Does he mention his emotions and how he is feeling? Does he become sarcastic and make fun of the psychiatrists? Is he truthful? Does he lie in his status message? Begin each status message with "Brent is…" Each status message should be one sentence in length.

The Underdog
by Joshua Davis

Joshua Davis has accumulated a lifetime of failures. In elementary he electrocuted himself while trying to construct a fully operational replica of a battleship in his bathtub. In high school he started a rock band, and at their first and only performance he forgot the lyrics— the group disbanded. In college he attempted to create a feature length film. He sold his film to a company in Nicaragua. The company went bankrupt and Joshua was never paid for his film. As an adult, Joshua Davis is a 129-pound data entry clerk whose wife wants only three things in life — direct sunlight, a dining room and a bathtub. None of which is in their tiny apartment in San Diego. He's not exactly living his dreams.

Desperate to make his wife happy and to do something that he actually enjoys, Joshua doesn't do what most adults would normally do— get a higher paying job. Instead, this guy decides to make money by competing in every outlandish competition he can enter. In his first outlandish competition, Joshua competes in the U.S. National Arm Wrestling Championship and he gets 4th place! (He was 4th out of four contestants total at the competition.) But! Fourth place means that he got a spot on Team USA and would compete in the World Championships. In Poland he competed against the Russian Ripper.

After the arm wrestling championships, Joshua continued on his quest to compete for money. He tries bullfighting in Spain, sumo wrestling 500-pound men and backward running in India. He even competes in the Sauna World Championship sitting inside a blistering 220-degree sauna, just to get his wife a bathtub.

DISCUSSION QUESTIONS

1. Which outlandish competition would you like to try?
2. Which competition would you never try?
3. In the introduction, Joshua asks, "We tell our children that they can grow up to be champions if they really put their minds to it. But is it true?" What do you think? Can we all grow up to be what we want to be?
4. Why does Joshua attempt these competitions? What does he hope to accomplish?
5. Despite losing all of his sumo matches, Joshua is still an inspiration to the audience. Why?
6. How does his wife, Tara, respond to Joshua's attempts to compete in these competitions?

PROJECT: PUBLIC SPEAKING (IF JOSHUA CAN ARM WRESTLE...)

Visit Joshua Davis' Web site, www.underdognation.com, for a list of some of the world's most outlandish competitions. Let your teens choose a competition from the list and prepare an oral report. Each speech should include an explanation or definition of what the sport is and how it is played, rules of the competition, how the sport began or the history of the sport, current records, and champions of the sport. Time to practice those public speaking skills! You never know when they will come in handy. Maybe one day you'll participate in a national orators' competition!

Sacagawea Speaks
by Joyce Badgley Hunsaker

Who in here has played 20 questions? We're going to play something like that—however, instead of you asking questions, I'm going to give you tenfacts (not 20) about someone and you must guess who it is.

- The person I am thinking of is a woman.
- She saw almost everyone in her clan killed by the Minnetarees.
- This woman was married at the age of 14.
- When this woman went into labor, she was given 2 rings of a rattlesnake broken and added to water to help her.
- She had a baby she named Pomp though her French husband named him Jean Baptiste.
- She adopted her sister's son, Bazil.
- With her French husband she accompanied a group of white men to the Big Water Where the Sun Goes Down. They give her the nickname "Janey."

- William Clark, one of the white travelers grows so fond of her son, Pomp, that he requests to adopt him. She declines.
- The other traveler, Meriwether Lewis, dies while traveling to Washington, D.C.
- She is Native American.

Any guesses who the woman was? *If they can't guess, give them extra clues and speak the names of the white travelers, Lewis and Clark, together. After many hints, eventually tell them the answer.*

DISCUSSION QUESTIONS

1. How was Sacagawea chosen for this expedition?
2. What languages did Sacagawea speak?
3. What was the woman's belt Sacagawea received? Do we have anything like that in our culture?
4. Why didn't Sacagawea and Otter Woman speak the Shoshoni language? Do you understand Charbonneau's reasoning?
5. List some of the odd medicines Sacagawea took to cure her various ailments.
6. Why did Sacagawea find it odd that the dog accompanying the expedition did not carry supplies?
7. What was Pompey's Pillar? What is so significant about the land formation?

PROJECT: EXPEDITION SUPPLY LIST

This is a project for nearly every subject and works great to teach teamwork. Split your class into groups of around 2–3. Instruct your students to choose a location to go on a hypothetical expedition. After the place is chosen, each group needs to do significant research on the area, determining: weather, terrain, wildlife, and, if humans dwell there, what languages are spoken. Based on this information and the guide provided in *Sacagawea Speaks* under the chapter "Expedition Supply List," have each group create their own supply list.

Once the list is created, have each group present the list to the class. They need to include the following information in their presentation:

- Explain why each item was chosen (use the information you found in your research on weather, terrain, wildlife, and languages).
- List at least 5 items you wanted to bring but cannot. Explain your reasoning.
- How do you plan to pack and transport the supplies?

Fortune's Bones
by Marilyn Nelson

We don't know very much about Fortune. We know that he was a slave in Waterbury, Connecticut, in the 1700s. He had a wife, Dinah; two sons, Africa and Jacob; and two daughters, Mira and Roxa. His owner was Dr. Preserved Porter, a physician who specialized in setting broken bones. We know that at some point during his life, Fortune's back was broken but he survived and worked for many more years. We know that after his death he continued to serve his owner, Dr. Porter and Dr. Porter's children, grandchildren and great grandchildren who also became physicians. Dr. Porter didn't bury Fortune. Instead, he boiled him — boiled the skin and muscles right off those bones. Then he labeled those bones and studied them. Fortune's name was forgotten and the descendants of Dr. Porter named the skeleton Larry. At some point Fortune was boarded up in the attic and completely forgotten until a work crew rediscovered him while renovating the house. Who was this skeleton? George Washington? A war hero? Was he murdered? Did he drown? Did he hang? Only a hard search through local historical records gave Fortune back his identity. This is the *Manumission Requiem*, poetry and music written to honor the slave Fortune, whose bones were never freed, even after death.

DISCUSSION QUESTIONS

1. What does the word "manumission" mean?
2. What does the word "requiem" mean?
3. Why is this book called *The Manumission Requiem*?
4. How does Dinah feel about cleaning the room where Fortune's bones are stored?
5. What are the songs in this book doing? What purpose do they serve?
6. Whose voices do we hear in these songs?
7. How do you think Fortune would feel if he knew that his bones would be used for science rather than buried?

PROJECT: SLAVE NARRATIVES

Visit http://xroads.virginia.edu/~hyper/wpa/wpahome.html to view samples of several slave narratives from *The American Slave: A Composite Autobiography* by George P. Rawick, ed. Click on the "Annotated Index of Narratives" link to access the samples of slave narratives. Either read these narratives aloud to your group of teens or assign the narratives to your teens to read aloud to the rest of the group. It is important to review the section "Reading the Narratives" with your group first as these narratives were collected during the 1930s by white people in the Jim Crow South era and some of the notes made by the interviewers may be offensive to us today. Be sure to discuss the unspoken feelings and hidden meanings found in some of these narratives.

Between a Rock and a Hard Place
by Aron Ralston

On Saturday, April 26, 2003, Aron Ralston set out on one of his usual hikes, climbing the red rocks and sandstone just outside the Canyonlands National Park in southeastern Utah. As he's climbing down into a canyon, he grabs a stone the size of a large bus tire and begins to drop down when he feels the stone responding to his adjusting grip and begin to move from its position. Aron drops down quickly but sees the boulder falling down toward him. He's only standing on a small ledge so there's no place to go. The rock crushes his right hand and traps his right arm. Aron is alone and trapped with a crushed arm for six days with little food and water. The longer he is out there the more certain

Showing your teens a wide range of biographies helps them think beyond the traditional sports and historical options.

he is that he is going to die. He starts recording himself with his digital camera saying his farewells to his family. On the 6th day he realizes what he has to do to save his own life. He cuts off his own arm. This is his autobiography, complete with pictures recording his entire ordeal.

Discussion Questions

1. Why does Aron love hiking, climbing and adventure seeking?
2. What are Aron's first thoughts after he realizes he is trapped?

3. Why won't Aron yell for help more than once a day?
4. What are the signs that Aron's body is dying?
5. List two ways that Aron keeps himself occupied since he can't move around or do anything physical?
6. What does Aron say to his video camera? Who does he most often address?
7. When does Aron decide to amputate his hand? Why does he make this decision?
8. Who are the first people Aron meets after he is free from the rock? What is their reaction? How is Aron's account of this meeting and their account of this meeting different?
9. Other than losing his hand, how did the accident and entrapment change Aron's life?

PROJECT: HIKING SAFETY

Now is a great time to discuss hiking safety with your teens. Get hiking safety tips from books in your library or various Web sites online. You might also consider asking an expert hiker or park ranger to speak to your teens about hiking safety. As a hands-on activity, bring in sample hiking supplies, some essential and some not essential, and let your teens pick out which items they should always pack when preparing for a hiking trip.

Classroom Integration

Biographies transcend curriculum subjects and do not have to be tied down to your literature classes. Your social studies or current events lesson could include biographies like *a long way gone* or *The Diary of Ma Yan*. If your curricula requires that you provide lessons on career choices, let your teens pick out career based biographies like *Angels of Mercy: The Army Nurses of World War II* by Betsy Kuhn, *Firefighterette Gillete: A Firefighter Who Crashed & Burned: A Success Story* by Kathy Gillete, or even *The Underdog*, the autobiography of Joshua Davis' continuing search for his life's calling. For almost every historic time period there are a wide variety of biographies from which to choose, even the biography of a man's bones (*Fortune's Bones*). And if you are preparing to teach your literature students a lesson on biographies, remind your students that biographies don't have to be about the famous or infamous. Sometimes seemingly ordinary people have riveting stories to tell such as *The Burn Journals* or *Between a Rock and a Hard Place*.

More Great Books

Angels of Mercy: The Army Nurses of World War II by Betsy Kuhn
The Beast of Chicago: An Account of the Life and Crimes of Herman W. Mudgett by Rick Geary
Between a Rock and a Hard Place by Aron Ralston
The Burn Journals by Brent Runyon
Che: A Graphic Biography by Spain Rodriguez
Chinese Cinderella: The True Story of an Unwanted Daughter by Adeline Yen Mah

Dark Dreams: The Story of Stephen King by Nancy Whitelaw
The Diary of Ma Yan by Ma Yan
E=Einstein: His Life, His Thought, and His Influence on Our Culture by Donald Goldsmith and Marcia Bartusiak
Einstein: Visionary Scientist by John B. Severance
Ethel and Ernest: A True Story by Raymond Briggs
Firefighterette Gillete: A Firefighter Who Crashed & Burned: A Success Story by Kathy Gillete
Fortune's Bones: The Manumission Requiem by Marilyn Nelson
Hole in My Life by Jack Gantos
Houdini: The Handcuff King by Jason Lutes and Nick Bertozzi
In My Hands: Memories of a Holocaust Rescuer by Irene Gut Opdyke with Jennifer Armstrong
Isadora Duncan: A Graphic Biography by Sabrina Jones
Jack the Ripper by Rick Geary
J. Edgar Hoover: A Graphic Biography by Rick Geary
King of the Mild Frontier by Chris Crutcher
a long way gone by Ishmael Beah
Louis Braille: A Touch of Genius by C. Michael Mellor
Lucky by Alice Seabold
Maus: A Survivor's Tale by Art Spiegelman
The Murder of Abraham Lincoln by Rick Geary
Nat Turner by Kyle Baker
Perfect Example by John Porcellino
Persepolis: The Story of a Childhood by Marjane Satrapi
Phineas Gage: A Gruesome but True Story About Brain Science by John Fleischman
The Radioactive Boy Scout: The True Story of a Boy and His Backyard Nuclear Reactor by Ken Silverstein
Sacagawea Speaks: Beyond the Shining Mountains with Lewis & Clark by Joyce Badgley Hunsaker
The Underdog: How I Survived the World's Most Outlandish Competitions by Joshua Davis
Within Reach: My Everest Story by Mark Pfetzer and Jack Galvin
You Remind Me of You: A Poetry Memoir by Eireann Corrigan
You Want Women to Vote, Lizzie Stanton? by Jean Fritz

4

Crimes

This chapter includes books about stupid criminals, books about juvenile delin-
quents, and books about teens just messing up. It's an opportunity to discuss
morality, laws, why we live by them, what happens when we don't, and the
fairness or unfairness of the criminal justice system.

What is it about crimes and criminals that holds our attention so much? We are fascinated by bank robbers, organized crime, and jewel thefts; the number of crime shows
on television continues to grow. Most mysteries involve a crime making us ask that question: "Who did it?" We pay no attention to the billions of people around the globe who
spend their days obeying the rules. Instead, our news media brings us stories of those
who broke those laws, broke into homes, kidnapped children and murdered their neighbors. Sometimes we cheer when the criminals are brought to justice and sometimes we
cheer when they get away. Bonnie and Clyde, Al Capone, Jesse James, Billy the Kid, Baby
Face Nelson, Lizzie Borden, and Charles Manson are all names that send shivers down
our spines or have us shooting imaginary bullets from our finger guns. Either way, we're
hooked. Criminals are our heroes and our villains, and true crime is our beloved genre.
So, go ahead; indulge that guilty pleasure and use it to hook your teens. From true crime
novels to noble thief stories, this genre will catch the interest of your students and won't
let go.

Book Ideas with Booktalks,
Discussion Questions, and Project Ideas

They Broke the Law — You be the Judge
by Thomas A. Jacobs

How would you punish these teens?

- Adam, 15, is overheard describing the best way to kill all of the people in his
  school he doesn't like.
- Adelina, 13, is in trouble for robbing and assaulting another girl.
- Andrew, 17, is accused of assaulting his own brother.

- Brandon, 14, broke into a house.
- Brianne, 17, stole a car and a credit card.
- Charles, 16, is caught possessing cocaine and a gun.
- Joshua, 15, is in trouble for skipping school.
- Natalie, 14, gets caught with beer at a party.
- Samantha, 14, doesn't pay her cab fare.
- Tanya, 14, steals a pregnancy test kit from a drug store.

In *They Broke the Law* you get to read about the crime and then you decide how these teens should be punished. Are the real punishments too harsh or too soft?

DISCUSSION QUESTIONS

They Broke the Law is a very interactive book. For each case, Jacobs provides questions for discussion on the possible sentences as well as questions to respond to the judge's decisions. There are also questions at the end of the book in the section "Closing Arguments" that stimulate general discussion over the cases as a whole. Please see the questions in *They Broke the Law* for discussion.

PROJECT: ROLE-PLAYING

They Broke the Law provides a detailed suggestion for role-playing each of the cases. These role-plays require at least two teens—one to be the judge and one to be the teen. Other teens may also play the parts of parents, family members or victims if you prefer to use larger groups. For detailed instructions on role-playing these cases, read the "Using Role-Plays" section of *They Broke the Law*.

In Defiance of Hitler
by Carla Killough McClafferty

Face the left side of the room: He grew up as a spoiled only child. His father was a stockbroker and his mother was emotionally unstable and suffered many nervous breakdowns. He was very intelligent and was considered somewhat of a know-it-all. Expelled and reaccepted into Harvard, he was also a bit of a troublemaker. And this man, Varian Fry, would be the one chosen.

Face the right side of the room: There were 200 people, both Jews and non–Jews, on the initial list ranging anywhere from artists to sculptors, biochemists to harpsichordists, and playwrights to the man who wrote the true but critical biography of Hitler. These were the people the Emergency Rescue Committee deemed worthy of rescuing. Varian Fry was the one chosen to rescue them from the Nazis.

Face the entire room: Mr. Fry bought a plane ticket to France for a month, to assess the situation and hopefully get started. Upon arrival he soon discovered that the situation was far worse than America knew and he could no longer simply focus on rescuing the refugees on his now seemingly short list. After more than a year of rescuing over 2,000 refugees, he was forced to leave by the law enforcement and the American Embassy.

Stupid criminals, daring escapades and rebellious heroics appeal to teens and provide an easy starting point for discussion.

There is a time and place to defy the odds, to stand for something — even if it is considered a crime.

Educators and Librarians, please take time to review the back of the book. It contains many useful resources that may add value to your booktalk including further reading, Web sites, and source notes.

Discussion Questions

1. What did you think of the way the book portrayed Varian Fry before he went to France for the Emergency Rescue Committee? Did it change while he was in France?

2. If you had to choose people to help you with a dangerous mission, such as saving Jewish refugees from the Nazis, how would you decide who to trust?
3. Why do you think the American Embassy wanted him to leave?
4. In the chapter "Expelled," Varian has a conversation with de Rodellec du Porzic. What is de Rodellec du Porzic's perspective on the outdated notion of human rights?
5. What does de Rodellec du Porzic think is a more reasonable relationship between society and the individual? Do you agree or disagree? Why?
6. Give three reasons why you think it was difficult for Varian Fry to assimilate back into American culture.
7. Define the word "vigilante." Was Varian Fry a vigilante? Why or Why not?

PROJECT: RIGHTEOUS CRIMINAL

In Defiance of Hitler depicts a righteous time to commit a righteous crime. There are other heroes in history that had to commit crimes to do what was ultimately right. Have each student choose a historical figure that went against what was accepted in society to do what was right, such as present scientific information that was accurate or defend the lowly members of society. This is a great opportunity to discuss vigilantes.

Assign each student a 3–5 minute presentation as his chosen historical figure. Encourage creativity (costumes and props)! An interesting twist on this would be to allow students to choose historical figures who broke the law without righteous cause. In this case the student would need to try to see the situation from the lawbreakers perspective, trying to understand the reasoning behind the criminal actions.

True Notebooks
by Mark Salzman

Murder — that's why most of these teens are in Central Juvenile Hall. Murder. Most of them are gangbangers who've been in juvenile hall more than once. Most of them are awaiting sentencing. Most of them are being tried as adults, and most of them will be sent to the adult prison before they turn 18. They are angry, scared, depressed, and they terrify Mark Salzman, an author who agrees to visit a writing class at Central. Plus he's not sure he's qualified to judge poems about AK-47s. But their writing surprises Mark. It's not that their writing is so wonderful. It's that these boys write about their fears, their regrets and their dreams. Mark agrees to start his own writing class at Central and *True Notebooks* is the story of the first years of this class told through the writing of these prisoners. Mostly they write about trying to find a reason to believe in themselves when no one else will, when they lose all hope and are faced with spending the rest of their lives in prison with no chance of freedom.

DISCUSSION QUESTIONS

1. Why does Mark Salzman not want to visit the prison writing class? What do you think of his list of reasons not to visit?
2. What convinces Mark to start teaching a writing class of his own?

3. What do you think of Sister Janet Harris? Do you think she is naive? Do you agree with her tactics with the prisoners?
4. What makes this writing class so difficult for Mark?
5. Why does Mark keep volunteering for the class?
6. Mark only refuses to go to the writing class once. Why? What makes him so angry?
7. Do you sympathize with the teens in Central Juvenile Hall? If you were the judge, would you sentence them to the adult prison or keep them at Central?
8. Do you think the writing class helps these teens? How?
9. What makes it so difficult for these teens to stay out of trouble?

PROJECT: CREATIVE ESSAY

Reading about writing is the perfect time to write. Once your teens have read about these teens in prison, about their lives as gang members and their lives as prisoners, ask your teens to write a creative essay about what they think it would be like to be in prison for life. How would they feel? Would they be scared? Angry? Hopeless? Would they try to escape? What would they do? What would they think?

Voices from the Streets
by S. Beth Atkin

There are the Crips, the Bloods, First Nation, Latin Queens, Boston Red Dragons, TNS. Do you know how old they are? Saroeum was only 14 years old when he joined a gang. Elena was 13 and Brandy was 12. In order for Brandy to join her gang she had to be "beat in." She had to fight six guys and two girls at the same time for three minutes. Elena describes her initiation beating as "walking in." It was still a beating. When she decided to leave the gang she was "walked out." The beating lasted twice as long.

Why would anyone want to join a gang? Elena joined her gang for protection from her abusive boyfriend. Brandy did it to get her mother's attention. Sareoum joined in order to be accepted and loved. He did it to have a family. Despite the violence and the shootings, these teens wanted to belong. When they had no one else to turn to, they turned to a gang and the gang gave them what they needed. Acceptance.

But they got more than they bargained for. Saroeum began robbing homes; sometimes the homeowners were killed during the robbery. Elena attended three funerals in just a few months and became the target of a rival gang member. Melissa, 15 years old, found herself pregnant. Patrick suffered three skull fractures and almost lost his vision in one eye. These are the stories of teens who found themselves in street gangs and their struggles to break out of them.

DISCUSSION QUESTIONS

1. In Brandy's chapter "No One Around," she says, "I missed out on my childhood because of my mom." Do you think this is true?
2. In several of these stories, the teenagers don't want their younger brothers or sisters to be in gangs even though the teens are in them. Why?

3. Why don't these teens turn to their own families?
4. Why is it so difficult to leave these gangs?
5. Out of all of these stories, are there any teens you think will return to a gang? Why?
6. Which teens do you think will stay away from gangs permanently? Why?

PROJECT: DEBATE: PARENTAL FAULT OR TEEN RESPONSIBILITY?

Reading about teens struggling to get out of gangs is a good time to practice debate skills. In *Voices from the Streets* several teens discuss why they joined a gang in the first place, often citing a lack of attention or structure from their families as the reason. Divide your teens in half and ask them to debate this issue. Ask half of your teens to argue that the teens' families are responsible for their induction into gangs, and ask the other half of your teens to argue that the families are not responsible, that the teens are responsible for their own actions. You can either have your teens debate from the arguments based in this book or you can ask your teens to prepare for the debate by researching this topic your library's online databases.

Crime Scene
by Richard Platt

Booktalk Option A: *Before beginning this booktalk, locate the section "Answers in Blood" (or some other story you find particularly interesting).* I'm going to start listing off different jobs within a certain profession. When you think you know what the profession is, raise your hand.

- photographer
- geneticist
- artist
- toxicologist
- dentist
- psychologist
- coroner
- anthropologist
- investigator

Start calling on people who have raised hands until someone guesses forensic science. After it is guessed (or you end up revealing it), jump right into telling the story from "Answers in Blood," then read the information below.

On the timeline of forensic science, the first recorded examination was on Julius Caesar and it revealed that, though there were 23 stab wounds, only one to the chest was fatal. In 1247 a Chinese lawyer and investigator writes a book explaining how to distinguish a suicide, homicide, and natural death. The first dental identification recorded occurred in 1776 by Paul Revere. He recognized General Warren's corpse by the false tooth made from a walrus tusk.

Forensic science has been around for literally thousands of years and has recently become popular through various television shows. *(If you have an interactive audience, this would be a great time to see if they could name a few.)* *Crime Scene* covers every possible step, tool, and occupation within the forensic science profession.

Booktalk Option B: *Before beginning your talk, mark 3–4 stories, such as "The*

Docklands Bomb," "Dingo Attack or Murder?," "Ivan the Terrible," and "Answers in Blood." Read or summarize each story and leave off the ending to each one. If you're interested to know if the dingo really did eat the woman's baby or if you want to know who really bombed Graham's car and left the bloody sheep's head on their fence, take a look inside *Crime Scene.*

Discussion Questions

1. If you had to choose one of the jobs in the book, which would you choose? Why?
2. Discussing and reading about death is difficult for a lot of people. Is it difficult for you? Why or why not?
3. In the section "Dingo Attack or Murder?," how much money did the mother receive after she was released? Do you think that was enough?
4. What is "Computer Forensics"?
5. In the "Breakthroughs in Forensic Science" section in the back of the book, list three things that surprised you?

Project: Forensic Science Career Analysis

Split your class into groups of 2–4. Using the different careers listed in the book, assign each group a different occupation within the forensic science field. Provide each group a posterboard and instruct them to list the duties within that occupation, then, based on any one of the stories from the book, have them describe in detail what someone with their respective occupation would have to do if they had to work the crime scene. Have the students present their different occupations to the class.

Hole in My Life
by Jack Gantos

Author of the Joey Pigza series and over 30 children's and teen books, Jack Gantos wanted to be like all of those great American authors who took off on adventures as young men. He wanted the spice of life on which to live when he became a great author. Off he went into the wild blue yonder; and in an attempt to get back home (and to score $10,000 for college) he agreed to help sail a 60-foot yacht loaded with hashish from the Virgin Islands to New York City, where he and his partners sold the drug until federal agents finally caught up to them. For his part in the conspiracy, the 20-year-old Jack Gantos was sentenced to serve up to six years in prison. But in prison he finally moved from dreaming of becoming a writer to actually writing, and his new found dedication helped him endure the worst experience of his life.

Discussion Questions

1. Have you read the Joey Pigza series? What have you read by Jack Gantos? Are you surprised to learn that Gantos is a convicted criminal?
2. Why did Gantos go to prison?

3. What decisions did Gantos make that lead him to commit his crime? What could he have done differently?
4. Could his parents have made a difference? How do you think they contributed to Jack's decision to get involved in illegal activities?
5. How did going to prison change Jack's life?
6. What was prison like for Jack? How was he afraid? Was he ever happy in prison?
7. Why do you think Gantos writes children's books?
8. What have you learned from Gantos?
9. Why is the title of this book, *Hole in My Life?*

PROJECT: LETTER TO THE AUTHOR

Write a letter to Jack Gantos. What would you say to him? Would you ask him more information about his prison life? Would you ask him questions about how and why he writes books? Would you ask him about his Joey Pigza series? What would you tell Gantos about yourself?

Mysteries Unwrapped
by Susan Sloate

Alcatraz: fortress, prison, Native American occupied territory, museum. The island of Alcatraz has been many things but its most famous use was as a high security prison — the highest security prison in the United States, in fact. This island held the country's most dangerous criminals. Al Capone, Machine Gun Kelly and the Birdman of Alcatraz all stayed within the boundaries of this notorious island. But did you know that the island was once an American fortress to protect its borders against Japan and Russia during California's gold rush years? Did you know that it was a military prison during the Civil War? Did you know that after the high security prison shut down, Sioux Indians claimed the island as their own? Did you know that when Alcatraz was a prison, the prisoners were not allowed to speak? Did you know that several prisoners tried to escape Alcatraz but turned themselves in when they discovered just how cold the water surrounding the island really was? Alcatraz is a tiny, barren, ugly island with a fascinating history, and while you may never visit Alcatraz yourself, you can read about the mysteries of Alcatraz in this book, *Mysteries Unwrapped: The Secrets of Alcatraz.*

DISCUSSION QUESTIONS

1. Why is the island named Alcatraz? Who named it?
2. How did the United States first use the island? How successful was this first use of Alcatraz?
3. How did the island become a high security prison?
4. What were some of the strictest rules for the prisoners?
5. What was life like on the island for the employees' children?
6. Did any prisoners ever successfully escape from Alcatraz?
7. Why did Native Americans occupy Alcatraz?
8. How is Alcatraz used today?

PROJECT: ALCATRAZ HEADLINE TIMELINE

Ask your teens to search for newspaper and magazine headlines featuring Alcatraz using online databases or even the Virtual Alcatraz Museum at http://www.nps.gov/history/museum/exhibits/alca/overview.html. Find as many headlines as you can, then ask your students to cut and paste these headlines onto a poster board as a timeline. Does the attitude in these headlines change over time? Can your students see the various uses for Alcatraz hidden in these headlines? How far back can your teens find news headlines?

Outlaws, Mobsters, and Murderers
by Diana Claitor

As expected with a book on criminals, this book describes some gruesome tales and there are a few photographs that show unsettling scenes. Please take the age and maturity of your students into consideration before deciding to incorporate this book into your booktalks.

There have been scandals in baseball for a long time. Can anyone name any? In 1919 a whole team decided to lose the World Series for extra cash.

Crime has been around throughout history and this book, *Outlaws, Mobsters, and Murderers*, discusses some of the major criminals, their crimes, and the outcomes of their cases. Can you name some famous criminals throughout history? *Allow students to answer, and if the criminal they name can be found in the book, be sure to tell them.*

This book is filled with some of the most gruesome and scary stories—from The Big Clown to Jesse James, James Earl Ray to Jack the Ripper. And justice is always served.

DISCUSSION QUESTIONS

1. List two of the criminals you read about.
2. Were there any examples in which you did not think the punishment fit the crime?
3. What makes stories like Diane Downs or Charles Manson so creepy?
4. In the story "A Mother's Love," what do you think of Ma Barker?
5. What do you think leads people to be criminals?
6. Why do you think people are so interested in crimes and criminals?
7. Do you think there will ever be a society that does not have crime? Explain your answer.

PROJECT: A WORLD WITH NO CRIME

If you have a large group, split it into groups of no more than 5. Instruct the teens to brainstorm different theories on how to create a society that does not have any crime. More laws? If so, what kind? A specific government system? Provide the students at least 20–30 minutes to discuss their ideas and then bring the class back together. Allow the different groups to discuss their ideas for the class and why they think they would or wouldn't work. This is not an official speech but an opportunity for students to think critically about their culture and their world. If it's appropriate, allow the rest of your class to question various theories provided by the groups.

More Great Books

The Beast of Chicago: An Account of the Life and Crimes of Herman W. Mudgett by Rick Geary
Crime Scene: The Ultimate Guide to Forensic Science by Richard Platt
The Fatal Bullet: The Assassination of President James A. Garfield by Rick Geary
Getting Away with Murder: The True Story of the Emmett Till Case by Chris Crowe
Gut-Eating Bugs: Maggots Reveal the Time of Death! by Danielle Denega
Hole in My Life by Jack Gantos
In Defiance of Hitler: The Secret Mission of Varian Fry by Carla Killough McClafferty
Killer at Large: Criminal Profilers and the Cases They Solve! by D. B. Beres
Killer Wallpaper: True Cases of Deadly Poisonings by Anna Prokos
The Murder of Abraham Lincoln by Rick Geary
Mysteries Unwrapped: The Secrets of Alcatraz by Susan Sloate
Outlaws, Mobsters, and Murderers: The Villains — The Deeds by Diana Claitor
People's History: Locked Up: A History of the U. S. Prison System by Laura B. Edge
The Radioactive Boy Scout: The True Story of a Boy and His Backyard Nuclear Reactor by Ken Silverstein
The Saga of the Bloody Benders by Rick Geary
Spyology by Spencer Blake and Dugald A. Steer
The Stupid Crook Book by Leland Gregory
Teens Take It To Court: Young People Who Challenged the Law and Changed Your Life by Thomas A. Jacobs
They Broke the Law — You Be the Judge: True Cases of Teen Crime by Thomas A. Jacobs
Thieves!: Ten Stories of Surprising Heists, Comical Capers and Daring Escapades by Andreas Schroeder
Toe Tagged: True Stories from the Morgue by Jaime Joyce
True Notebooks: A Writer's Year at Juvenile Hall by Mark Salzman
Voices from the Streets: Young Former Gang Members Tell Their Stories by S. Beth Atkin
When Objects Talk by Mark P. Friedlander Jr. and Terry M. Phillips

5

Food and Crafts

Manga cookbooks, food as art, and even the history of candy — we cover it all.
And lest you (or your teens) think crafts are for babies and old ladies, we've
got some rockin' crafts that will get your most reluctant teens interested!

If you are not a crafter or chef, you may not think this chapter is for you but food
and craft books traverse academic disciplines and they are just plain fun. Many international cookbooks can be used in a country studies lesson. There is a wide range of books
to support your school's interior design or home economics classes. You can find nature
or experiment-focused craft and food books to support your science curriculum. Even
your shop class can find craft books to spark the imaginations of your students and his-
tory-of-food books provide a unique view of past cultures. Whether you're a teacher
looking for an idea to get your class out of a rut, a school librarian trying to bring attention
to an underused library section, or a public librarian needing to spice up a discussion
group or event, try out a few of these books with your teens. You'll see the spark of curiosity brighten your students' interest and attention.

Book Ideas with Booktalks, Discussion Questions, and Project Ideas

Change Your Room
by Jane Bull

Anyone totally bored with your bedroom? Wish you could make a cool bedroom
your way? The library has several teen books on decorating your bedroom including this
one called *Change Your Room*, which may just be the most colorful book I've ever seen.

This book covers ways to decorate and organize your closet; how to make creative
storage and organize your stuff; how to paint your walls, dressers and everything else in
your room; ideas for painting your boring chairs; even ways to decorate your doorknob
and how to decorate all of the details like cool picture frames.

While mentioning the different decorating ideas that this book covers, we also show the
teens the color pictures in the book so teens can get an idea of just how colorful the decoration
ideas are.

1. What is the difference between harmonious colors and complementary colors?
2. Which of the five hue or shade ideas do you like the most (harmonious hues, silver spectrum, wild contrasts, sunshine shades or comic colors)? Is there a design that you don't like?
3. Which of the organization and storage ideas could you use most?
4. If you could decorate your own doorknob, how would you decorate it?
5. Why do you think so many people enjoy decorating their bedrooms? Why is your bedroom so important to you?

PROJECT: ROOM DECORATIONS

Projects are easy with this book. Just choose a craft idea from the book, gather your supplies and let your teens decorate. A few ideas from *Change Your Room* include:

- picture frames: start with a basic cardboard frame but add toys, buttons, glitter, cloth, jewels and any number of other decorative items
- lamp shades: decorated with paint, jewels, toys or cutouts
- paper pots: paper-mache pots that can be decorated any number of ways
- handy hangers: make cardboard hangers for your clothes using magazine cutouts to create funky faces

The Cookbook Set

Cookbooks are not a traditional discussion group choice. However, there are several cookbooks written specifically for teens and these books should not be overlooked. Rather than trying to create a discussion group session using a single cookbook, try hosting a cookbook review discussion and let your teens choose a cookbook from your collection. To introduce this topic, show the teens several cookbook options, including meals featured in these books. A few choices include:

Clueless in the Kitchen
by Evelyn Raab

In *Clueless* you'll find recipes for a breakfast pizza for 1, x-ray vision soup, turkey carcass soup, mom's dreaded meat loaf, fried rice with whatever, vegetarian cowboy beans, antidepressant brownies, idiotproof 1-bowl chocolate cake, and a cup of coffee. This cookbook also tells you how to stock a kitchen, what cooking tools and pantry items you'll need. This book tells you the basics like frying an egg, cutting vegetables, and planning meals. If you truly are clueless when it comes to the kitchen, you might give this cookbook a try.

Cooking Up a Storm
by Sam Stern

British teen, Sam Stern, has his own series of cookbooks. So, if you're into all things British or even if you just like mimicking the British accent, see what you think of Sam's recipes. He offers ideas for cooking like his zucchini and cream cheese sandwich, peanut butter and jelly sandwich, chocolate chipperdoodles, scones, gazpacho, flash omelettes, camping pasta, and comfort mash. Sam's books are very colorful, full of easy cooking tips and lots of pictures of Sam.

The Manga Cookbook
by The Manga University Culinary Institute

This one is for the Manga fans. This book uses mostly visuals (Manga style) to show you how to cut, cook and eat these recipes. *The Manga Cookbook* also shows you how to set the traditional Japanese table, the *ichijyuusansai*, consisting of soup, three side dishes and rice. You'll find recipes like, usagi ringo (rabbit shaped apple slices), tamago tomodachi (egg buddies), tako sausage, Naruto rolls, rice burgers, soboro bento, miso soup, sushi rice, California rolls, and 3-color dango (sweet dumplings).

DISCUSSION QUESTIONS

1. How easy are the recipes to make? Do the recipes call for everyday familiar ingredients or ingredients that are difficult to find in a grocery store?
2. How complete are the recipes? Do the instructions tell you how long it will take to make the item? Are the nutritional facts listed? Are the instructions easy or difficult to follow? Does the author use language you know or does she use professional culinary vocabulary?
3. How is the cookbook organized? Is it easy to find recipes? Does it include extra information such as necessary pantry items and cooking tools? Does it offer lessons for basic cooking to help get you started or does the cookbook assume that you are already a professional in the kitchen?
4. Are the recipes tasty? Or do they sound disgusting?
5. What do you think of the voice of the author? If the cookbook is intended for teenagers, does the author write in a language that you can relate to? Is the language forced? Does the author use too many slang words or do they make no effort to write to teens at all?
6. If you are preparing a dinner party for friends, which recipes would you use from your cookbook?

PROJECT: POTLUCK SNACKS

Let your teens prepare at home a recipe from the cookbook of their choosing and bring it in for everyone to try. Have plates, napkins, cutlery, and drinks on hand for the group. Also ask your teens to clearly label their food dish and list all of the ingredients used in the recipe so teens can steer clear of any food allergies they may have. You may also ask your teens to talk about their food dish. Why did they choose and prepare this particular dish? How long did it take to prepare (no extra points for slaving away in the kitchen all day!)? How difficult or simple was it to make? How healthy or indulgent is this recipe? How easy was it to follow the instructions in the recipe? Be sure to leave enough time to let your teens enjoy the food!

Play with Your Food
by Joost Elffers

How many times have we heard our parents yell, "Don't play with your food!"? A lot, right? But we've all seen the funny face in the fruit or the contorted body in the vegetable. We've had fun molding those mashed potatoes into a tower, right? *Show teens the picture of the camel making a face and the pepper making the same face beneath it.* In fact, we love giving life to inanimate objects, turning clouds into pictures, boulders into giants. *Show the picture of* The Vegetable Gardener *by Guiseppe Arcimboldo.* What do you see in this picture? *Most likely they'll state the obvious, that they see a bowl of vegetables. Next, show them the picture upside down.* Now what do you see? *If they're looking at all closely they'll see the gardener!* The author of this book loves turning fruit and veggies into all kinds of little critters. Can you guess what they are? *Show teens pictures from the section* "Vegetable Zoo: A Garden Parade" *and ask the teens to tell you what the fruits and vegetables have been transformed into. A few suggestions include the pineapple turtle; the pepper seal; squirrel and rabbit; the pear mice and teddy bear; the lemon pigs; the okra, peanut, cherry insects; the artichoke wolf; and the cucumber alligators.*

DISCUSSION QUESTIONS

1. According to the author, Joost Elffers, "It seems inherent in human nature to seek correspondences between ourselves and the creatures or objects that surround us." What does he mean?
2. Elffers also says, "*Looking* and *seeing* can be two entirely different things." What distinction is he making between these two words?
3. What is the difference between the terms "personification" and "anthropomorphism"? Which term more correctly defines the transformations found in *Play with Your Food*?
4. Take a close look at the paintings *The Vegetable Gardener* and *Vertemus (Emperor Rudolf II)* by Guiseppe Arcimboldo. What do these paintings depict?
5. Do you think the *Vegetable Zoo: A Garden Parade* is art?
6. According to Elffers, "Eyes can be the indicators of emotion, personality and mood." Look through the *Vegetable Zoo.* What types of eyes convey anger, fear, joy and sadness?
7. Can ears on these vegetables convey emotion as well?

PROJECT: FOOD AS ART

For supplies you'll need a wide variety of fruits and vegetables. To prepare, visit your local grocery store or farmers' market and grab anything from the vegetable section that has animal transforming potential—funny looking yams, oddly shaped brussel sprouts, mutated strawberries, anything will work. You'll also want to have on hand various beans, seeds, and small fruits like grapes or olives. Depending on how much you trust your teens and on the regulations and polices set by your institution, you may also have a knife or 2. If you can't use knives, try toothpicks or scissors as an alternative.

Let your teens view all of the fruits and vegetables in their natural states and ask them if they see any humanizing aspects in the food. Do any of the veggies look like animals? Could they be turned into something else? Some teens may be determined to turn a vegetable into their pet, but the key with this project is to start with the vegetables and fruits and let these items decide what they should be. Once you have discussed the potential in each piece of food with your teens, let them pick a piece and start the transformation.

You may want to display these pieces of art for the rest of the school or library to view, but don't keep them on display for too long as they'll start decaying and attracting insects!

Nature's Art Box
by Laura C. Martin

Are you tired of the same old craft projects with popsicle sticks, paper bags and yarn? *Nature's Art Box* offers a slew of craft ideas that use only items that you can pick up in your backyard (or your next trip to the beach). You can make a chess set out of pine cones, corn husks, seashells, stones and fungus. You can create miniature horses, porcupines and snails out of twigs, pine cones and moss or make an okra pod canoe or a variety of Christmas ornaments. You can make a necklace out of cantaloupe seeds or design your own miniature zen garden and sand paintings. You can even learn to make dyes using egg whites and beeswax, make your own ink using vinegar and tea, or design your own paint colors using flowers and soil.

DISCUSSION QUESTIONS

1. What is a craft? What does "to craft" mean?
2. Read the section called "Cave Paintings." What would you have done if you had discovered the cave?
3. What does it mean to "look with the eyes of an artist"?
4. Why does the author include a section called "Nature Skills"? What are the dangers of searching for your own craft supplies outdoors?
5. Do you think this book is a true nature craft book? How often do you need supplies that are not found in nature? Only a little? More than you would like? Does the book offer alternatives for store bought supplies?
6. Which craft idea would you most like to try? Are there any that do not interest you at all? Why?

PROJECT: PICK A CRAFT!

There are so many crafts to choose from in this book! One way to make this more than just a set of crafts is to take your group of teens out into the wild to find their own craft materials. Follow the rules in the book about which items that are best found out in nature (pine cones and flowers) and which items are better bought in a craft store (such as moss). You will want to have your store-bought items on hand before your nature walk. Ask your teens to pick out a few potential crafts to try before the walk and to review what supplies they will need. This way they will know what they are looking for during the walk. Also, if you are taking a walk in a public park or on private property, make sure you follow all of the rules for picking flowers and disturbing natural areas.

ManCrafts
by the editors of *Popular Mechanics*

It seems as though there are oodles of craft books out there for girls—books about scrapbooking with ribbons, the best way to cut out hearts, and how to make your own tutu. Finally, there is a book about how to do "manly" crafts. This book is filled with everything! Not only does it describe crafts to do with axes, but you can read how to pick out a good ax. Did you even know there was

Don't be frightened by power tools! They are for the amateur and professional — and are useful for nearly all projects in *ManCrafts*.

such thing as a good ax and a bad ax? You can learn to hammer tin, build furniture, work with leather and even draw cartoons or bind books.

Who in here can figure out how to play pretty much any video-game? Who in here can build a coffee table? The skills in this book will teach you to do things that can be used in the real world, and they don't involve a monitor and keyboard. Oh, and just because you're not a dude, that doesn't mean you can't learn these skills.

DISCUSSION QUESTIONS

1. What is a coping saw? List three things you could create by using it.
2. List two of the tools needed when working with leather and describe their function.
3. If you learned how to bind books, what books would you want create new covers for?
4. What is block printing and what is it used for?
5. Where would you find tin for the tin-can crafts?
6. Braiding and knotting sound really feminine — what sort of masculine things could you make using this skill?

PROJECT: PICK A CRAFT! (THE MANLY APPROACH)

Just like the other craft books, what better project to suggest than one included in these books. Sometimes the jump between reading about a project or craft and actually doing it seems insurmountable, particularly if students have not had any experience doing this sort of work. Completing a project with peers (preferably one not involving an ax — that one more than likely should be done at home with adult supervision) will hopefully empower the students to try some other projects at home. Also, testing a project or two in class will only demonstrate the cool factor of the crafts and the book.

Chow
by Janice Wong

For most people food has a lot of memories attached to it. *At this point provide your class a memory from your own life that makes you think of a certain food. For example, Tara's aunt used to make tapioca pudding and let her eat it out of goblets — as a child, Tara always felt so special eating pudding out of an "adult" glass.* I'm going to say a certain kind of food and when you hear the food, if it brings a memory to mind, raise your hand and share it. *I have listed a few examples of foods you can ask below but, based on your location, try to pick foods you think are most common for family dinners or holidays.*

- macaroni and cheese
- chocolate chip cookies
- roasted turkey
- grits
- cupcakes

Chow is book full of memories and full of recipes. The author writes about her family of Chinese heritage, who lived in Canada and opened two Chinese restaurants. Her father loved cooking and her mother was quite the baker; between the two of them, they compiled and created many delicious and easy recipes. Each recipe includes at least one memory.

DISCUSSION QUESTIONS

1. What is the setting of most of the author's memories?
2. What was very peculiar about Dennis Wong's birth?
3. What is a rooster husband?
4. What was the Chinese Exclusion Act and why do you think it existed?
5. Why did Wong's father open a restaurant instead of going into chemistry?
6. Why was it difficult for people of Asian descent to find a job in the West?
7. In your family do you have any foods that make you think of past memories?

PROJECT: MEMORY COOKBOOK

Have students make a list of least five foods to which they have fond memories attached. Instruct them to take the list home and retrieve the recipes. With recipes in hand, each student will handwrite a small cookbook that includes the recipes and at least a paragraph with each one explaining their respective memories. Each teen will create a cover, title their book, and bind it with whatever supplies you have available (yarn, staples, tape). For extra points have students bring in a sample of one of their memory-filled dishes to share with the class. Spend this day sampling dishes and allowing students look at the other cookbooks and share their memories.

Sweet!
by Ann Love and Jane Drake

Does anyone know what the first candy was made from? The answer is honey! Since prehistoric times people have been eating honey to sooth their sweet cravings. At first they would climb up tree trunks, swat stinging bees and grab chunks of honeycomb. That's a lot to go through for a sweet tooth! Do you know how bees make honey? A bee collects nectar from flowers, stores it in a special stomach, throws it back up into the mouth of another bee. That bee then throws it up into the honeycomb cell where other bees fan it with their wings. Yum! Today we make most of our candy with sugar from the sugarcane plant and corn syrup from corn plants, but we still love honey.

Do you know how gummy bears are made? They are thickened using gelatin. Gelatin is actually made from animal skins, ligaments and bones! Yum! And did you also know that one of the first brands of chewing gum was actually made from chicle, which was originally a substitute for rubber? Yum! Saltwater taffy was created when a taffy shop was flooded with seawater during a storm! Fudge was born when someone tried to make caramel and messed up. "Fudge" was a popular slang word for "foolishness." From penny candy to jelly beans to candy canes and lollipops, *Sweet!* reveals how candy was discovered, invented and carefully turned into the sweet deliciousness we love today.

DISCUSSION QUESTIONS

1. According to the candy timeline, what is the first evidence of humans eating candy?
2. Why are we programmed to love candy so much?
3. Read the section "Sweet Country." What are all of the different candies that are popular around the world? Are there any that do not sound appetizing to you? Are there any that you would like to try?
4. What did humans do to get honey before they learned how to keep bees in bee boxes?
5. How did people first use gummy candies?
6. What are medieval subtleties?
7. How was chocolate first consumed?
8. Which is better for you: milk chocolate or dark chocolate? Why?

PROJECT: CANDY FROM AROUND THE WORLD

There are two ways to complete this project. The first method is to purchase candy from an international store or section of your local grocery store. Many grocers are now offering popular candies from Asia and Mexico. Get a varied selection and then let your teens taste these international treats. Be sure to have information on each type of candy. Where is this candy popular? Where was it made? How is it made? What are the ingredients? Ask teens what they think of each piece. Is it sweeter than the candy they are used to? Is it fruity or bitter?

The second method is to let your teens make a popular candy from different countries. Take a look at the "Sweet Country" section of *Sweet!* and assign the different candies to your teens. Let your teens find recipes online for these candies as well as some background information about the candy. As your teens hand out their homemade candy, let your teens tell the group about the candy.

Craft Set

Craft books can be painfully cheesy and have us and our teens cringing as we try to look at the photographs to get ideas. This set will help you throw off the cheesy shackles and encourage teens to tackle crafty projects that actually interest them, not just a way to pass the time!

The Craft Queen's Guide to Hip Knits
by Catherine Tough

If you think knitting is for little old ladies with blue hair, you've got another think coming! This book is filled with 19 real projects that aren't lame; like fingerless mitts so you can use your iPod and have warm hands, lamp shade covers to fix up your room, and a scarf you can't buy at Gap. *Show the photos as you list them.* This book is filled with the instructions from start to finish, and there's not one blue hair in the whole book!

Make It You
by Shannon Mullen

Put your knitting needles down and go to your (or your momma's) sewing machine! If you're tired of the same old clothes that everyone else at school is wearing or your room looking like everyone else's, you seriously need to check out this book. You can make your own raw-edge or reversible belt, bags made out of the material YOU choose, or pillows and blankets. *Again, be sure to show pictures as you list examples.*

99 Ways to Cut, Sew, Trim, & Tie Your
T-Shirt Into Something Special
by Faith and Justina Blakeney, Anka Livakovic, and Ellen Schultz

I've shown you ways you can decorate your room on the cheap and even make your own clothes, but this next book is the cheapest (and coolest!) of all. If you're like me, you have a ton of T-shirts—maybe from summer camp, a sports team you were on, or even a club you're involved in. And your tees are not exactly original, everyone has the same ones. With this book you can choose from 99 different ways to make your shirt rockin' and totally original. While some T-shirts call for sewing, a lot of them only require scissors and the ability to tie knots. You'll actually want to wear that T-shirt from the bake sale you did last year!

DISCUSSION QUESTIONS

1. Why learn to make your own stuff when you can just buy it at the store?
2. Is it OK not to follow the rules in the book? (*The answer to the question is always YES! Creativity comes from trying new things!*)
3. What kinds of crafts do you like to do?

4. What projects in the books do you plan to try?
5. Instead of buying supplies at a craft store, where are some other places you can find things like fabric or T-shirts for cheap? *(Thrift stores and garage sales are great places to find fabric and T-shirts!)*

PROJECT: INSTRUCTION MANUAL AND SPEECH

Instruct students to decide on a skill they already know how to do and have them create an instruction manual, with at least three photos! Skills can range anywhere from whittling to cooking, juggling to putting on make-up — just make sure to approve their skill before they begin working. After completing the instruction manual, they will need to prepare a "how-to" speech that lasts 5–7 minutes in which they directly show the class how to do the skill. Some skills will have limitations, such as cooking, but work around those as much as possible!

More Great Books

The Art of the Catapult: Build Greek Ballistae, Roman Onagers, English Trebuchets, and More Ancient Artillery by William Gurstelle
Change Your Room by Jane Bull
Chow: From China to Canada: Memories of Food and Family by Janice Wong
Clueless in the Kitchen: A Cookbook for Teens by Evelyn Raab
Cooking up a Storm: The Teen Survival Cookbook by Sam and Susan Stern
The Craft Queen's Guide to Hip Knits by Catherine Tough
Decorate Yourself by Tom Andrich
Entertaining Edibles: 50 Fun Food Sculptures for All Occasions by Sidney Escowitz
Everything I Ate: A Year in the Life of My Mouth by Tucker Shaw
Fueling the Teen Machine by Ellen L. Shanley and Colleen A. Thompson
Gastroanomalies: Questionable Culinary Creations from the Golden Age of American Cookery by James Lileks
Ghoulish Goodies by Sharon Bowers
Girlosophy: Real Girls Eat by Anthea Paul
Gross-Out Cakes: The Kitty Litter Cake and Other Classics by Kathleen Barlow and Britney Schetselaar
Insatiable: The Compelling Story of Four Teens, Food and Its Power by Eve Eliot
Make it You: Sew Hip by Shannon Mullen
Mancrafts: Leather Tooling, Fly Tying, Ax Whittling and Other Cool Things To Do by the editors of Popular Mechanics
The Manga Cookbook by The Manga University Culinary Institute
Nature's Art Box by Laura C. Martin
99 Ways to Cut, Sew, Trim & Tie Your T-Shirt Into Something Special by Faith and Justina Blakeney, Anka Livakovic, and Ellen Schultz
Origami with Dollar Bills by Duy Nguyen
Planet Yumthing: Do-It-Yourself by Ela Jaynes and Darren Greenblatt
Play with Your Food by Joost Elffers
Real Food Real Fast: Quick & Healthy Eating from the British Teen Cooking Sensation by Sam and Susan Stern
Show Off: How To Do Absolutely Everything One Step at a Time by Sarah Hines Stephens and Bethany Mann
Slumber Parties: Things to Make and Do by Jennifer Traig
Student's Go Vegan Cookbook by Carole Raymond

Sweet! The Delicious Story of Candy by Ann Love and Jane Drake
Teens Cook Dessert by Megan, Jill and Judi Carle
Teens Cook: How to Cook What You Want to Eat by Megan, Jill, and Judi Carle
The Teen's Vegetarian Cookbook by Judy Krizmanic
What the World Eats by Faith D'Alusio and Peter Menzel
While You're Waiting for the Food to Come by Eric Muller

6

Art

Photography, graffiti, the art of the skateboard, graphic art, high art, popular art, art by teens, art by old people, and art by dead people!

Teen art books are reminiscent of all of those picture books we poured over when we were just learning to read. Do you remember reading the words with the help of your mother, father, or teacher? We would read the words on the page but then scour over the pictures pointing out the portrayed actions and checking to make sure that the characters were indeed doing what the words proclaimed. We spent more time analyzing the artwork than we did reading the book. If you lead a discussion group, revisiting art books with your teens provides a break from the monthly routine of reading and discussion and lets your teens rekindle that innate instinct to analyze the images they see. In addition to the break from routine for your teens, booktalking art books gives you a break from preparing and memorizing that traditional talk. If you intersperse an art book or two into your talks, you provide yourself and your teens with a few minutes of quiet show and tell as you let your teens see some of the preselected pictures. Whether you are a public librarian or work in a school setting, art books supply fodder for debates, project ideas, and interdisciplinary studies and gives teens a break from the intense focus of reading skills while still developing their critical analysis aptitude.

Book Ideas with Booktalks, Discussion Questions, and Project Ideas

Graffiti Set

Graffiti L.A. and *Graffiti World*
by Steve Grody and by Nicholas Ganz

For this booktalk begin with a short discussion of how your teens define graffiti. Start with the simple question "What is graffiti?" Surely some teens will automatically tell you that graffiti is a crime used by gangs to ruin buildings and public areas. Other teens may tell you that graffiti can be murals or pieces of artwork. Both views are correct. After the short discussion, show your teens pictures from the two books. For these particular books we'll avoid suggesting specific pictures and let you decide which images are best suited to your teens based on age, maturity, and the general views of your community as some images may be considered suggestive.

DISCUSSION QUESTIONS

1. What is the difference between tagging and graffiti art?
2. *Graffiti L.A.* focuses on graffiti found around the Los Angeles area while *Graffiti World* provides images of graffiti from around the globe. Do you see any style differences between the L.A. art and the rest of the world? Or is the graffiti the same?
3. What are the popular views concerning graffiti in the rest of the world? Is it seen as a crime or works of art? Is graffiti considered a delinquent art everywhere?
4. Why is graffiti considered a crime? What rules do taggers break by creating their artwork?
5. What is the difference between graffiti and murals?
6. What is your favorite style of graffiti? Do you prefer the images or the textwork?
7. Who creates graffiti?
8. Where can you find graffiti art?

PROJECT: GRAFFITI AS ART DEBATE

Rather than tackling the cultural ramifications of teaching your teens graffiti art techniques with your principal or library director, let your teens debate whether or not graffiti is art or crime. Divide your teens into two groups and ask them to research their respective stances. If your library has access to the online database *Opposing Viewpoints*, be sure to have your teens access this valuable resource to gather evidence for their arguments. Ask your teens to choose images from *Graffiti L.A.* and *Graffiti World* as evidence as well.

Boards
by Jacob Hoye

Begin this booktalk by asking your teens if any of them enjoy skateboarding. If you don't have any skateboarders in your group, this book may not be the best choice. However, if you know you have several skateboarders, this is a good book to use to connect with them. Some questions to consider asking to begin the booktalk include: Do any of you skateboard? Where do you skate? Do you ever get into trouble for riding where you shouldn't? Why do you think skateboarders get into trouble for riding in public places so much? What does your skateboard look like? Is it just plain or have you decorated it? Why?

This book is called *Boards: The Art & Design of the Skateboard* and it shows us some of the most popular and one-of-a-kind designs for skateboards. *At this point, go ahead and show the group some of your favorite designs from the book. Again, for this book we'll avoid suggesting specific pictures and let you decide which images are best suited to your teens based on age, maturity and the general views of your community, as some images may be considered suggestive.*

Discussion Questions

1. To what other art media are skateboards compared? Do you think this comparison is correct? What are the differences between skateboards as art and these other media as art?
2. According to Marc Johnson what are the two primary intentions for creating deck artwork?
3. As far as artist Sean Cliver is concerned, "You can't go wrong with scantily-clad chicks—cheapest marketing tool in the book." True? Untrue? Do his boards draw your attention or prompt you to move on to another artist?
4. 5boro artists say, "We are influenced by motion and its cause." What do they mean? Why would skateboard artists be influenced by motion? What is the "cause" of skateboard motion?
5. Tony Larson calls the board a disposable object. If so, why do these artists spend so much time creating their deck art?
6. Which skateboard designs draw you in? Which skateboard would you choose for yourself?

Project Option 1: Show and Tell

Ask any of your teens who have skateboards if they would show off their designs to the rest of the group. Most likely, many of your skateboarding teens will not have purchased skateboards with designs on them. Instead, they will have created their own designs using stickers, markers, etc. Why did they design their skateboard art as they did? Why did they choose those images or words?

Project Option 2: Design Your Own

If you do not have many skateboarding teens in your group, let your teens design their own skateboard decks. For supplies you'll need several pieces of cardboard or white posterboard cut into life-sized skateboard shapes. You'll also need glue, construction paper, scissors, markers, paint and possibly even discarded magazines if your teens like to cut out pictures to use in collages. Begin with a discussion about skateboard art and how each skateboard is a representation of the skateboarder (of each teen, in other words) and how skateboard art is often inspired by movement, freedom and even rebellion against authority. Then, let your teens loose to design their own skateboard deck.

Custom Kicks
by Kim Smits

Many teens enjoy drawing on their shoes, jeans and other articles of clothing. They want to make it their own, personalize it. For this booktalk ask your teens if they have ever created art on their clothes. Then show your teens pictures of your favorite custom kicks from the book. For each shoe design that you show, be sure to describe the shoe as well. What does the artist say about the design? How did they make it?

Discussion Questions

1. Who are the artists who design these shoes? Why do they prefer to create art on a shoe?
2. Have you ever decorated your shoes? Why did you do so?
3. What is the most common type of customized shoe in *Custom Kicks*? Why do you think this is?
4. What type of shoe do you think would be the most challenging to customize?
5. Which custom designs do you like?
6. Do you think customizing shoes is art?

Project: Create Your Own Custom Kicks

Ask your teens to bring in an old pair of shoes. These could be shoes that are in their closet that they never wear any more or a pair of shoes purchased at a thrift store. Stress to your teens that they shouldn't spend a lot of money purchasing shoes if they are buying a pair. The shoes can be tennis shoes, dress shoes, high heels, clogs, wellies, snow boots, or any other type of shoe. Also ask your teens to bring in design ideas. What do they want their new shoes to look like? How do they want to design them? Before your teens begin work on their real shoes, have them create one-dimensional posterboard cutouts of the shoes and let them experiment with these templates first. Once your teens think they have their design planned out and ready, let them design their own custom kicks. A list of supplies is provided with the book.

The Guerilla Art Kit
by Keri Smith

Have you ever seen a seemingly random quote printed in chalk on the sidewalk? Have you ever seen a sticker on a public mirror or a Post-it note on a wall? Have you ever seen a tree decorated by someone unknown? Have you ever left your mark on a piece of public property? You are not alone. This book, *The Guerilla Art Kit,* will show you how to create temporary surprise pieces of art — art that will brighten up a stranger's day, encourage fellow students, make passersby laugh or think or get angry. What do you want to tell the world? What do you have to say? It doesn't have to be important. It doesn't have to be unique. It doesn't have to be political or even honest. But if you have something to tell the world, think about transforming your words into guerilla art. You never know who will see it, read it and love it.

Discussion Questions

1. What is guerilla art?
2. Have you ever seen a piece of guerilla art in public? Did it take you by surprise? Did you point it out to anyone else? Did you recognize it as art at the time?
3. What is the point of guerilla art? Does guerilla art come with a message?
4. Why create artwork that is temporary?

5. What is guerilla art etiquette? Why is this etiquette important?
6. Which art exercise do you want to try first?

PROJECT: YOUR OWN GUERILLA ART

For this project discuss with your teens which of the projects they want to try. It is important to have this discussion to make sure that your teens will not get into trouble with the library or school when implementing their art. Also discuss how the artwork should be carried out. What preparation do they need to complete beforehand? When should they install their artwork? How will they know that their artwork has made a difference? Once all of the particulars have been worked out, let your teens begin their own guerilla art project! This project can be done as an entire group, in small groups or as individuals.

Lewis & Clark Revisited
by Greg MacGregor

Who can tell me why Lewis and Clark are significant to American history? *Hopefully, you will have some students raise their hands, however be prepared to answer your own question in case they don't.* The photographs in this book were taken at the beginning of the 21st century to follow an adventure taken at the beginning of the 19th century, nearly 200 years prior when the United States of America was a little over 25 years old. What aspects do you think have changed throughout the United States?

Read entry number 10, 15, and 53. If you happen to live near any of the entries, read those instead! Also, this is a great book to pair with the "Sacagawea Speaks" *booktalk in the* "Biography and Memoirs chapter."

DISCUSSION QUESTIONS

1. Explain why you think Lewis and Clark were so important to American History?
2. If Lewis and Clark were able to take the trip today, what do you think would surprise them the most?
3. Who was the one man who died on their expedition?
4. What did the adventurers primarily eat?
5. What was the name of the Indian woman that accompanied them?
6. What was your favorite photograph? Why?

PROJECT: PHOTOGRAPH YOUR ADVENTURE

This is a great project to do on the next field trip your group or class takes. Take as many pictures on your next field trip as you have students in the class. When you return to class, print the pictures off and assign one picture to each student. Instruct the students to write a journal entry based on the picture and their memories of the trip. Compile the pictures and journal entries together in a book.

Variation: This variation on the project is a great way to show how one's perception of a shared experience can drastically change from another. In this project, take enough pictures for five students to be assigned to one picture. Instruct the students, without discussing it with others, to journal their experience correlated with the picture. After all of the journal entries are submitted, combine them in a book with the pictures and read them aloud.

Andy Warhol
by Susan Goldman Rubin

Can anyone tell me who Andy Warhol is? What is he famous for? What did he paint? Have you ever seen one of Andy's paintings? Everyday as a child, Andy would color with crayons and a piece of paper. His mother would offer a prize to him and his older brothers for the best picture of the day and Andy always won. Also, everyday Andy would have soup and a sandwich for lunch. Can anyone guess what kind of soup Andy ate everyday? Yes! He had Campbells soup every single day for lunch for 20 years! No wonder he painted the soup cans. Andy didn't want to be an artist when he grew up. He wanted to be a tap dancer and was a huge fan of Shirley Temple. But his natural talent was painting and that's what he did despite flunking art school in college. Andy never did what people wanted him to do. He painted what he wanted to paint and no one could tell him to do things differently. Andy painted what he saw in life and in our culture. He painted his cats. *Show the picture* Lavender Sam. He painted shoes. *Show the picture of Andy's prints for* A la Recherche du Shoe. He painted Campbells soup cans. *Show the picture* "100 Cans." He even painted a paint-by-numbers canvas just to make fun of its lack of originality. *Show the picture* Do It Yourself (Sailboats). Andy painted whatever he wanted and he never worried about whether anyone would actually like it. He just painted.

DISCUSSION QUESTIONS

1. What was one of the major influences for Andy's soup can paintings?
2. Why did Andy fail his college art classes?
3. How did Andy's last name change from Warhola to Warhol?
4. What were Andy's first jobs? How did this influence his fame as a pop artist?
5. Why did Andy paint the *Do It Yourself (Sailboats)* painting?
6. What is pop art?
7. Out of all the artwork featured in this book, which of Andy's painting do you like the best? Why?

PROJECT: POP ART

Ask your teens to find a piece of pop culture and bring it in to the group meeting or class. These pieces could be candy wrappers, food cans from home, clothing with brand names, comic books, shoes, pictures of celebrities, or any other popular items currently in stores. Provide canvas and art supplies for your teens and let them paint their pop culture items.

When creating our own Focus book, we asked our local library's video center and they helped us create a photo shoot. What a unique opportunity for us and the teens!

Focus: Love
by Lark Books

Think of places where you might see hearts in your everyday life. *Allow students to name different ideas. Most of them will probably be really obvious places, like cards at the grocery story or candy. Then show them various places different people have found hearts. Simply go through the book ahead of time and choose some of the most obscure photos (like the hearts found on animals) and show them to the class.*

DISCUSSION QUESTIONS

1. Who took the photographs?
2. What were your favorite pictures?
3. How do you think being a photographer would make you look at the world differently?
4. Do you think some photos were more symbolic than others? Explain.
5. In the author's opinion, what has the heart symbolized?
6. What does the heart shape symbolize to you?

Project: Create your own Focus book

Using a different shape, have students photograph or sketch the various places they find your new shape. This could be done as a class, in groups, or individually. Also, encourage students to set up shots; in the book, a lot of the pictures look like hearts simply because they had the right angle or because they placed two objects together that don't necessarily go together. If you could plan this on your next field trip, it would be a great way to keep them busy during lulls. For the library educator this is a great project to display your teens' artwork and to decorate your teen area!

I'll Tell What I Saw
by Michael Mazur

Has anyone read Dante's *Divine Comedy*? *If students raise their hand, allow them to talk about what they remember it being about.* It is an epic poem written in the early 12th century about the author's trip through three spiritual places: Inferno (Hell), Purgatorio (Purgatory), and Paradiso (Paradise). The illustrator of this book takes specific sections of Dante's *Divine Comedy* and combines it with his original artwork. I'm going to read you a segment from the book and I want you to imagine it your mind.

Read painting Inferno III *70–87*

After reading, allow students to talk about what they imagined. What does the sky look like? What does the river look like? What about the old man in the boat? *Show them the picture.* Does the picture looked how you expected it to look? What is different?

DISCUSSION QUESTIONS

1. What is Dante's *Divine Comedy* about?
2. In the prologue, why do you think one section is black and the other white?
3. What pictures and words resonated with you?
4. Were there any that you pictured differently?
5. What does light primarily symbolize?
6. Compare the *Map of Hell* to the *Plan of Paradise*. How are the colors chosen different? Do they change the way the pictures feel?

PROJECT: ARTISTIC INTERPRETATION OF CLASSICAL LITERATURE

Like the artist has done in this book, encourage your students to do the same. If your class or group is reading the same book, students can come up with their own artistic interpretation of the story or a section of the story — through music, drawing, or playwriting (assuming the piece is not originally a play). Be sure you allow time for your students to perform or present their art. This project can also be done individually, reading their own choice of classic literature and artistically interpreting the work. With this option students will learn more about different works during the presentations.

More Great Books

Andy Warhol: Pop Art Painter by Susan Goldman Rubin

Art Attack: A Short Cultural History of the Avant-Garde by Marc Aronson

Art Fraud Detective: Spot the Difference, Solve the Crime by Anna Nilsen

The Art of Marvel by Lee Stan

Bling: The Hip-Hop Jewelry Book by Reggie Osse and Gabriel Tolliver

Boards: The Art & Design of the Skateboard by Jacob Hoye, ed.

Brush Up Your Shakespeare: An Infectious Tour from the Most Quotable and Famous Words and Phrases from the Bard by Michael Macrone and Tom Lulevitch

Custom Kicks by Kim Smits

Focus: Love: Your World, Your Images by Lark Books

Graffiti L.A.: Street Styles and Art by Steve Grody

Graffiti World: Street Art from Five Continents by Nicholas Ganz

The Guerilla Art Kit: Everything You Need to Put Your Message Out into the World by Keri Smith

I'll Tell What I Saw: Select Translations and Illustrations from the Divine Comedy by Michael Mazur

Imaginary Museum: Poems on Art by Joseph Stanton

I See the Rhythm by Toyomi Igus

Lewis & Clark Revisited: A Photographer's Trail by Greg MacGregor

MAD Cover to Cover: 48 Years, 6 Months, & Three Days of MAD Magazine Centers by Frank Jacobs

Mechanika: Creating the Art of Science Fiction by Doug Chiang

Wake Up Our Souls: A Celebration of Black American Artists by Tonya Bolden

Whatcha Mean, What's a Zine?: The Art of Making Zines and Minicomics by Mark Todd

Words with Wings: A Treasury of African-American Poetry and Art by Belinda Rochelle

7

Short Stories and Poetry

Short stories are great for students who think reading a whole book is just too much work. Many teens think poetry is lame; these books should change their minds!

A lot of times the reason teens may not find reading appealing is because they've been exposed to bad books or books far above their reading level. Short stories are the reluctant reader's dream; they provide everything a novel does but without the time commitment. For your slower readers short stories can provide small victories while helping students practice and eventually enhance their skills. They are also excellent discussion group fodder! Poetry, on the other hand, can be tricky. When it's time to read poetry in school, few students stifle their groans. Trying to make poetry appealing for pleasure reading is nearly insurmountable. The trick is, like with short stories, choosing poems that students can relate to and simply cannot help but laugh at. Teen angst poems (and stories, for that matter) do appeal to a specific population of teens and should always be presented, but humorous poetry is the key to every teen's heart. For example, after students hear "Goldilocks and the Three Bears" from Roald Dahl's *Vile Verses*, they all rush to be the first to check it out. And like short stories, these small victories will hopefully accumulate into a love of poetry. Once the love of poetry is instilled in the teen, it is an excellent means to present history and classical literature.

Book Ideas with Booktalks, Discussion Questions, and Project Ideas

Worlds Afire
by Paul B. Janeczko

To start this booktalk we begin by reading one of the poems such as "Mabel Conrad, Animal Trainer." *Then, we continue by quoting from the back cover:* "Others have their own version of the story: Harry King, war veteran, went to the circus to take his mind off things. Eddy Carlyle, sideshow fan, came to see the freaks. And eleven-year-old Polly McDonald," who wanted to stay outside with the animals, went in anyway because "Aunt Betty didn't want to miss the Greatest Show on Earth."

And then the firefighters were called, but they were too late to save Harry or Eddy, or Polly and her aunt Betty, because the canvas tent, "waterproofed with gasoline and paraffin, "caught fire" like one huge candle/ just waiting for a light."

These haunting poems draw their power from a true event: the Hartford, Connecticut, circus fire of July 6, 1944, in which 167 people were killed and more than 500 injured.

DISCUSSION QUESTIONS

1. Dixie Levine, the gorilla attendant says, "Nobody comes to the circus for the truth." What does she mean?
2. Did Martin K. Davies, the bandleader, survive the fire?
3. Read the poem "Bill Conti: Parent." Why do the fallen get stepped on? Why aren't they helped up? What happens to Bill?
4. Read the poem "Mrs. Estelle Sutton: Mother of Carl and Joan." At the end of her poem she says, "Now he'll have to hear about us from strangers." Who does she mean when she says "us"? Who does she think died in the fire?
5. Who is the burning man?
6. How does the poet wipe away the fire at the end of the book?

PROJECT: HISTORICAL POETRY

World's Afire brings to life the true account of a tragic event, the 1944 Hartford, Connecticut, circus fire. For this project ask your teens to write a poem based on a true event in your local community. What events have made the news in the past few years? Is there an historic event that is famous in your community? Ask your teens to research the news archives of your community (your local special collections librarian can help with this project) and pick a headline event. Once your teens have researched this event and gathered all of the news articles they can find, ask them to turn that event into a poem. The format of the poem is up to you, but ask your teens to consider the voice of the poem. Who is speaking? Is it in the first or third person? What is the time period of the poem? Are the teens writing as if the event is taking place right now or did it happen in the past? What aspect of the event should they focus on? Are they covering the entire event or just one detail of the event? Let your teens read the poems aloud after giving a brief summary of the event they chose.

Be Afraid, Be Very Afraid
by Jan Harold Brunvand

This booktalk is short and sweet but hooks them every time. If you need to throw in one last booktalk before the bell rings, this talk is perfect.

Phantom hitchhikers, mad men with hooks, poisonous spiders in house plants, snakes in banana peels, the babysitter's worst nightmare, arms falling off, maggots inside your head, stolen kidneys, being buried alive, and Bloody Mary. All of the urban legends that keep you and your friends awake at night are in this book, *Be Afraid, Be Very Afraid*, compiled by Jan Brunvand.

DISCUSSION QUESTIONS

1. Read the first story in "Along Came a Spider … or a Snake, or Rat: Spiders in Cacti" section. What about this story doesn't seem true to you? What about the e-mail in the same section, "Plantlife." What about this story couldn't possibly be true?
2. Are there any stories in *Be Afraid* that you haven't heard of before? Are there any that you have told to others in the past?
3. Which type of story do you find the most intriguing; the stories with murderers, insects, snakes, ghosts, gruesome deaths and accidents, or another type of story?
4. Do you think there are any truths to these urban legends?
5. How do you think these stories get started?
6. Does the background information provided by Brunvand make the stories less frightening or even more intriguing?

PROJECT: STORYTELLING

Let your teens become storytellers. Ask your teens to pick one of the legends from *Be Afraid* and prepare the story to be told out loud. Before your teens pick their stories, review good storytelling skills with them. Be sure to discuss how to use voice to create atmosphere, how to pace the story such as starting out slow to create mystery and speeding up when the story starts climaxing, and using gestures and facial expressions to enhance the story. Your teens should have the story memorized, and they should practice telling their story before they try it out on their peers.

Technically, It's Not My Fault and Blue Lipstick
by John Grandits

For these concrete poems, we pick a poem from the collection and read it to the group, showing the teens the layout of the poem as we go. It's a good idea to pick a poem that is fun to follow on the page. Be sure to have the words of the poem posted on the back of the book to make it easier for you to read as the pages of the book will be turned toward your teens. A few suggestions are: "Skateboard," "The Autobiography of Murray the Fart," "It's Not Fair" or "Spew Machine" from Technically, It's Not My Fault, *or "Bad Hair Day," "Zombie Jocks" or "Tattoo & Tongue Stud" from* Blue Lipstick.

DISCUSSION QUESTIONS

1. What is a concrete poem?
2. Which poem to do you think best represents a concrete poem? Why?
3. Are there any graphics that don't really seem to represent the poem correctly? What would have been a better representation?
4. Who are the narrators of these poems? How old do you think they are? What is their relationship to each other? What do they like and dislike? What do you know about them?
5. Which poem do you like best and why?
6. If you were to create a concrete poem about your day, what shape would it take?

PROJECT: CONCRETE POEMS

Ask your teens to create their own concrete poem. You can keep this project open-ended so your teens can pick whatever topic they want, or you can give your teens a topic and see just how varied their interpretations are. Some topics to consider are: current events, "A day in the life of," breakfast or dinner, school life; or if you are in a school, you might consider picking a topic that is being taught in the students' other classes as a curriculum tie-in. What are the social studies or history classes studying? Are the science classes dissecting frogs or experimenting with gravity? Asking your teens to create concrete poems using these subjects will not only give you a unique lesson on concrete poems but will also help your students study for their other classes. After all, you have to know your subject before you can put it into poetry, right?

I Never Saw Another Butterfly
by Hana Volvkova

For this booktalk we give a little background on Terezin and the children who lived and died there. Once our teens understand who is writing these poems and drawing the artwork, we read some of the poems and show some samples of the art. We also try to tell our teens what happened to the children who created the artwork as we go along. Below is a small synopsis and some sample poems and art to consider sharing with your teens.

Terezin was a Nazi concentration camp that imprisoned over 60,000 Jews between 1942–1944. Inside Terezin, one Jewish artist, Friedl Dicker-Brandeis, taught the children art. She would tell stories and the children would draw the objects she mentioned in those stories. The children also drew pictures of Terezin and of their homes. They wrote poetry about their lives and their experiences. The children of Terezin created about 5,000 drawings and collages while Friedl drew very little. She saved the paper and paints for the children. Friedl died in Auschwitz on October 6, 1944. Of the 15,000 children living in Terezin, only 100 survived. Included in this book are samples of their drawings and their poetry.

Read the poem "The Butterfly" by Pavel Friedmann. Pavel died in Auschwitz on September 29, 1944. *Show teens the drawing* Terezin Barracks. This drawing of Terezin barracks is by Sonja Waldsteinova. Sonja survived and returned to Prague after the liberation.

Read the first paragraph of "Lights Out." Twelve-year-old Helga Weissova kept a diary for the 2½ years she spent at Terezin. She also painted many, many pictures. She currently lives in Prague and is an artist.

Show teens the two page spread abstract watercolor by Nely Silvinova. She lived in Terezin for two years and died in Auschwitz on October 4, 1944.

Read "I am a Jew" and show the artwork on the same page. Franta Bass died in Auschwitz. The artist of this picture is unknown.

DISCUSSION QUESTIONS

1. Read the poem "At Terezin." What can you learn about Terezin from this poem? What was life like for its inhabitants?

2. Study the drawing signed "Helga Weissova heim 24." What is going on in this drawing? Who are the characters featured here?
3. Read the poem "Fear." What is happening in this poem? What is the poet afraid of?
4. What is the tone of these poems? What do you think these children and teens were feeling in Terezin? Were they hopeful, desperate, scared, wishful?
5. Which poem do you think evokes the strongest reaction? Which poem affected you the most?
6. What do you see in these drawings? What is life like according to the pictures?

Project: A Picture Is Worth a Thousand Words

While many of the drawings in this collection are accompanied by poems on the same page, the poems and drawings were not originally drawn and written together. Instead, they were placed together by the editors of this book. Pick a drawing from this collection and write a poem to describe what is happening in the artwork. What colors are used? What is the subject of the drawing? Is there any action taking place in the drawing? Is the drawing hopeful or scary? How do you put the artwork into words?

The Inner City Mother Goose
by Eve Merriam

For these poems begin by asking teens to finish some traditional nursery rhymes for you. When they finish the traditional version, read the Inner City *version found in Eve Merriam's collection. Here are some examples you could use:*

- Finish this nursery rhyme: Hey diddle, diddle.... *Let the teens finish the rhyme for you.* Here's a new version by Eve Merriam. *Read "Hey Diddle Diddle."*
- OK, can you finish this one? Jack be nimble, Jack be quick.... *Let the teens finish the rhyme.* Here's Eve's version. *Read "Jack Be Nimble, Jack Be Quick."*
- What about this one? Mary, Mary, quite contrary.... *Hopefully, teens can finish 1 or 2 lines of this rhyme.* Here's the inner city version. *Read "Mary, Mary."*

Discussion Questions

1. According to the introduction, old nursery rhymes were sometimes created to be codes for the peasants when they wished to discuss something the gentry shouldn't hear. What is different about those hushed coded messages and Eve Merriam's poems?
2. In some of the poems, such as "Lucy Locket" and "Diddle Diddle Dumpling," the last line of the poem does not fit into the rhythm or rhyme of the rest of the poem. Why does Merriam do this? Are there any other poems that end with a nonrhyming line?
3. Who is Nobody in the poem "Who Killed Nobody?"
4. For many of the poems it is easy to recognize their traditional counterparts. Which poems do you recognize? Are there any nursery rhymes that you don't recognize?
5. Why did Eve Merriam rewrite these traditional nursery rhymes?

Let your teens rewrite their own nursery rhymes. Ask your teens to pick a topic related to their school life, such as classes, riding the school bus, eating lunch in the cafeteria, walking through the halls, great teachers, bad teachers, the principals and administration, the school board, funding, textbooks, etc. Then ask them to choose a traditional nursery rhyme and turn that rhyme into a modern rhyme about their topic. Be sure to encourage them to make the poem still recognizable when they are finished. Some aspects of the poem should remain the same such as the rhythm or the rhyming. Any nonsense words should remain the same as well.

The World According to Dog
by Joyce Sidman

Option A: Raise your hand if you have had a pet that was your best friend. *Call on students who have hands up to say what kind of pet they had.* To a lot of people, a dog is not just an animal or a pet they feed and water; a dog is a confidant, a sidekick, and a member of the family. *Read the story "The One Who Listens."* Not only are dogs our friends and members of our family but they also are teachers. Has anyone in here ever learned something from a dog? *Read "How to Meet a New Idea (Based on the Study of a Dog)."*

Option B: *For this talk print off the words in the poem "Dog and Squirrel: Steps in Flirtation." Call on two students to volunteer and have one read the part of the dog and the other read the part of the squirrel (in italics). This is a great option if you notice your group is getting restless.*

DISCUSSION QUESTIONS

1. What kind of poems are "Awakening" and "Tag?"
2. What was your favorite poem? Prose?
3. Have you ever had a pet that was more than just an animal? Explain.
4. Why do you think people get so attached to animals?
5. How could this book be considered art?

PROJECT: PET POETRY OR PROSE

As a class, discuss ways that pets can seem like more than just animals. Provide the class at least 20 minutes to write their own poetry or prose that reflects a meaningful relationship with a pet. Even for students who have never had a pet who was a friend, they can write how they would imagine it to be — the stories do not have to be autobiographical. For some this project may be a way of reflecting on positive experiences, and for others it may be a way to see another point of view. If there is time allow students the opportunity read their prose or poetry for the group.

Troll's Eye View
by Ellen Datlow and Terri Windling

Who is the main character in Cinderella? *What about* Snow White and the Seven Dwarfs? *And who was the main character in* Sleeping Beauty? *Between each question, allow the teens to answer.* Well, it seems like the beautiful "good guys" get all the attention. What about the witch in *Rapunzel?* Or did you ever think the witch in *Hansel and Gretel* was really a kindly old woman? In *Troll's Eye View* we get the story from the so-called villains. *Read the first four paragraphs of the story* "Up the Down Beanstalk: A Wife Remembers" *by Peter S. Beagle. If you're unsure if your teens know the story of* "Jack and the Beanstalk," *you may want to review it before starting the story.*

DISCUSSION QUESTIONS

1. In the story "Wizard's Apprentice," why do you think Nick wanted to stay with Mr. Smallbone, even though he was mean to Nick? Would you have stayed with the evil wizard?
2. In "An Unwelcomed Guest," what was the "scary" name Jenny the cat gave herself? If you were to give yourself a villainous name, what would it be?
3. Who does the poem "Faery Tales," describe?
4. Read the poem "Observing Formalities." How important are formalities and manners to you?
5. Who is your favorite villain from a fairy tale?

PROJECT: WRITE YOUR OWN VILLAINOUS STORY

After reading this book of short stories and going over discussion questions, their minds are more than likely buzzing with ideas. Using poetry, prose, or comic strip style, allow your students to create their own stories from the point of view of the villain. This is a great project to do before an open house — not only does it display the teens' creativity, but hopefully the students will be enthusiastic to show off their work.

Invasion of the Road Weenies and Other Warped and Creepy Tales
by David Lubar

David Lubar is a genius when it comes to the warped and creepy and the stories in this book will not disappoint. This book has had 6th graders falling out of their seats laughing and teachers in the back of the room giggling too. It works for the young teens and the older, and it is a perfect way to start your booktalks or perk up a dead booktalking session. My favorite story to read is "Copies"; *it is the perfect length and the end is delightfully creepy and disgusting — a perfect pairing for teen audiences!*

When doing this book remember to put away your responsible adult hat and let loose. If you're throwing yourself into the character and truly having fun with this story, the students will pick up on it and feel free to laugh and enjoy it.

Short stories are the perfect basis for book discussions, allowing students who didn't read the entire book to get involved.

DISCUSSION QUESTIONS

1. What was your favorite story? (*Allow students to summarize their favorite story. This is a great question to start with because it will break the ice and provide the students a chance to laugh again at the weirdness.*)
2. Were there any stories you thought were inappropriate? Explain.
3. Did you figure out the endings of any of the stories before you finished reading? Which ones?
4. What characteristics do you think make a really good creepy story?
5. If you were to make up your ending to one of the stories, which one would you rewrite? How would you end it?

PROJECT: ILLUSTRATING THE CREEPY

While full of the amazingly creepy and warped, this book is missing the wonderfully disturbing illustrations to accompany the stories. Have each student choose the story they wish to illustrate and provide them the time and resources to create. (If multiple students want the same story, you could always draw them from a hat.) The only requirement is that the characters they draw accurately reflect the way David Lubar describes them — other than his descriptions, they're free to interpret. If you have ample time, encourage students to do multiple illustrations for different parts of each short story.

Shelf Life
by Gary Paulsen

Show of hands: How many of you out there think reading is lame because it takes way too long to get through a book? Then you definitely need to stick with the short stories in *Shelf Life*. This book is full of short stories by awesome authors like Margaret Peterson Haddix and Gregory Maguire. In this book you'll find pirates, a creature named The Thing That Lasts, and what it's like to live on Mars. Each story has something hidden inside—if you decide to check it out, I'd love to know if you find it. *Spoiler: a different book title is mentioned in each short story.*

Discussion Questions

1. What is mentioned in each story? *The answer is at least one book title.*
2. Can you name any books mentioned in the first story? *Go through each story and try to identify the different book titles.*
3. Why did Gary Paulsen want to produce this book?
4. Which story did you like most? Why?
5. In the story "Escape," what escape mechanism did they talk about? Do you have ways that you escape from your own reality?
6. In the story "Follow the Water," would you have made the same decision Georgiana did at the end? Explain.
7. In the story "Testing, Testing, 1 … 2 … 3," why was Patrick considered an idiot?
8. At the end of the story "The Good Deed," why does Risa want to make sure Heather wasn't reading with her to do a good deed?
9. What was the true story in "Barcarole for Paper and Bones"?

Project Option 1: Discussion Groups

This book makes a wonderful book for discussion groups. Instruct students to write down two discussion questions or topics based on any of the stories in the book. If you have a small class, go through the students' questions together; if you're in a large group, split them into groups of 4–5. Be sure to walk around and help spark conversation.

Project Option 2: Hidden Title Story

Just like the authors in this book, have students write their own short stories and hide their favorite book title in the book somewhere. The short story doesn't necessarily need to be about the book they're mentioning, it simply needs to be mentioned in the story. If you have time, share the stories aloud in the class.

Project Option 3: Personalized Reader Story

Similar to Paulsen's short autobiography in the introduction, have students write their own story about how they came to read. Is it their 3rd grade teacher who was really passionate about books? Or maybe their parents read to them every night and made them excited about reading? It may even be they saw the big high school boy on the bus reading when they were in kindergarten and that made them want to read! Whatever their reading story is, write it down. If you have the time, take your students to visit a younger grade level and share their stories with them.

Vile Verses
by Roald Dahl

This is a favorite among teens, and even when we visit a school multiple times, they request this booktalk. We start off by asking the students who hate poetry to raise their hand; needless to say, most of the teens do. All we ask of them is that they pretend to listen. We then quickly summarize the traditional story of "Goldilocks and the Three Bears" as a group.

I'm going to read you a poem about this story that you are so familiar with — but just know, the author has a different perspective of the little girl with the golden curls. *At this point read Dahl's poem, "Goldilocks and the Three Bears," as quickly as you possibly can. Don't be embarrassed to practice ahead of time because the quicker you can read, the more engrossed the teens will inevitably be.*

DISCUSSION QUESTIONS

1. What was your favorite poem?
2. What other Dahl books have you read? Did you recognize any of the poems from his books?
3. Many of the poems are simply a different perspective of a classic children's story. If you had to rewrite a children's story, which one would it be? Explain.
4. There are seven parts to the book. How does each poem fit into the title of its respective part?
5. What is so unique about the illustrations?

PROJECT: POETRY PRESENTATIONS

For this project instruct each teen to choose a favorite poem from Dahl's book to perform. Discuss important techniques for performing poetry and encourage students to use different voices for different characters. Spend time practicing among the other teens in the class, and when the poems are perfected, schedule a time to visit elementary classes to perform these works.

Classroom Integration

It seems there are poems or short stories on nearly every topic out there — pop culture, environmental concerns, pets, and even plain creepiness. Use this to your advantage!

To get students excited and interested in poetry, find poetry that appeals to them. The complete weirdness of *Inner City Mother Goose* or *Vile Verses* may not necessarily need to interest you, but if it gets your students reading poetry, that is a victory. After they grow more comfortable with poetry, try slowly working in the heavier required reading. Hopefully, the silliness will have broken down some of the intimidation that is associated with poetry.

Short stories are the same way! This is a great medium to start the reluctant reader or even to start your literature class. By beginning a semester with short stories and working your way toward books like *The Grapes of Wrath* and *To Kill a Mockingbird*, students will be far more confident and even genuinely interested. The small and seemingly instantaneous victories achieved when reading short stories will transfer as students become more self-assured in their abilities to not only read but evaluate their reading.

More Great Books

Angry Management by Chris Crutcher
Ask the Bones: Scary Stories from Around the World by Arielle North Olson and Howard Schwartz
Be Afraid, Be Very Afraid: The Book of Scary Urban Legends by Jan Harold Brunvand
Behind the Wheel: Poems About Driving by Janet S. Wong
Being Dead by Vivian Vande Velde
Blue Lipstick by John Grandits
The Brimstone Journals by Ron Koertge
Bronx Masquerade by Nikki Grimes
The Eternal Kiss: 13 Vampire Stories of Blood and Desire by Trisha Telep, ed.
Every Man for Himself: Ten Short Stories About Being a Guy by Nancy E. Mercado, ed.
Falling Hard: 100 Love Poems by Teenagers by Betsy Franco, ed.
Fortune's Bones: The Manumission Requiem by Marilyn Nelson
Geektastic: Stories from the Nerd Herd by Holly Black and Cecil Castellucci, ed.
Half-human by Bruce Coville, ed.
i never saw another butterfly by Hana Volavkova, ed.
The Inner City Mother Goose by Eve Merriam
Invasion of the Road Weenies and Other Warped and Creepy Tales by David Lubar
Keesha's House by Helen Frost
Love, Football and Other Contact Sports by Alden Carter
More Bones: Scary Stories from Around the World by Arielle North Olson and Howard Schwartz
Necessary Noise: Stories About Our Families as They Really Are by Michael Cart, ed.
Nevermore: A Graphic Adaptation of Edgar Allan Poe's Short Stories by Dan Whitehead, ed.
Partly Cloudy: Poems of Love and Longing by Gary Soto
Poems from Homeroom: A Writer's Place to Start by Kathi Appelt
Primate Behavior by Sarah Lindsay
Prom Nights from Hell by Meg Cabot, et al.
The Restless Dead: Ten Original Stories of the Supernatural by Deborah Noyes, ed.
Revolting Rhymes by Roald Dahl
Shelf Life: Stories by the Book by Gary Paulsen, ed.
The Surrender Tree: Poems of Cuba's Struggle for Freedom by Margarita Engle
Technically, It's Not My Fault by John Grandits
13: Thirteen Stories that Capture the Agony and Ecstasy of Being Thirteen by James Howe, ed.
Tough Boy Sonatas by Curtis Crisler
Troll's Eye View: A Book of Villainous Tales by Ellen Datlow and Terri Windling, eds.
Vile Verses by Roald Dahl

What are You Afraid Of? Stories About Phobias by Donald R. Gallo, ed.
The World According to Dog: Poems and Teen Voices by Joyce Sidman
Worlds Afire by Paul B. Janeczko
Young Oxford Book of Nasty Endings by Dennis Pepper
You Remind Me of You: A Poetry Memoir by Eireann Corrigan

8

Graphic Novels

No manga here (although we do enjoy manga)— these graphic novels contain history, science and current events portrayed through comic-style art.

Graphic novels often get a bad rap. As librarians and educators working with teens, we know the value of a good manga series or the draw of those classic comics. This graphic medium encourages those reluctant readers to do what we hope most—read! But this format is all too often a touchy subject, and as educators we find ourselves defending the graphic novels from those who find the subject matter too violent or too suggestive. We struggle with a series that has been perfectly appropriate for our collection until that latest issue, which goes just a bit too far. However, we know that for some teens these comic-style works are truly the holy grail when convincing them to read; thus, we continue to search for the balance of age-appropriate subject matter and addictive introductory reading material. The books in this chapter offer an alternative to fiction graphics, to manga, and comic books. These works are graphic adaptations of history, current events, poetry, and classic short stories. They offer biographical facts brought to life by an artist's sketch, poetry rendered real, and historic documents given new dimension. If you have a teen who just can't get that biography report finished or hates reading that history text-book or if you have teens who find poetry boring and dead, give them one of these books and let them explore the life of Abraham Lincoln or the poetry of Edgar Allen Poe in a less intimidating, more visually interesting format.

Book Ideas with Booktalks, Discussion Questions, and Project Ideas

Pitch Black
by Youme Landowne and Anthony Horton

Youme Landowne is an artist who went to college and has lived and studied in the United States, Kenya, Japan, Haiti, Laos, and Cuba. When she met Anthony Horton, he was living in the subway tunnels of New York City. What would make these two seemingly different people spend hours and hours riding the New York City subway system together? They're both artists and now these two people are the creators of *Pitch Black*, a graphic novel biography of Anthony's life in the subway tunnels—a whole other world six stories below New York City. Just because you don't see it, doesn't mean nothing's there.

Discussion Questions

1. Take a closer look at all of the people drawn in *Pitch Black*. What do you notice about them?
2. Look closely at the art, signs and words in the background of the subway. What do you think Landowne and Horton are trying to say?
3. How could The Center be worse than living on the streets?
4. If Anthony Horton's first trip into the tunnels was so terrible, why would he be willing to go back? Would you be willing to go into the tunnels?
5. Read through the "Things That Should and Should Not Be Done When You Are Living Underground" section. Which rule do you think is the most important one to follow? Why?
6. Read through the "People I'll Never Forget" section. Can you name the people who helped shape the person you are?
7. Back outside of the tunnels, Youme says, "It feels weird out here. Like it's too bright." Anthony responds, "You have no idea." What do they mean?
8. What do the authors mean when they say, "Our memories and dreams walk beside us, informing everything we think we see"?

Project: Graphic Biography

This is a great project for your art class or for your manga or comic book club. First, ask your teens to divide into pairs. Then give your pairs time to get to know each other and discuss any connections or similarities they may discover about each other. Ask your teens to create a biographical graphic story. This story could focus on either the event, hobby, or interest that connects the pair, or it could focus on a biographical story about one or both of the teens. Both teens should participate equally. For example, instead of letting one teen do all of the drawing because it is her story and she knows how to draw the scenes, make sure that the teen describes her story in enough detail so the other teen can accurately draw the scenes as well.

Houdini
by Jason Lutes and Nick Bertozzi

During a time when people weren't sure if magicians were really clever or controlled by demons, Harry Houdini (real name: Ehrich Weiss) took center stage with his ability to escape any form of bondage—handcuffs, straitjackets, and containers of all shapes and sizes. Though he knew how capable he was, he attributed all of his success to hard work, claiming anyone could perform his feats with enough practice.

Step-by-step, *Houdini: The Handcuff King* shows what happened when Harry Houdini claimed to be able to jump from the Harvard Bridge into the Charles River while bound and shackled. This is a true story of a man who knew the boundaries and tried everything to push them.

Discussion Questions

1. What do you think of Harry Houdini? Did your perception change from reading this book?
2. While it has never been proven that Houdini's wife helped him, it is one theory. Can you think of other methods he may have used to escape entrapment?
3. Who was Houdini's boyhood idol? What did Houdini discover about him?
4. A reporter asks Houdini what the root of his fame and success is; how does Houdini respond?
5. After speaking to the reporters, what was the reporter saying on the phone that made Houdini so angry? Have you ever overheard someone talking about you? Explain.
6. Houdini claims to have worked diligently since he was a child to avoid entrapment. Is there anything you work very hard to achieve? Explain. Are you still working toward it?
7. Why do you think the audience wants to watch Houdini jump off the bridge? Would you have gone to watch? Why or why not?

Project: Graphic Biography, Historical Adaptation

Split your class into groups of 3–4. Instruct each group to choose a historical figure (or you could choose one for them based on your current history topic). After doing considerable biographical research, each group must choose a single event in the history of their assigned historical figure. At this point each group must draw a 12-pane representation of their selected event. Encourage the students to work together by evaluating the talents of the various people in their group — drawers, writers, researchers.

Beowolf
by Gareth Hinds

If you have read Beowolf, *you remember the violence; since this book is a graphic novel, the bloodshed is even more vivid. Please take this into account before deciding to incorporate into your presentation.*

The most magnificent banquet hall ever imagined was built in the kingdom. A monster, cursed and exiled, grew angry and for 12 years devoured all who entered the banquet hall. No warrior could defeat the monster — he preyed on them all ... until a hero came from far across the sea. He lay in wait for the monster, equipped with only his strength and confidence.

This story, over 1,000 years old, is legend. Both the art and the text weave a tale that has been told around campfires and in the classroom. It is a tale of a hero who protected a land that wasn't his own with a strength that knew no bounds. The hero was Beowolf.

DISCUSSION QUESTIONS

1. Who was the original author of *Beowolf*?
2. Describe the beast who was devouring all who were in Heorot.
3. What weapons did Beowolf use to fight Grendel?
4. How did the fight with Grendel end?
5. Who was the 2nd battle with? Why did Beowolf have to fight it?
6. What weapons did Beowolf use in the final fight?
7. At the end of the tale, what happened to the treasure the dragon was guarding?

PROJECT: CLASSIC LITERATURE ADAPTATION

Like many of the other graphic novel projects, this project will work best for your art class or manga or comic book club. Split your group into groups of 2–3. Instruct them to select a piece of classic literature or poetry and create a minimum 12-pane adaptation. Depending on the work they choose, they may need to only focus on a specific chapter or event in the story or poem. After completing the projects, host a book party. Not only will they be able to display their art and storytelling skills to their peers, this will also provide the students the opportunity learn about other classic works.

The Fatal Bullet
by Rick Geary

Two men, very similar but so very different. Both grew up on the frontier. Both were the youngest in their families. Both lost a parent at a young age. Both considered entering strict religious sects and becoming preachers. Both were eventually drawn to politics. One became president of the United States. He didn't really mean to. He was simply attending the Republican convention and his name was suggested, and then his name was shouted and then his name was put down as the Republican candidate: James A. Garfield for president. The other wanted such praise. He wanted to be acknowledged as the brilliant man that he was. He tried to get appointed as the Consul to France. He didn't get it. So, he assassinated the president. Two sides of the same coin. How could such similar experiences create such different men?

However it happened, it is clear that on Saturday, July 2, 1881, James A. Garfield and his two oldest sons were on their way to meet Mrs. Garfield and the younger children for a vacation. They were at the train station when Charles Guiteau shot President Garfield from three feet away. And he missed. He fired a 2nd bullet and it ploughed into the president's back, fracturing two ribs, chipping his spine, penetrating a major artery and then stopping just behind the pancreas. Amazingly, President Garfield lived for 2½ months because a bubble formed in the artery that let the blood keep flowing. But, on September 19, 1881, that anuerysm burst and President Garfield finally passed away.

Charles Guiteau, meanwhile, was arrested. He was confident, though, that he was doing the world a favor. He thought he would be honored as a hero, exonerated from all wrong-doing and finally get that appointment to France. Alas, Charles Guiteau was executed on June 30, 1882. Poor, poor, misguided, crazy Guiteau. Crazy, crazy man.

Discussion Questions

1. How can two people with such seemingly similar childhood experiences become such different men?
2. Describe the difference between the characters of these two men.
3. How does the author depict these two men? Do you think the author is objective in his descriptions or is he trying to influence his readers?
4. Why do you think Guiteau believed he wouldn't be punished for his crime?
5. What did Guiteau really want from life?
6. Why did it take so long for Congress to form the Secret Service? How do you think this has changed the presidency?

Project: Melodrama Adaptation

While in the strictest sense, a melodrama uses music to influence the audience's mood, the term has taken on a more general meaning that defines a work characterizing extravagant gestures and emotions and the predominance of plot and physical action. Melodramas also often include 1-dimensional characters—good versus bad, hero versus villain. The dichotomy of the hero, James A. Garfield, and the villain, Charles Guiteau, make this graphic novel an easy choice for an impromptu melodramatic adaptation.

The easiest way to adapt this graphic novel into a melodrama is to use a narrator to read the text. The narrator reads the text aloud, and each time a character is introduced, another teen volunteers to play that part by completing whatever action is being described by the narrator. The actors simply follow the directions of the narrator. The graphic panes of the novel will help teens get an idea of what they could be doing for these actions. For example, when the narrator says that Garfield rode through a battle on horseback, then the Garfield actor must improv galloping through the battle on horseback. When the narrator speaks the lines said by specific characters, the actors simply repeat those lines. The actors should make their actions as campy and grandiose as possible in order to get the true flair of melodrama. Sound effects from the teens not acting are encouraged.

If you don't have time to recreate the entire graphic novel (and you probably won't), begin with "The Day of Infamy" on July 2, 1881, and recreate the day that Garfield was shot as well as the days following.

Ethel & Ernest
by Raymond Briggs

She was shaking a dust cloth out the window and he thought the pretty girl was waving at him. They were soon married. They were very poor, living below the poverty line, and were ecstatic when they moved into a small home with indoor plumbing! They dreamed of electric lights, a garden, and children. Through pictures, their story depicts a simple love story set in England that made it through World War II, the near destruction of their home, the Korean War, and the moon landing.

1. What did Ernest do for a living?
2. What major event happened to the family in the 1930s?
3. Why did they put blackout curtains in their living room?
4. What major event happened to Great Britian in the 1930s?
5. What happened to their son after Germany declared war on Great Britian? Why?

Old books and oodles of craft supplies provide a creative base for graphic novels your teens create.

6. In the 1940–1950 section, why was Ernest crying when he got off work?
7. When the bomb was dropped on Hiroshima, why did Ethel say, "You can't fight a war with bombs like that"?
8. What was Ethel's response to man landing on the moon?
9. Why do you think this story has a powerful impact on people?

PROJECT: AUTOBIOGRAPHY AND ALTERED BOOK

First, have students create their own autobiography in graphic novel form with a minimum of 12 panes. Afterward, create original book covers from old books and instruct students to attach their graphic novel strips inside the book. Various art and craft supplies can be used to alter the inside pages in other ways; encourage students to use the art previously in the book in conjunction with their new creations!

American Born Chinese
by Gene Luen Yang

Jin Wang is the son of two Chinese-born parents who came to the United States for an education. He thought he lived a normal American life until he started school at Mayflower Elementary — his clothes smelled different, the lunch his mom packed was weird, his name was different, and kids asked him if his family eats dogs. When it seemed like things couldn't get any worse, he made a friend — a new student from Taiwan, Wei-Chen Sun. They never knew how much of an impact they would have on one another.

DISCUSSION QUESTIONS

1. Briefly describe the Chinese parable Jin Wang's mother tells him. What does it mean?
2. The old woman at the Chinese Herbalist gives Jin Wang some very important advice

when he says he wants to be a transformer when he grows up. What was the advice? How does this advice carry through to the end of the story?

3. Why did Jin Wang avoid Suzy Nakamura?
4. Why does Danny not like the visits from his cousin Chin-Kee?
5. What did the monkey king have to do to get out from under the mountain of rocks? How was this symbolic to Jin Wang-Danny?
6. What was the moral of this story? How can it apply to your life?

PROJECT: CREATIVE WRITING: ALLEGORIES

The book *American Born Chinese* is full of fulfilled allegories. As a class compile a list of various life lessons like the one from the book that focuses on being yourself. Instruct students to write their own 1–2 page allegory that depicts a moral they have chosen from the list. On the due date have the students read their stories in front of the class.

Satchel Paige
by James Sturm and Rich Tommaso

"I went head-to-head with Satchel Paige once. Tall and lanky, he took his time; adjusted his shoe laces, tucked in his shirt — nobody hurried Paige. The batter standing there in the batter's box, his grip getting tighter and tighter on the bat but nobody's gonna hurry Satchel. And when he was ready to pitch, nobody saw that fastball. Not even the batter. But I went head-to-head with Satchel once. And I got the best of him. Sometimes, I read about Satchel in the *Chicago Defender* or the *Pittsburgh Courier*. I read about him pitching his fastballs, barnstorming across the country playing three games in one day. I read about him playing white baseball teams and nobody getting past his fastball. I work in the fields, pay my debts to the landowners. I send my son to school everyday and keep to myself. It's a free world, even if the landowners don't want it to be. I take my son to watch Satchel and his team play against the Tuckwilla baseball team, the team the landowners play on. I take my son to watch Satchel Paige get the best of those white men and then I tell my son about the time I got the best of Satchel."

DISCUSSION QUESTIONS

1. What does the title *Satchel Paige: Striking Out Jim Crow* mean? How does Paige strike out Jim Crow?
2. Who is the narrator of this story? Can you figure out his name? How does Satchel Paige affect the narrator's life? What can you deduce about the narrator's life from the story?
3. What are the difference between white baseball players and black baseball players during the time of this story?
4. How does the narrator rebel against the white land owners?
5. How does Satchel Paige rebel against the white ball players?
6. What is the subject of this story — Satchel Paige, the narrator or the Jim Crow culture? What do you learn from reading this story?

PROJECT: COMPARE AND CONTRAST

Compare and contrast the lives of the narrator and Satchel Paige. Using a Venn diagram, write down aspects of each character's life as either unique to each character or a shared experience for both characters.

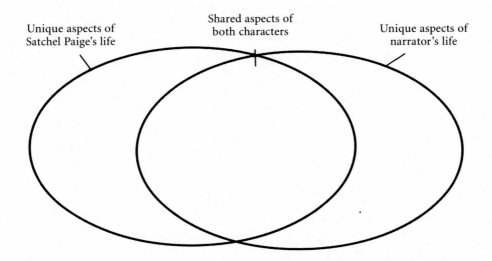

Unique aspects of
Satchel Paige's life

Shared aspects of
both characters

Unique aspects of
narrator's life

Thoreau at Walden
by John Porcellino

What am I going to do with my life? What is this life about really? Why do people run from task to task hurried, troubled and unhappy? What do we really need to live? Why must there always be noise and why must we always be busy? These are questions that Thoreau asked himself.

Why would he move away from people? What does he do all day in the woods? How can he stay healthy living on just beans and grains? Why didn't he pay his taxes like a good citizen should? Why would he give up a good teaching job just because he didn't want to whip his students? These are the questions that Thoreau's neighbors asked each other whenever they saw Thoreau in town.

But Thoreau was determined to not live by everyone else's expectations. He wanted to enjoy life, to enjoy the wilderness and nature. He wanted to find truth in nature without the contraptions and rules forced on him by the rest of society. Thoreau was a transcendentalist. Transcendentalism is a philosophy that focuses on personal intuition over social conformity.

Live your life to the beat of your own drum. Have you ever heard that saying? Thoreau said it and he lived it. This book is an introduction to the philosophy of Henry David Thoreau and his life at Walden Pond told through Thoreau's words and accompanied by drawings of John Porcellino.

Discussion Questions

1. Porcellino draws several series of panels with no words. What do these wordless drawings convey? What do they say to you?
2. What is the difference between viewing this life as a hardship and viewing this life as a pastime?
3. Why did Thoreau move to a cabin in the woods?
4. Thoreau and Porcellino paint the idea that living alone in the woods is peaceful, simple and easy. What challenges do you think Thoreau faced living in the woods? What was Thoreau's view of these challenges?
5. What did Thoreau think of the people living in the town?
6. Why didn't Thoreau pay his taxes? How did he feel when someone paid this tax for him?
7. How do you think Thoreau's writing inspired people to create national parks and wild spaces?

Project: This Day in Thoreau's Journal

Search for your birthday in Thoreau's journals. His journals span several years so you may be able to find several years with your birthday. What was Thoreau doing that day? Was he walking through the woods? Listening to birds? Observing people? Speaking to a group? Traveling? Does he tell a story? Does he complain? What does he hear? What does he see? Once you think you understand what Thoreau is writing about, try to draw the journal entry in three graphic panels or less. You can find Thoreau's journal at your local library or online at http://www.walden.org/institute/thoreau/writings/journal/Journal.htm or http://hdt.typepad.com/henrys_blog/.

Graphic Storytelling and Visual Narrative
by Will Eisner

For this booktalk you need access to a marker board or poster board. If you are not an artist, do not fret; simply call on various students to draw the different items. I'm going to draw a character on the board, and I want you to describe his personality. *Draw an evil, sneaky looking man. If you need help, refer to chapter 4. After it is drawn, call on various students to describe what they think his personality is like and then ask them to explain why they think he looks evil.*

When drawing, it's easiest to convey characters by making them resemble an animal. For example, if I were to draw a woman with big hair like a lion, what would you think of her? What about a fat man that had big round eyes and chubby cheeks like a bear cub? Will Eisner discusses this technique and many others to help you create the best graphic novel or comic book ever! And most of his suggestions are written in graphic novel form. *Flip through the book so the students can see it's filled with comics.*

Discussion Questions

1. In your own words, describe the function of a story.
2. How are stereotypes helpful when creating images?

3. What are some different kinds of stories you can tell with images and words?
4. What is reader retention?
5. What are ways to achieve reader retention?
6. Why is it easier when the writer and the artist are the same person?

PROJECT: HOW-TO GRAPHIC STORY

In many classes students are required to do a "how-to" speech, teaching the class to do something they have experience doing. Instead of a speech, use the tools learned in Eisner's book to create at least an 8-pane instructional story. Though some students claim they are not artists, encourage them to draw what they can — many comics draw stick figures as characters and use various distinguishing features (like a hat or cane) to tell them apart. On the back of their comic, instruct each student write one tool they used from the book to help them communicate their ideas more effectively.

More Great Books

Action Philosophers: Volumes 1 and 2 by Fred Van Lente and Ryan Dunlavey
American Born Chinese by Gene Luen Yang
The Beast of Chicago: An Account of the Life and Crimes of Herman W. Mudgett by Rick Geary
Beowolf by Gareth Hinds
Che: A Graphic Biography by Spain Rodriguez
Ethel & Ernest: a True Story by Raymond Briggs
Famous Players: The Mysterious Death of William Desmond Taylor by Rick Geary
The Fatal Bullet: The Assassination, of President James A. Garfield, by Rick Geary
Graphic Classics: H. P. Lovecraft by Richard Corren, Matt Howarth, Mason Crumb, and Gahan Wilson
Graphic Storytelling and Visual Narrative by Will Eisner
Houdini: The Handcuff King by Jason Lutes and Nick Bertozzi
Isadora Duncan: A Graphic Biography by Sabrina Jones
Jack the Ripper by Rick Geary
J. Edgar Hoover: A Graphic Biography by Rick Geary
The Lindbergh Child by Rick Geary
Logicomix: An Epic Search For Truth by Apostolos Doxiadis and Christos H. Papadimitriou
Maus: A Survivor's Tale by Art Spiegelman
The Murder of Abraham Lincoln by Rick Geary
The Mystery of Mary Rogers by Rick Geary
Nat Turner by Kyle Baker
Nevermore: A Graphic Adaptation of Edgar Allan Poe's Short Stories by Dan Whitehead, ed.
A People's History of the American Empire by Howard Zinn
Perfect Example by John Porcellino
Persepolis: The Story of Childhood by Marjane Satrapi
Pitch Black by Youme Landowne and Anthony Horton
The Saga of the Bloody Benders by Rick Geary
Satchel Paige: Striking Out Jim Crow by James Sturm and Rich Tommaso
There's a Hair in My Dirt! A Worm's Story by Gary Larson
Thoreau at Walden by John Porcellino
The United States Constitution: A Graphic Adaptation by Jonathan Hennessey
The Wall: Growing Up Behind the Iron Curtain by Peter Sis
Write Your Own Graphic Novel by Natalie Rosinsky

9

Science

In this chapter, we explore the fascinating genre of scientific nonfiction, from the science of death to pondering questions such as "Can you really drill a hole through your head and survive?"

Every so-called boring school subject is filled with countless interesting topics; just take a look at your Trivial Pursuit cards. Science is one of those subjects that is truly overflowing with interesting topics—from novas to artificial intelligence, extreme weather to cadavers, and rare insects to the Loch Ness monster. What isn't to love? To make room for all the potential, we have added chapters for animals and nature, while this chapter focuses on everything else.

With science books you'll almost always have the shock factor going for you. Be sure to slow down and wait for students to comprehend what you're saying—talking about how cadavers are like superheroes can be a little shocking. Science books are also excellent choices to use for pairing—what better way to introduce simple machines than to read *Amazing Leonardo da Vinci Inventions You Can Build Yourself*!

Book Ideas with Booktalks, Discussion Questions, and Project Ideas

Amazing Leonardo da Vinci Inventions You Can Build Yourself
by Maxine Anderson

Have you ever had to do a chore that you just didn't want to do, and wished you could invent a machine to do it for you? Have you ever had an idea for an invention? What is your idea? Who can tell me why Leonardo da Vinci is famous? What was his most popular painting? Did you know that he was also an inventor? He filled hundreds of notebooks with ideas for inventions ranging from flying machines to armored tanks, and he did all of this in the 15th century. This book takes some of da Vinci's inventions and tells you how to make them. One of his notebooks shows a man walking on top of water using what looked like snowshoes and holding poles. You can learn to build your own walk-on-water shoes with just some Styrofoam, a yardstick, a kitchen knife, a pen, some duct tape and two sticks long enough to use as poles. You can build your own 15th century armored tank or even a helicopter. *Be sure to show the pictures of the armored tank and the helicopter from the book.*

Discussion Questions

1. What was the Renaissance? Do you know what it means to be a "renaissance man" like Leonardo da Vinci?
2. Leonardo kept a notebook with him at all times to sketch what he saw around him or to draw sketches for invention ideas. How do you think this made him a better artist?
3. What is a perspectograph? How does it work and what does it do? How does is improve artwork?
4. A lot of times Leonardo would dream up and draw his inventions, but he couldn't actually create them because the technology was lacking. What inventions do you dream of creating that cannot yet become a reality?
5. Why would Leonardo want to invent walk-on-water shoes? If you had a pair of these shoes, what would you do with them?
6. Why would Leonardo want to invent a parachute if human flight was not yet a possibility?

Project: Amazing Leonardo da Vinci Inventions You Can Build Yourself

The author, Maxine Anderson, makes this project super easy by giving you tons of projects to build. Choose any of Leonardo's inventions in the book and build away!

Outbreak
by Bryn Barnard

The author of this book, Bryn Barnard, has been vaccinated for diphtheria, tetanus, pertussis, measles, mumps, rubella, smallpox, typhoid, polio, influenza, cholera, yellow fever, rabies, hepatitis A, hepatitis B, and Japanese encephalitis. His water is filtered and chlorinated. He washes his hands several times each day. Why? Because these diseases have wrecked havoc on the world, killing millions of people in cruel and painful ways. And this author doesn't want the same to happen to him.

The Black Death, for instance, caused victims to become feverish and grow painful black welts that had a nauseating stench. One third of Europe's population was killed. Thirty to ninety percent of those who get smallpox die. In China people vaccinated each other by blowing dried smallpox scabs up a patient's nose, causing a mild case of the illness. People treated had a 1 in 50 chance of dying but the survivors were immune for life.

Tuberculosis used to be a cool disease. It was thought that if you got this coughing sickness, you were passionate with an artistic fire. The pale skin, flushed cheeks and the bloody handkerchief were envied marks of passion and genius. In Japan tuberculosis was thought to be love sickness. Too bad it is actually a bacteria passed to humans through domesticated animals that causes you to hack up blood and bits of lung.

Toxoplasma gondii is a disease that infects half of the world's population today, and most infected people don't even know they have this disease! Why? Because there aren't any real physical symptoms, like bleeding eyes or sneezing or coughing. Instead, all of the symptoms affect your personality. This disease slows down your reaction time making driving more dangerous, and it changes your personality making you act like a different person. How do you get this disease? From not washing your hands after you change the kitty litter.

DISCUSSION QUESTIONS

1. In the author's opening paragraph, he says, "You're born pristine and alone, but it doesn't last. With your first independent breath your body becomes a cooperate venture with other creatures: a colony, a host. You become infected." What does he mean by that? How does that make you feel?
2. How did the Black Death change Europe?
3. How was smallpox like a biological bomb when Europeans first explored the Americas? What caused the biological catastrophe?
4. What is inoculation and why does it work? Would you have been willing to take the 17th century Chinese version of inoculation for smallpox?
5. Throughout history people have tried many cures for disease and have failed, including experimenting with noise. Why would someone try making loud noises as a cure?

Jill uses some old packing materials to create her own walk-on-water shoes.

6. Why do you think people would believe that tuberculosis was hereditary rather than contagious?
7. Tuberculosis was sometimes thought to be love sickness. Why?
8. Tuberculosis was almost eradicated with the development of antibiotics which killed the tuberculosis bacterium. Why is this disease now considered one of the 21st century's greatest health challenges?
9. Why would Columbia University physician, Harold Neu, say, "Bacteria are cleverer than men"?
10. What is the best way to keep diseases from spreading?

PROJECT: PAPIER-MACHE DOCTOR'S MASK

This is a great project to collaborate between classes if you are in a school setting or just to have fun with if you are in a public library. Whether you are using this book in your science class or history class, the art class can get in on the wonder that is *Outbreak* by creating papier-mache Black Death doctor's masks. These masks were worn by physicians during the Middle Ages and featured glass lenses and a long beak. The long beak was filed with rags soaked in vinegar to keep out the stench of rotten flesh. You can see a picture of the mask in the "Smithereens" chapter of *Outbreak*.

Toe Tagged
by Jaime Joyce

Facts:

- Stefanie Rabinowitz was 29 years old with a husband, Craig, and a 1-year-old daughter.
- On April 30, 1997, in the early morning hours, Craig called 911 to say that his wife was in the bathtub, she wasn't moving and he couldn't wake her up.
- Police found Stephanie in the bathtub, dead.
- She wore a watch, a ring, and some other jewelry.
- Around Stefanie's neck were found scrapes where skin had been rubbed away.
- There were tiny red marks from hemorrhaging found under Stefanie's eyelids.
- There was undigested food in Stefanie's stomach that had only had 3 hours of digestion before death.
- There was a double dose of sleeping pills in Stefanie's system.

What do you think? Was Stephanie's death an accidental drowning or was it murder?

Here's what the medical examiner was able to conclude from these facts:

- The sleeping pills belonged to Stefanie's husband, not Stefanie.
- The red marks around Stefanie's neck and under her eyelids meant she had been strangled, she didn't drown.
- The food in her system meant that she had been dead by 10:30 p.m. but her husband said she didn't get into the bathtub until 11:45 p.m.
- Craig is a lying murderer who killed his wife for her one million dollar life insurance policy.

Getting away with murder is never as easy as you think it is.

DISCUSSION QUESTIONS

1. What is the difference between coroners, medical examiners and forensic pathologists?
2. How do you become a forensic pathologist? Would you want to?
3. What are the three clues that forensic pathologists use to figure out how long a body has been dead? Why do these clues work so well?

4. Pathologists don't just examine the body, they also examine the clothes. Why?

5. Putting together the clues of a crime is like putting together a puzzle. What happens if you put the puzzle together incorrectly?

6. In the case of Janice Johnson, forensic pathologists only had to figure out what could have happened to Janice rather than what certainly happened. How did that prove Clayton Johnson was innocent?

7. In the case of Stefanie Rabinowitz, the medical examiner decided that Stefanie died before 10:30 p.m. but her husband didn't call until after midnight. Why do you think he took so long to call the authorities? Why did this hurt his testimony?

PROJECT: AN INTERACTIVE AUTOPSY

The Australian Museum has an interactive autopsy to explore! Visit http://www.deathonline.net/movies/mm/autopsy.cfm to watch an autopsy on a drawn body. Your teens get to take out organs and weigh them as well as watch useful videos and examine autopsy tools.

Questions to ask your teens as they experiment with the interactive autopsy:

- Describe the autopsy table.
- What is rigor mortis and how will the forensic pathologist test for it?
- What is lividity and how will the forensic pathologist test for it?
- What is the Rokitansky method?
- How much do each of the organs (except the stomach and intestines) weigh?

Stiff
by Mary Roach

Read the first four paragraphs of the introduction to Stiff *for this booktalk. Students typically seem shocked with the cavalier yet logical points made in that short segment. And, as with other books, reading directly from the book makes the book seem even more legitimate to the students. After reading the first four paragraphs, end the booktalk with:* However, a cadaver cannot have these adventures until it is no longer a person; a person can never be a cadaver. Once they are a cadaver, the possibilities are endless. They can help the military, go to medical school, solve murder mysteries, or just become worm food. It's up to you. But remember, you only get one choice. Death doesn't have to be boring.

DISCUSSION QUESTIONS

1. What do you think Roach means in the introduction when she writes that a cadaver is not a person?

2. Why do you think medical schools are so respectful of cadavers?

3. What happens to a cadaver's brain if not in a cooler?

4. After a plane crash, how can corpses help tell the story?

5. In chapter six how does Duncan MacPherson, the ballistics expert, explain why some people fall immediately after being shot even though it takes 10–12 seconds to lose consciousness?

6. What is a "beating-heart cadaver"?
7. What would you want done with your body? Why?

PROJECT: AN INTERACTIVE AUTOPSY SHORT STORY

The project "An Interactive Autopsy" that we suggest to go with the book *Toe Tagged* is also applicable for this book. It will give students a great opportunity to virtually *do* what they've been reading. In addition to this project, have them write a creative story imagining they were not merely virtually taking out the organs and weighing them but actually doing it. Encourage them to use their senses to help with the story: What do they smell? Are any smells so repugnant they can taste them? What are the sounds? What do the organs feel like? If possible, make time to read them aloud in class.

Robo sapiens
by Peter Menzel and Faith D'Aluisio

Before this booktalk, please take the time to mark the pictures you will need to show.

What are Homo sapiens? *(Field answers until you get the appropriate response.)* What is a robot? Based on those definitions, how would you define Robo sapiens?

As defined by this book, Robo sapiens are a hybrid of humans and robots "with intelligence vastly superior to that of purely biological mankind." *Show the photograph of Honda P3.* This robot works in a set of programs. For example, he may be programmed to open a door, walk through it, and shut the door behind him. He is not controlled by a human during the process and, therefore, cannot be changed or stopped — the robot is simply fulfilling a program requirement.

Show photo of DB. DB, which stands for Dynamic Brain, works quite differently. These researchers are using the robot to study human brain function. DB does not fulfill various programs like Honda P3. Instead, DB mimics. For the authors DB watched a woman dancing, and after watching, similar music was played and the robot tried to imitate what he had seen the woman doing.

Show photo of the robot in the "Getting Ahead" chapter (she doesn't have a name). They're also creating robots that can use body language to communicate. Most robot researchers are working with the brain but these researchers are working specifically with the face. *Turn the page and show the photograph of the face without the skin.* The purpose behind this type of project is the idea that humans will be able to communicate better with robots that have animated faces. This book is full of information on specific robots like those I showed you and many more — from robots that look and act like dinosaurs to those who will help explore the solar system.

DISCUSSION QUESTIONS

1. Define robot in your own words.
2. What is artificial intelligence?
3. Many people believe the future for robots with artificial intelligence will be end of human civilization. What do you think?

4. Define biominetics in your own words. What is an example of why we would want machines to act like living creatures?
5. Explain some of the future possibilities for robots.
6. Describe how robots can help with prosthetic needs.
7. If you could have one of the robots in the book, which one would it be? Explain.

PROJECT: DESIGN A FRIEND

The book *Robo sapiens* provides a plethora of options for robots—from sympathetic facial expressions to vacuuming the floor. This assignment could be for small groups or individuals; this would also work great for a library display case! Instruct each student to come up with a robot idea—if they were to create a robot, what would it be? Just like the explanations on each robot in the book, be sure the students come up with the following information:

- name
- origin of name
- purpose

- creative inspiration
- approximate height

To make it even more interesting, encourage the students to design (on paper or a 3-D version) the look of the robot!

Variation: Depending on the size of your group, you may also want to structure the project like a science fair, but instead of physically building the robots, they would be judged on their designs.

Monster Hunt
by Rory Storm

Raise your hand if you can define cryptozoology. *Poll the class for potential answers.*

Kryptos in Greek means "hidden," *zoion* means "living creature" and *logos* means "study." If we put them together, what is cryptozoology the study of? *Only ask that last question if they couldn't figure out the definition when you asked the first time.*

I'll tell you about a couple hidden creatures, also known as cryptids, and we'll see if you can guess them.

Cryptid #1: He is one of the most famous and oldest crytids—even Native Americans have claimed his existence. The average footprint of this monster is about 15½ inches; the longest recorded footprint was 27 inches. His nicknames are Skunk Ape and Cripple Foot. *Take guesses and show a picture. If they can't figure it out, reveal the answer: Bigfoot.*

Cryptid #2: This creature is a reptile and lives in water. It's about 40–80 feet long. Its nickname is Nessie and lives in Loch Ness, Great Glen, Scotland. *Take guesses and show a picture. If they can't figure it out, reveal the answer: Loch Ness Monster.*

More information about cryptids and the people who study them can be found in *Monster Hunt.*

DISCUSSION QUESTIONS

1 Is cryptozoology a real study?
2. Describe the most recent sighting of Mothman.
3. What is the most famous cryptid of all time? Where does this creature reside?
4. List some creatures that live on different continents but have a lot of similarities.
5. What is the largest marsupial that ever lived? What does this marsupial have to do with the Bunyip?
6. Why does Africa seem like a great place to discover cryptids?
7. What was the most frightening cryptid to you?
8. What was the most surprising thing you learned in *Monster Hunt*?

PROJECT: CRYPTID DISCOVERY PRESENTATIONS

This is a great group project that will fit into nearly every subject matter. Split your group into groups of two people (this project can also be done individually). Instruct each group to choose a monster from the book. After reading the section on their respective creature, each group needs to do research on the location and other reported sightings of the creature.

Using photographs and the results from their research, each group needs to create a poster that contains information on their specific cryptid. Create a grade sheet that appeals to the specific class; for example, if it is for a language arts class, the research and structure is most important and the grade sheet should reflect those standards. For science more weight will be placed on the scientific facts and a burden of proof.

Brain
by Michael S. Sweeney

Tell the students to listen very carefully and remember the words in the order that you say them: pillow, tree, hat, shelf, sink, hair, statue, cloud, plate, canvas.

Our brains tell our lungs how to suck in air, our eyes how to see, and our toes how to wiggle. It helps us eat, feel, and remember. Can anyone remember the words I said in the correct order? *Call on a few students; if someone gets it correct, move on to the next section. If not, try this next activity. On separate notecards, have the ten words listed above written. Again ask the students to listen and try to remember the words in the correct order. This time show the words on the respective notecards as you say them aloud. Call on students to try and remember them in the correct order.*

The brain is the most intricate, complicated organ in the body and its development and functioning are absolutely fascinating. Just like with anything else, things can go wrong in the brain. Read the short story in chapter 8 about Henry Gustav Molaison titled "A Memorable Amnesic."

DISCUSSION QUESTIONS

1. What were some of the older theories of the brain?
2. How is the brain protected?

3. What is phrenology?
4. Explain how humans feel pain.
5. How do optical illusions work?
6. What happens in the brain when we are sleeping?
7. What was the most fascinating thing you learned?
8. What happens to the brain as you get older?

Project: All About the Brain — You Be the Teacher

There are ten chapters in the book (including the epilogue). Divide your class into ten groups and assign each group one chapter in the book. Using handmade 3-D examples, posters, and student-created worksheets, each group must teach the class their chapter within approximately 10–20 minutes. Each respective group must produce a quiz sheet of ten questions that they plan to answer during their presentations (be sure to approve the quiz sheets beforehand). The quiz sheets will be handed out before each presentation for the students to complete and turn in for grading to ensure the class is intellectually engaged in each group's presentation.

The Radioactive Boy Scout
by Ken Silverstein

It was a typical middle class neighborhood, 20 minutes from Detroit. And it was a typical summer afternoon with the sound of lawn mowers humming, children laughing as they jumped on their trampolines or swam in their pools, and mothers pushing their babies around their neighborhood in strollers. But June 26, 1995, was not a typical day in the Golf Manor neighborhood. Dotty Pease was driving home that afternoon when she saw a sight straight out of a science fiction movie: 11 men swarming across her front yard all wearing ventilated white moon suits. As neighbors gathered around the house, they watched these men take apart a shed in the backyard of Dotty's next door neighbor's home. No one could get a straight answer from the men. All the neighbors knew was that the men were from the Federal Environmental Protection Agency. If the people of Golf Manor had known the truth, their worry and concern would probably have turned into full-blown hysteria, for these men in moon suits were dismantling a homemade nuclear reactor, a nuclear reactor built by teenager David Hahn from instructions found in a 1960s chemistry textbook — a nuclear reactor that produced levels of radiation so high that it put the 40 thousand nearby residents at serious health risk. Why was he building a homemade nuclear reactor? To earn an atomic-energy merit badge from his Boy Scout troop.

Discussion Questions

1. What were the steps that David Hahn took to create his nuclear reactor?
2. Where did David find his radioactive material?
3. How did David get away with creating his reactor in the potting shed with no one noticing?

4. What was David's relationship with his father like? What was his relationship with his mother like?
5. How did the government find out about the David's nuclear experiment?
6. How did the government respond?
7. Did David seek any medical help after his experiments? Why or why not?

PROJECT: NUCLEAR ENERGY STUDIES

If you are a teacher, consider letting your students read this book in conjunction with studying nuclear energy in their science class. This way your students will have a greater grasp of nuclear energy and the dangers that David Hahn placed himself in as a teenager. If you are a public librarian, you might consider asking your teens to get into groups and assign each group a different source of energy to research. Energy sources could include nuclear, solar, wind, and coal. Let your teens loose in the library to find the answers to the following questions:

- How is the energy created or harvested?
- How is the energy stored?
- How many energy stations for this particular source are there in the United States today?
- How expensive is this energy to gather?
- What barriers currently exist to using this energy?
- Are there any negative environmental effects for using this energy?

After your groups have answered these questions, create a chart with your entire group to compare the different energy sources available. Discuss with your teens which sources of energy are best and which shouldn't be used.

Zero G.
by Peter Bond

For this booktalk simply read the story in chapter 2 called "Earth to Space in 8½ Minutes" and mark some photos to show the teens. Our favorites include photos of the shuttle shower, astronaut beds (and how they are strapped down), the toilet, and the rehydratable food. Be sure to not simply show the pictures but explain the innerworkings of each one — this book is full of a lot of information and fabulous photos, be sure to take advantage of both!

DISCUSSION QUESTIONS

1. Would you want to be an astronaut? Explain.
2. What are the qualifications to be an astronaut? Do you think there should be any others?
3. What is so significant about the Challenger? Had you ever heard of it before reading this book?
4. What do you think would be the most difficult part about living in a place with little or no gravity?

5. Explain what kind of food and drink they eat while in space?
6. How do they use the restroom?
7. Name one interesting fact or story you learned in the book?

PROJECT: SPACE SETTLEMENT

If you have a large class, split them into groups of 3–5 (if not, this project can be done individually or as one large group). Design a space settlement on the planet or moon of your choice using the information in the book — take into account weather, gravity, terrain, and what the citizens will do while living there. After getting it designed on paper, make a 3-D adaptation using whatever supplies you have. (You can find legos and other building materials at thrift stores). If time allows, present your settlements to the class and have your class vote on which settlement they would want to be assigned to visit.

Classroom Integration

Science is an all-encompassing subject — nearly every topic you cover in school may be tied back to science. If you're in *Romeo and Juliet,* you could talk about poisons or forensic science; for a geography lesson on Chile, you may discuss agriculture. If the drudgery of winter has seeped into your classroom and you need to liven it up, find the science counterpart and run with it! There are countless science topics with truly stunning and teen-friendly nonfiction books. Brainstorm the science relationship and pair it with the teen book.

If you work in a school where students attend classes taught by different instructors for different subjects, consider working with the science teacher to come up with a track that periodically integrates the subject or books you're working on with the topics they're studying in science. This will solidify the information with the students and make both classes more interactive.

If you don't have those freedoms at your school, go to your public library and school library and pull all of the books off of the shelf that have to do with your subject and set them up. Allow students to spend one day browsing the collection, and if possible, allow students to check out the books. It could be even better if you can integrate these books into the curriculum with a project or presentation. When working with teens the bottomline is think weird, wild, and undeniably interesting and you'll hit a home run — and science fulfills all of those qualifications!

More Great Books

Almanac of the Gross, Disgusting & Totally Repulsive: A Compendium of Fulsome Facts by Eric Elfman
Amazing Leonardo da Vinci Inventions You Can Build Yourself by Maxine Anderson
Brain: The Complete Mind by Michael S. Sweeney
Freaks of the Storm: From Flying Cows to Stealing Thunder: The World's Strangest True Weather Stories by Randy Cerveny

Geekspeak by Dr. Graham Tattersall

The Grand Tour: A Traveler's Guide to the Solar System by Ron Miller and William Hartmann

Grossology by Silvia Branzei and Jack Keely

Guinea Pig Scientists: Bold Self-Experimenters in Science and Medicine by Leslie Dendy, Mel Boring, and C. B. Mordan

Gut-Eating Bugs: Maggots Reveal the Time of Death! by Danielle Denega

How to Fossilize Your Hamster and Other Amazing Experiments for the Armchair Scientist by Mick O'Hare

Killer at Large: Criminal Profilers and the Cases they Solve! by D. B. Beres

Killer Wallpaper: True Cases of Deadly Poisonings by Anna Prokos

Light, Sound, and Waves Science Fair Projects: Using Sunglasses, Guitars, CDs, and Other Stuff by Robert Gardner

Monster Hunt: The Guide to Cryptozoology by Rory Storm

Mythbusters: Don't Try This at Home by The Discovery Channel and Mary Packard

Oh, Yuck: The Encyclopedia of Everything Nasty by Joy Masoff

101 Things You Wish You'd Invented and Some You Wish No One Had by Richard Horne and Tracey Turner

Outbreak: Plagues That Changed History by Bryn Barnard

Phineas Gage: A Gruesome but True Story About Brain Science by John Fleischman

Phobias: Everything You Wanted to Know but Were Afraid to Ask by Judy Monroe

The Radioactive Boy Scout: The True Story of a Boy and His Backyard Nuclear Reactor by Ken Silverstein

Really Useful Things: The Origins of Everyday Things by Joel Levy

Robo sapiens: Evolution of a New Species by Peter Menzel and Faith D'Aluisio

Stiff: The Curious Lives of Human Cadavers by Mary Roach

The Stunning Science of Everything: Science with the Squishy Bits Left In! by Nick Arnold and Tony De Saulles

That's Not My Science Book by Kate Kelly

Toe-Tagged: True Stories from the Morgue by Jaime Joyce

Travels with the Fossil Hunters by Peter J. Whybrow, ed.

When Objects Talk by Mark P. Friedlander Jr. and Terry M. Phillips

While You're Waiting for the Food to Come by Eric Muller

Zero G: Life and Survival in Space by Peter Bond

10

Animals

From insects and reptiles to cute and cuddly kittens, these books are filled with fascinating facts about the animal world surrounding us. Whether it's discovering why your pet cat makes that funny face or why certain ants explode, this chapter will make you die from cuteness overload and faint in creepy-crawly horror.

While this seems like a subchapter of "Science," we simply could not resist sharing all the possibilities with animals in its own chapter. After visiting the zoo what seven year old doesn't want to work there when he grows up? Though it seems something happens by the time that seven year old becomes a teen; sure there are still those teens that are crazy about animals, but the rest of them have heard just about all they can stand on mammals. These books are used to relight that flame of excitement when it comes to animals—who can resist but to look at just one more picture in *Gut-Eating Bugs*? And we simply cannot help ourselves when we read *Alex & Me*; we *need* our own parrot. Talking about animals does not have to center primarily around talking about kingdom, genus, or species—that kind of talk comes after the fire of curiosity is sparked by books that exploit the hidden truths of the animal kingdom.

Book Ideas with Booktalks, Discussion Questions, and Project Ideas

Gut-Eating Bugs
by Danielle Denega

All of the cases in this book are true! And they all feature dead bodies covered in bugs! A corpse is found at the bottom of a river. A family is found murdered in a cabin, and two hikers are found drowned in a desert. In all three cases bugs eating the decaying flesh of the bodies uncover the time of death and help solve the cases. You can be certain that if your body is ever left for dead out in the woods, blowflies will lay their eggs on your body within ten minutes of your death. And the maggots will most certainly tell the police when you died. Bugs may be creepy, crawly and give you the shivers, but to scientists and forensic entomologists, they are vital clues in many murder cases.

Discussion Questions

1. What is a forensic entomologist?
2. How does weather affect the life cycle of bugs on a dead body? Why?
3. How did black flies show when Hye-Yon Smith died? How did that prove that her husband was the murderer?
4. In true-life case #2, what two factors could have been responsible for the slower life cycle of the flies?
5. What does a Berlese funnel do?
6. When was the first recorded use of insects to solve a murder?
7. Before 1668 where did most people think maggots came from?
8. There are only about 62 forensic entomologists in the world. What do most entomologists do as their main work when they are not working on a crime scene investigation? Would you want to be a forensic entomologist? Why or why not?

Project: Act 1: Scene: Bugs!

Divide the teens into groups of five and ask them to choose between the Hye-Yon Smith case or the Mississippi family case. Have the teens write a script depicting the court scene for whichever case they choose. Each script should include at least the judge, the lawyer defending the suspect, the lawyer prosecuting the suspect, the suspect and a forensic entomologist. The script should focus on how the forensic entomologist proves the suspect to be guilty. If you want to get fancy, have the teens create visuals for evidence.

Alex & Me
by Irene M. Pepperberg

"You be good. I love you," were the last words Irene heard her dear friend Alex say to her before he died. Alex had been with her for 30 years—she taught him to speak and how to use the word "no." She put up with him when he was cranky or jealous of her other friends. When Irene was in a bad mood, Alex would say things like "Calm down!" They were emotionally attached. But even more important were the scientific discoveries Irene and Alex made.

We have two suggestions to finish this booktalk:

1. Search the Internet for video clips starring Alex the parrot and Dr. Irene M. Pepperberg. Before revealing to the class that Alex is, in fact, a parrot, show a video of Alex not merely performing but answering questions and reasoning (there are many examples).
2. Search for a short article on Alex and Dr. Pepperberg that briefly describes their work and ask for a volunteer to come up and read it.

Discussion Questions

1. In what ways did Dr. Irene Pepperberg correctly utilize the scientific method?
2. Dr. Pepperberg claims that Alex does more than mimic what he hears; give three examples.

3. How were Alex, Griffin, and Arthur different?
4. Do you think animals have personalities? Why or why not?
5. Why would it be important for us to know if animals (birds, monkeys, etc.) have more intellectual power than we currently assume?

PROJECT: THE SCIENTIFIC METHOD AND BEYOND

Discuss the scientific method thoroughly and be sure to focus on the various ways Dr. Pepperberg followed the scientific method. Split the students into groups of 2–3 and assign them a variation of the the steps in the scientific method:

- Come up with a question they believe needs answering.
- Gather up-to-date information about the topic from at least 3 resources.
- Based on the information gathered, form a hypothesis.
- Construct an outline for how they would hypothetically do an experiment to answer their question.

They won't be actually completing the experiment so there is no need to analyze or interpret data. In their groups, present their projects to the class. The retest will be symbolized by allowing the class to offer different suggestions to make the experiment more precise or thorough.

The World of the Spider
by Adrienne Mason

Before giving this booktalk, go through the book and find pictures that accompany the various aspects of spiders listed below. Place sticky notes on the pages you want to show the class and number them — as you're going through your booktalk, you can show the correct pages.

Imagine a peaceful place, like a grassy meadow. There are tall daisies and the grass is blowing gently in the wind. You're running through it and decide to lay down. W. S. Bristowe, a British arachnologist, determined that within one acre of grass there were 2,265,000 spiders; therefore, you just imagined yourself laying on thousands of spiders.

It has been said that at any time in any place, there is a spider within a meter of you. Though you may not see it, it is probably performing a courtship dance, spinning an intricate wonder with silk, laying young in a small sac, or injecting a special lique-fying venom into its prey and sucking out the juices.

Humans, part of the 4,000 species of mammals, share this planet with close to 38,000 species of spider — 4,400 species alone are various jumping spiders (that means there are 400 more species of jumping spiders than all species of mammals). Our arach-nid friends have successfully occupied nearly everywhere — mountains, deserts, caves, seashores, and ponds.

How do all of these spiders come to be? The spider, from egg sac to adult spider, is really quite complicated. The mating process itself may involve the male playing his web like a guitar or presenting his spider girlfriend with a delicious silk-wrapped beetle. Unfortunately, sometimes it's not so romantic — the Nephila female is so large (100 times larger than the male) that when he ventures onto her web, she does not take notice of him as a mate or a meal because he is so small.

After conception, the eggs are wrapped in a carefully constructed egg sac. When the growing baby spiders become too large for the sac, they use a small egg tooth to find their way out. Some spider mothers care for their helpless young after birth; however, other hatchlings are equipped with all they need.

DISCUSSION QUESTIONS

1. Besides the stereotypical web, what other kinds of homes do spiders create?
2. What are the two body parts of the spider called?
3. List three clues a spider might be preparing to molt.
4. Describe what happens after the female receives the male's sperm.
5. How do spiders fly?
6. List and briefly describe the three main types of predatory spiders.
7. In the food web is a spider the predator or prey? *Trick question: Both!*

PROJECT: FOOD WEB

After discussing the definition of a food web and how it works, divide the class into groups of about 5. Have each group come up with their own food web and each student represent a different creature. Be sure that each group knows the spider should be predator and prey in their web.

Using string, follow the food web from student (creature) to student (creature) ending at the top predator. After building the string web, have the student representing the spider let go of the string. What do the students think happens to the creatures below the spider in the food web? Above?

Instruct each group to draw their food web on a poster board and illustrate what happens to the various creatures on the food web when the spider is removed.

Essential Cat
by Caroline Davis

This is a simple booktalk for a pet care guide. We've found that this particular booktalk creates a connection moment when all of the teens in the room realize that they have a shared experience. And if you, as the booktalker, have a cat or cats, then you've probably had this experience as well. This booktalk is told from Jill's point of view. Please rewrite this booktalk to include your own pet cats, your neighbor's cats, your siblings' cats or whoever you know with cats.

Who has cats? *Let the teens answers. If you are booktalking to younger teens, you'll get rather excited responses.* What's your cat's name? *Spend some time with this question. Let your teens tell you about their pet cats.* I have two cats, Simon and Natasha, and they make this weird face all of the time, where their mouths form this weird open square shape and their eyes take on a dazed expression — kind of like … *mimic the Flehman reaction face for your teens! We've always had teens recognize this facial expression as something their own cats do regularly.* Has anyone ever seen your cat do that? In my house we call it the bad kitty smell face, because it looks like they've just smelled something bad. But according to the *Essential Cat* book, this face is called the Flehman reaction, which allows the cats to taste smells through a special organ in the roof of their mouth. *Show your teens the picture of the cat making the Flehman reaction face.* This book can tell you all kinds of things you never knew about your cat. So, if you want to understand the many mysteries of your cat's behavior then check this book out.

From "aw" to "ew," there is the perfect animal book for every teen.

DISCUSSION QUESTIONS

1. What is the difference between a pedigreed, cross-bred and non–pedigreed cat?
2. If you have a cat of your own, what behaviors do you recognize from this book?
3. How can you tell if a cat is anxious or worried? Curious? Bored?
4. Why do cats like to perch in high places?
5. Why do dogs often chase cats? How can this be prevented?
6. Who were the first pet cats? Why were they domesticated?

PROJECT: RESEARCHING A NEW PET

While not all of your teens will have pets in their own homes, most of them do wish for a pet and would like to own some type of animal. Let your teens dream by asking them to research pet care for the animal of their choice. Your public library will have dozens if not hundreds of books on caring for all sorts of pets from cats and dogs to horses, cows, spiders, snakes and other reptiles, even guinea pigs and mice. For this project teens must pick out a pet care guide for the animal of their choice from the library. Then they should answer a few basic questions.

- How do you properly choose which animal is right for you? Where do you find these animals?
- How do you care for the animal while it is young?
- What health concerns should you watch out for? How do you keep your animal healthy?
- What are the feeding habits of your animal?

- Does the animal stay inside or does it roam outside? What type of living accommodations should you make for your animal?
- What do you do if your animal is injured or gets sick?
- What concerns should you watch out for as the animal gets older?
- Can you train your animal? How?
- How do you know what your animal is feeling? What signs should you look for?

You can ask your teens to answer these questions in a variety of formats. Do they present orally to the rest of the group? Should they create a tri-fold poster? Should they write a research paper? The delivery method for their research is up to you.

Shark Life
by Peter Benchley

Peter Benchley was hanging out underwater in a shark cage filled with floating chum, trying to attract a great white shark — not a big deal, not terrifying, not anything really out of the ordinary until a shark actually showed up. It starting biting on the cage, you know, just out of curiosity, but then it grabbed a piece of horse meat and started looking for more and then the rope connecting the cage to the boat got stuck in the shark's mouth. Benchley knew that if he didn't get that rope out of the shark's mouth, he would be dragged to the bottom and smashed to death.

Then there was the time he was in the Bermudas filming yellow tuna. A fishing line got caught around his ankle causing a bloody mess, which attracted an oceanic whitetip shark that made a very honest attempt at eating him. Benchley's only defense was a broomstick handle that accidentally saved his life.

Or there was the time that he swam on the back of a 16 foot manta ray, which threatened to take him too deep into the water.

Shark Life: True Stories of Sharks and the Sea is a collection of tales from the author of *Jaws* about his encounters with sharks, moray eels, whales and even dolphins. Benchley promises us that shark attacks are rare, that we have nothing to fear, but what good are these promises when he also tells us stories of arms disappearing, of arteries severed and bodies chomped in half at the waist?

DISCUSSION QUESTIONS

1. Benchley discusses the difference between conditioning sea animals and training them. What are these differences?
2. What are the dangers of conditioning wild animals?
3. Benchley describes the summer of 2001 as the Summer of the Shark. Why? Why did the media pay so much attention to sharks that summer?
4. Do you think all of the attention to shark attacks that summer was warranted?
5. Read the story "The Day All the Sharks Died." What is Benchley trying to tell us with this story?
6. Benchley describes several ocean species that humans fear such as barracudas, moray

ells, octopi, sting rays and squid. Why do you think humans are so afraid of these animals?

7. Do you have any personal experiences with the ocean or sea life?

PROJECT: DEAR DIARY

Let your teens research their favorite species of shark. Where does the shark live? Is it a coastal shark or a blue water shark? What does it eat? How does it breathe? Is it aggressive toward humans? Is it attractive to fishermen?

Once your teens have researched their choice of shark, ask them to write a diary entry from the shark's point of view that includes either an encounter with a human or a fishing boat. How does this shark spend its day? What does it find to eat? What does it see and smell throughout the day? What other fish and sea animals does this shark encounter? What happens when the shark encounters the humans or fishing boat?

The Dangerous Book for Dogs
by Joe Garden, Janet Ginsburg, Chris Pauls,
Anita Serwacki, and Scott Sherman

This is a great book to do when you notice your audience yawning, staring at the ceiling, or looking generally unenthusiastic.

- Raise your hand if you have a dog.
- Has anyone in here ever tried to give your dog medicine by hiding it in peanut butter or food and the dog somehow found a way to eat all around the pill but not the pill?
- Has anyone ever tried to put a costume, be it reindeer antlers at Christmas or a Zorro cape at Halloween, and your dog has always found a way to wiggle out of it?

You might think these actions are instinct, but really, they come from this book, *The Dangerous Book for Dogs*. In fact, the instructions for drinking from the "water bowl" in the bathroom (known to humans as a toilet) are in this book. *In the chapter "Questions About the World," there is a question regarding drinking from the water bowl. Read the question and the following response.*

DISCUSSION QUESTIONS

1. Do you have any experiences with dogs that helped you relate to what you read in this book?
2. In the "The Root of Barks" chapter, do you think the different descriptions of the barks are correct? What are other ways dogs use to communicate?
3. What dog was supposedly the first dog on the North American continent? Briefly summarize his story.
4. What are some popular novels about dogs listed in the book? Can you think of any additional books about dogs?

5. List some of the jobs that dogs can have. Have you ever met dogs that have these jobs?
6. Why do you think humans are so fascinated by dogs?

PROJECT: CREATIVE WRITING

Create your very own "Dangerous Book." Based on the original *The Dangerous Book for Boys*, *The Dangerous Book for Girls* and *The Dangerous Book for Dogs* have been written, and it's time for your students to create their own. Perfect for a long-term writing assignment, instruct your students to first choose who (or what) they want to write their "Dangerous Book" about—maybe a rat, fly, or even a laptop. With a minimum of an introduction, table of contents, and three chapters, students must write about their own being (or object), focusing primarily on creativity and grammar. To celebrate completing such a large a project, have a binding party for your class where the students will bind their books with homemade covers. Be sure to display these in a prominent place in the school—a project like this is one that lower grades can look forward to completing.

Meerkat Manor
by Tim Clutton-Brock

The saga of a meerkat: She was born the smallest of her litter. She was banished from her family by two female cousins fighting for dominance. She was saved from certain death by one of her cousin's sudden and untimely demise! And in a feat of meerkat glory, she returned triumphant to her family and earned the dominant position. But the saga wasn't over. Still vying for dominance, the females in her family killed litters of pups, with dead meerkat babies left and right. She was the stricken mother who could not be called queen without successful and live litters. And then, in the nick of time, Flower triumphs again and manages to keep her last litter of pups alive, saving herself and her group from losing their range to rival gangs of meerkats. This is the story of Flower, a little, itty-bitty meerkat ruling her family, defending her territory and hanging out with the scientists.

DISCUSSION QUESTIONS

1. Who are the people watching the meerkats? Why?
2. How did the research group convince the meerkats to become accustomed to them?
3. Who leads a pack of meerkats?
4. Why do meerkats use lookouts?
5. How did Flower become the leader of her gang?
6. How do meerkats form families? How do they protect their territory?

PROJECT: MEERKAT MANOR SERIES

Meerkat Manor gained fame as a popular television series on Animal Planet. For this project let your teens watch a few episodes of *Meerkat Manor* so they can see Flower and her gang in live action.

The Animal Dialogues
by Craig Childs

"I went on a hike with a buddy of mine, and in the midst of looking at different things, we unknowingly got separated. We're both fairly good trackers and knew we could find each other again. Not long after we were separated, I heard footsteps again. I paused, trying to decide if it was a bear, but clearly it wasn't. The footsteps were confident and abrupt. They, no doubt, belonged to my friend. Interestingly, I could tell he hadn't heard me yet, so I began tracking him. I thought, 'How fun will it be to sneak up behind him, jump on his back, and scare him?' I heard the sounds of birds and other creatures but I was concentrating very intently on following my companion and staying out of view so I could startle him at the most opportune moment. Suddenly, I heard his footsteps stop. I stopped. I heard walking again, but it was farther up ahead than I thought and it was quieter. I wondered if he knew I was there. I walked very carefully, only putting pressure on my heel and the outside of my foot with each step. He walked on and I followed — though I couldn't tell if he knew I was behind because he was still walking so softly. Suddenly, I heard someone yell behind me. I turned and looked and it was my companion hollering about a huge rattlesnake he just saw. Quickly thinking, 'If he is behind, who or what is in front me?' I suddenly realized I had been tracking a jaguar."

DISCUSSION QUESTIONS

1. Have you ever seen a bear? What new facts did you learn about bears?
2. How would you have responded in the story of the jaguar?
3. What did you think of the story about the hawk and rabbit? How could the way the clean snow unmarred by rabbit prints be symbolic of life and death?
4. Have you ever been in a car that hit a deer? Did the story, "Deer" make you think of the experience differently?
5. What was your favorite story? Explain.
6. Have you ever had an interesting run-in with an animal?

PROJECT: CREATIVE ANIMAL WRITING

Instruct students to individually choose their favorite story from the book. With this story in hand, they need to rewrite the story from the point of view of the animal: what is the animal thinking, feeling, and wanting? To do this effectively, they will more than likely need to do some extra research on their respective animal's behavior, however, don't encourage students to get too distracted by the research so that it inhibits their creativity.

The story needs to end in relatively the same manner as the story by Craig Childs, but the pathway, from the beginning to the end, should be narrated by the animal. As with many of the other creative writing projects, try to allow students the opportunity to read their stories to the class.

More Great Books

Alex & Me by Irene M. Pepperberg

Always Faithful: A Memoir of the Marine Dogs of WORLD WAR II by William Putney

The Animal Dialogues: Uncommon Encounters in the Wild by Craig Childs

A Big Little Life: A Memoir of a Joyful Dog by Dean Koontz

Chased by Sea Monsters: Prehistoric Predators of the Deep by Nigel Marven and Jasper James

Dancing with Cats by Burton Silver and Heather Busch

The Dangerous Book for Dogs: A Parody by Rex & Sparky by Joe Garden, Janet Ginsburg, Chris Pauls, Anita Serwacki, and Scott Sherman

Essential Cat by Caroline Davis

Exploding Ants: Amazing Facts About How Animals Adapt by Joanne Settel

Grayson by Lynne Cox

Gut-Eating Bugs: Maggots Reveal the Time of Death! by Danielle Denega

How to Speak Dog by Sarah Whitehead

March of the Penguins: Companion to the Major Motion Picture by Luc Jacquet, Jerome Maison and Donnali Fifield

Meerkat Manor: Flower of the Kalahari by Tim Clutton-Brock

Monster Hunt: The Guide to Cryptozoology by Rory Storm

My Season with Penguins: An Antarctic Journal by Sophie Webb

Rats: Observations on the History and Habitat of the City's Most Unwanted Inhabitants by Robert Sullivan

Shark Life: True Stories about Sharks & the Sea by Peter Benchley

Tales of the Cryptids: Mysterious Creatures That May or May Not Exist by Kelly Milner Halls, Rick Spears, and Roxyanne Young

The Tarantula Scientist by Sy Montgomery and Nic Bishop

That Gunk On Your Car: A Unique Guide to Insects of North America by Mark Hostetler

Whale by Joe Roman

The World of the Spider by Adrienne Mason

11

Nature

Looking for weird ocean life? Or maybe insane weather? It's all here. The intricacies in our sky, land, oceans, weather, and food web are just a few of the conversation-starting book topics!

Much like the "Science" and "Animal" chapters, "Nature" is filled with the odd curiosities in nature that are rarely discussed. It's true, every time a natural disaster occurs, we're all glued to our televisions in morbid curiosity, and who hasn't seen the news story about the person who has the flesh-eating bacteria. Nature is shrouded in mystery, unpredictability, and excitement — as educators we need to be using this to our advantage, particularly with teens. Nature and other science subjects are the perfect choice for the group with short attention spans, the dramatic, or those bored with life.

Book Ideas with Booktalks, Discussion Questions, and Project Ideas

Earth from Above
by Yann Arthus-Bertrand

Our co-booktalker, Jessica Friesema, loved showing this book to teens. Since this book is mainly a picture book, she would show a few pictures to the teens and then ask them if they could guess what is being portrayed in the picture. Some of these images are not easy to guess if you can't read the caption. Our favorite pictures to show teens are:

January 01: "A heart made out of mangroves in France"
March 04: "Locust infestation in Madagascar"
April 22: "Iceberg and penguin in Antarctica"
May 08: "Tulip fields in the Netherlands"
June 22: "A lagoon in Madagascar"
July 05: "Laundry drying in Chad"
August 12: "Timber raft in Canada"
September 09: "Modern graves in Egypt"
October 21: "Sunken boat in Kenya"
December 11: "Fishing nets in Spain"

Discussion Questions

1. What is sustainable development? What is it not?
2. Why are greenhouse gases a world wide problem? What do you think we should do to reduce them?
3. Why are forests important to the earth?
4. Why is fresh water so important to people? How did fresh water determine the development of civilization?
5. Why can't we use fossil fuels like oil, gas and coal indefinitely? What do you think we should use instead? What is stopping us from using other energy sources now?
6. What are the benefits of transportation? What are the negative effects?
7. What do you think it means to dehumanize a group of people or even a single individual?
8. Out of all of the pictures of the earth in this book, which is the most beautiful to you? Which is the most disturbing?

Project: Photo Journals

Ask your teens to take pictures of the nature, people or environment they see around them everyday. Pictures could include family, family habits or traditions, natural habitats, human habitats, pictures of pollution or damage to the environment. Ask teens to caption each photo and write one paragraph for each photo explaining why they took the picture. Once the photos are compiled, ask the teens to include an introduction to their journal in which they give their opinion on whether or not the earth is in danger by our habits and deeds or whether their community is mostly healthy.

Dangerous Planet
by Bryn Barnard

Do you know how the dinosaurs died? Have you ever heard of the Minoans? They were a peaceful civilization that controlled the Mediterranean world thousands of years before the Greeks and Romans. In 3,000 BC they were more advanced than any civilization for thousands of years to come with two writing systems, hot and cold running water, flushing toilets and cookware as advanced as we have today. Did I mention they were peaceful? No wars and they didn't even have locks on their doors. Too bad a tsunami wiped them out and humanity had to start over again.

Have you ever heard of Aksum, an ancient African Empire as powerful as Rome, Egypt and China? You probably haven't because a slight shift in climate wiped them out too.

Did you know that in 1816 the entire world experienced a year without summer all because of a volcanic eruption in the Indian Ocean? The old people called that year Eighteen Hundred and Froze to Death.

Bryn Barnard brings together just a small sample of some of history's most damaging natural disasters that changed the course of history wiping out entire species of animals and destroying entire civilizations.

Discussion Questions

1. According to *Dangerous Planet* what caused the dinosaurs' extinction? How did the asteroid cause so much devastation? What were the lingering effects of the asteroid?
2. What helped the mammals survive the devastation?
3. What do you think present day life would be like if the tsunami had not destroyed the Minoan culture?
4. Had you heard of Aksum before reading this book? What helped the Aksum empire thrive? What led to this civilization's downfall? Imagine a history in which Aksum continued to be a powerful empire. How would that success have altered world history?
5. Do you think the two storms that wrecked Kublai Khan's naval fleets were just bad timing and coincidence?
6. How did the eruption of Mount Tambora affect the world? How did it change history?
7. How did the Hurricane of 1888 create safer modern cities?
8. How are we making the planet more dangerous? What dangers are we ignoring that could change history again?

Allow students to use any materials available to create a diorama of their original alternative world.

Project: Alternative Worlds

Ask your teens to choose one of the events presented in *Dangerous Planet*. What would the present day world be like if that disaster had not occured? Let teens create their alternate world through a medium of their choosing. Options could include:

- a painting or drawing
- a diorama
- a tri-fold poster
- an essay
- a play or old time radio show

However your teens decide to present their alternate world, each presentation should show the changes to the earth, such as land masses and climate, plants and animals, and changes to humans including our habitats, diet, clothing, transportation and even which civilizations are now powerful and wealthy.

Freaks of the Storm
by Randy Cerveny

As with some of the other books, this is a great opportunity to do excerpts directly from the book. Reading from the book can instill a sense of "cool" reliability and legitimacy.

Weather is weird! It has driven bamboo through a brick wall, ripped the clothes off of people, and rained when there wasn't a cloud in the sky.

Read the first three "Item" sections at the beginning of the first chapter (depending on the age and attention span of your audience, you may want to only do one or 2).

DISCUSSION QUESTIONS

1. What was the story that surprised you the most?
2. Describe weird weather you have experienced.
3. Describe in your own words how thunder and lightening occur.
4. What are the three state variables (basic attributes) of our atmosphere?
5. Explain how wind works in your own words.
6. What is a primary source? What is a secondary source?
7. List three sources Randy Cerveny used in his book and label them as primary or secondary sources.

PROJECT: PRIMARY AND SECONDARY SOURCES

Before beginning this project, thoroughly review the difference between primary and secondary resources. Instruct the students to select one memorable weather event that has occurred in the last year. Using two primary and two secondary resources, have them create their own five paragraph newspaper article to present to the class. In addition to primary and secondary resources, this is an excellent opportunity to discuss the issue of reliable resources, particularly when searching the Internet for information.

Bitten
by Pamela Nagami, MD

Who in here has ever been bitten by a spider? *Encourage the students to raise their hands.* Keep your hand up if you're willing to tell the story. *Call on someone who still has his or her hand raised.*

Has anyone in here ever been stung by something? *Again, encourage the students to raise their hands if they have a story to tell. Call on someone to relay their personal story.*

It seems we can't get away from the creepy, crawly, and tiny flying creatures, especially those that bite and sting. *The first paragraph of chapter 1 "Invincible Invaders" is powerful! At this point open the book and read it.*

If you can stomach this book to the end, you'll discover that it's not just the bites and stings of spiders and wasps but a bite from the person sitting next to you could cause an infection so severe, you might have to have your hand amputated.

DISCUSSION QUESTIONS

1. Describe something you learned about fire ants.
2. In the chapter "Stingers from the Sea," what is something you will be more aware of next time you visit a large body of water? Have you ever known someone to come in contact with a man-o'-war or a jellyfish?

3. What are cone snails and why are they dangerous?
4. What is sleeping sickness? Do you run the risk of getting this in the United States of America? Explain.
5. Why are Komodo dragons dangerous?
6. Is rabies a problem in the United States? How?
7. What makes rat bites so dangerous?

PROJECT: NEWS REPORT: A SURVIVOR'S TALE

Your class will need to be in groups of at least three people and they will need access to a video camera and video-editing equipment. Using one of the survival stories from the book, have one person be the reporter, one person as the survivor, and the last person shooting video. They will need to create a script in which the reporter interviews the survivor on what happened, based loosely from the survivor's story from the book *Bitten*. They also will need to show a picture of what bit or stung the person and information on that species. Bonus points awarded for creativity!

Every Creeping Thing
by Richard Conniff

There are a lot of folks out of there who are afraid of nature. Is anyone afraid of something in nature? *Allow a smattering of the class to answer. If you tend to get the same answers, ask them to raise their hands for answers that haven't been said.* Being afraid of nature is a fear that dates back to the beginning of recorded history — more than likely this is because there is so much in nature that, even to this day, is a mystery to humans. The sloth, for example, has nearly odorless poo and its cleaning rituals are incredibly thorough, yet still, their fur contains various species of moths, ticks, mites, mosquitoes and biting sand flies. One researcher recorded 120 moths and 978 beetles from one sloth. Or the mouse is another example — though females can mingle from group to group, a male mouse will fight to death to remain the dominant mouse in his group, even going so far as to kill the infants of another male mouse. Nature is just plain weird, and after reading this book you'll see, it gets a lot weirder!

DISCUSSION QUESTIONS

1. Who is the author discussed in the introduction who is known to be a plagiarist?
2. Why do you think nature has always frightened humans?
3. What is the difference between a two-toed and three-toed sloth (other than the number of toes)?
4. In the chapter on mice, why were they trying to decide if they should applaud mice?
5. How did mice spread to nearly every inch of Earth?
6. What is a cormorant? Why do catfish farmers hate them?
7. Why do you think humans are so fascinated and afraid of sharks?
8. Describe one new fact you learned.

Project: Past Folklore, Present Fact

Divide your class into groups of 2–4 and assign them each a different creature from the book. Equipped with Internet access, books on folklore, and two pieces of poster-board, students must then find an old fable, legend, or myth about that specific creature and illustrate it on piece of the poster board. The other piece of poster board should reflect facts on their creature from the book and their own research. Each group must give a five minute speech on both posters that addresses the following items:

- Retell the folklore regarding your creature.
- Why were people afraid of your creature? Are they still? Why or why not?
- What facts did you find to prove or disprove the reason for fear?

Blizzard!
by Jim Murphy

The U.S. Weather Service is predicting a blizzard. What is the first thing your parents do? Do they run to the grocery store and grab milk and bread (when you really wish they would grab soda and potato chips)? Do they start chopping wood or purchase a few firewood bundles for your rarely used fireplace? Or do they just not worry about it because the forecast is really never as bad as they predict and your electricity and water run underground anyway, so it's not like you're going to lose power and not be able to watch TV for the next three days?

These days we've done a pretty good job preparing ourselves for bad weather in most cases, but it wasn't always so. In March 1888 the East Coast from Maine down to Maryland was sunny, warm and spring was in the air. The U.S. Signal Corps (the organization responsible for predicting weather back then) indicated that the weather would be a little colder, with a little rain and maybe some wind, despite the fact that there was a giant storm heading straight for them from the west and another giant storm heading straight for them from the south.

On Sunday morning the weather was looking a bit foreboding with giant black storm clouds looming on the horizon. By Sunday night the storms hit New York City. The temperature dropped to freezing within just a few minutes and the rain turned to snow and ice. That night trains moving up and down the East Coast were stranded by snow drifts, and passengers either waited it out or tried to walk to the nearest town, many of them dying of hypothermia on the journey. On Monday morning pedestrians in New York City found themselves being blown over by the wind. Some of them landed in snow drifts, suffocating as the wind held them face down in the snow. Snow drifts piled as high as rooftops on houses. The wind was so fierce that it wrecked ships and sent many sailors into the frigid waters.

Some would claim that this blizzard was just a snowstorm. But it brought New York and the entire East Coast to a standstill. This blizzard changed America. It changed how we prepare for disasters. It changed our transportation systems, our power systems and our weather prediction services. After the blizzard of 1888, American demanded never to be taken by surprise like that again. But you know, it seems that no matter how much we prepare, the weather always takes us by surprise. Despite our preparations, blizzards, hurricanes, and tornadoes all continue to prove stronger than our greatest efforts.

DISCUSSION QUESTIONS

1. Where did we get the word "blizzard"?
2. Many people went out into the blizzard to go to work or school. Why?
3. Whose responsibility was it to clear the streets of snow? Whose responsibility is it today?
4. *Blizzard!* tells the experiences of several families and individuals who faced the blizzard. Which story is the most surprising?
5. After reading the story of 17-year-old Sara Wilson, do you think her death could have been prevented? How?
6. New York City has always been home to many homeless people. Where did these people go during the storm?
7. How did the blizzard of 1888 change the transportation system in New York City? How did it change the power system?
8. What other storms have taken us by surprise?

PROJECT: WEATHER ON YOUR BIRTHDAY

What was the weather like on your birthday? Was it sunny, cloudy, raining, or snowing? What was the temperature? Was there any severe weather? Several online weather Web sites offer a historical look at weather. Visit www.wunderground.com to see what the weather was like in your hometown on your birthday. You might also consider visiting your local public library, as many libraries will keep records of the weather forecast for their areas.

Backyard and Beyond
by Edward Duensing and A. B. Millmoss

It's a beautiful summer day! The birds are singing, the bees are buzzing! And you are banished outside. Your mother has decided no more video games for you today! Not in this gorgeous weather! What do you do? Maybe find a pickup game of basketball? Grab your skateboard? Dig your bike out of the garage? Well, the next time you are forced to spend a few hours outside, try becoming a naturalist. What is a naturalist? It's a person who watches nature! Sound boring? It doesn't have to be. If you know what you are looking for and how to find it, you'll discover that your own backyard is filled with the signs of birds, night animals, and insects that you never knew existed all around you. Let's see how much you know about being a naturalist.

- When positioning yourself so that animals don't know you are there, do you hide behind or in front of a tree? You hide in front of the tree! Why? Because animals don't look there. You'll just blend into the tree itself.

- It's nighttime and you hear something digging around in your trashcans outside. You grab a flashlight and shine it out into the dark. You see bright yellow eyes shining back at you. What kind of animal is it? It's a raccoon! What about bright white eyes? That's a dog or a fox. What if you can't decide if the eyes are yellow or white because they seem to be a mix of both? You're looking at a bobcat!
- You see large tracks in the snow leading away from your house and into the woods. Could you tell what type of animals was in your yard?

With the help of this book, *Backyard and Beyond,* you'll learn how to identify tracks of animals, birdcalls, and signs to know when a storm's a comin.'

DISCUSSION QUESTIONS

1. What is the best way to "stalk" the nature hiding in your backyard?
2. What is the "stalker's walk"?
3. How can you tell the difference between tracks from a bounding gait and a walking gait?
4. When is the best time to look for birds? Why is stalking not an effective form of searching for birds?
5. How do you find a beehive?
6. List some of the insects you are likely to see if you are hunting them in your backyard?
7. Most birds' nests and squirrels' nests are found on the south-facing side of trees. Why?
8. The moon can be read for signs of approaching weather. List these signs and what weather they foretell.
9. Why do our eyes work differently at night? How do our eyes adjust to the night's limited light?
10. List the types of tracks to look for in your own backyard. What are the differences between the domestic cat tracks and a bobcat's tracks? What are the differences between a domestic dog's tracks and a red fox's tracks?

PROJECT: WEEKEND NATURALIST

Backyard and Beyond encourages us to learn about the wildlife surrounding us. The easiest project to accompany this book is to let your teens practice some of the author's techniques. Let your teens head out into the schoolyard, woods or park. Ask each of them to find a place to sit away from each other and let them observe the wildlife that begins to move around them. Afterward, have a discussion with your teens about what wildlife they saw.

Out of the Blue
by John Naylor

This is a booktalk to save for one of the first few days of Spring, the perfect storm in a school setting: the weather is fabulous, students are restless for their Spring Break, and you, admittedly, are just as anxious to get away. Take this booktalk outside! Granted, if you don't have the freedoms of rushing outside at the beginning of Spring, this talk will still work, but it will be so much better if you can!

When you're outside, especially away from the city or in a park, what are some things you notice? It seems we often spend a lot of time looking around us or down at the ground and not nearly enough looking up! What are some things we see when we look up? *Undoubtedly, you will get obvious answers, such as the sun and clouds. See if you can get more specific answers out of them. If you are able to take your teens outside, have them look up and begin describing specific things they see.*

Out of the Blue explains every possible thing you would want to know about the sky during an entire 24-hour period — in the morning, at lunch, at sunset, and through the night. It contains everything about mirages and rainbows, the best time to look at the moon and planets, and answers the timeless and complicated question about why the sky looks blue.

DISCUSSION QUESTIONS

1. Why is the sky blue? What makes it so difficult to explain?
2. What is polarized light? How can we recognize it in nature?
3. Explain the relationship between lake monsters and mirages.
4. What are the different colors at sunset? How do the colors in the sky seem to change when the sun is at the horizon and when it is just below the horizon?
5. What three things are essential if you are to see a rainbow? What three things can increase your chances?
6. If you want to see the man on the moon, when should you look?
7. Explain why it is not unusual to see the moon during the day.

PROJECT: OUR SKY IN A DAY

This is a great project to do as a class. You'll need a digital camera and access to a computer to retrieve the photos. For each hour that the school is open, have someone from the class go stand outside and take a picture (make sure it is the same spot and the same direction). If you can get in there before school or stay later, that will provide even more photos! After doing that for a day, compile the photos and, if you have the equipment, put them into a slideshow to view on an overhead. If you don't have the equipment, print them off and tape them on the wall in order. Analyze the changes that occur throughout the day and make observations based on the information from *Out of the Blue*. This project could also be done individually over a weekend.

Ocean
by Robert Dinwiddie, Sue Scott, and Fabien Cousteau

The next frontier for discovery is not in the Amazon or the deserts in Africa or even Antarctica. It's not in the sky, but under the water. Water covers about 75 percent of

Earth, controls our climate, and yet we know so little about what's under the beautiful waves that rise and fall from our shores every day.

Show various photographs and see if students can identify what is depicted in the photo. Photographs to show: "The Skeleton Coast" (chapter: "Coasts and the Seashore"), "Shelf Deposits" (chapter: "Shallow Seas"), "Monterey Bay Kelp Forest" (chapter: "Shallow Seas"), "Giant Filter-Feeder" (chapter: "The Open Ocean and Ocean Floor"), and "Ooze-Forming Zooplankton" (chapter: "The Open Ocean and Ocean Floor").

Does anyone in here not enjoy reading because it takes too long or you just don't like having to complete the book? This book is one you can pick and choose what you read. If you're interested in the ocean's basic make up, it's in here. If you're interested in hurricanes and other "water" storms, it's in here. And if you just can't stop looking at ocean life, it's in here too! Just read what you want, and skip the rest!

DISCUSSION QUESTIONS

1. What is Gondwana? What is Pangea?
2. What research did Benjamin Franklin do on oceans?
3. What is the global water cycle?
4. Why don't all coastlines look the same?
5. How does the giant filter-feeder shark eat?
6. How are iceberg shapes classified?
7. What is bioluminescence?

PROJECT: 3-D OCEAN RESEARCH

This book is packed with information and probably too large to expect students to read cover to cover. After allowing them to pick through and explore the amazing photography and content, instruct them to choose a topic they like. Have them then create a 3-D stationary presentation on their chosen topic using at least three sources. If you are close to the ocean, take a trip there to allow students extra time for research. If you have an aquarium in town, talk to them about displaying the presentation at their location. (If space is limited, you could make this a contest with the winner's presentation on display).

More Great Books

Adventures in Tornado Alley by Mike Hollingshead and Eric Nguyen
Backyard and Beyond: A Guide for Discovering the Outdoors by Edward Duensing and A. B. Millmoss
Between a Rock and a Hard Place by Aron Ralston
Bitten: True Medical Stories of Bites and Stings by Pamela Nagami, MD
Blizzard! by Jim Murphy
Creatures of the Deep by Erich Hoyt
Dangerous Planet: Natural Disasters that Changed History by Bryn Barnard
Earth from Above by Yann Arthus-Bertrand
Earth Shock: Hurricanes, Volcanoes, Earthquakes, Tornadoes and Other Forces of Nature by Andrew Robinson

Every Creeping Thing: True Tales of Faintly Repulsive Wildlife by Richard Conniff

Freaks of the Storm: From Flying Cows to Stealing Thunder: The World's Strangest True Weather Stories by Randy Cerveny

The Invisible Kingdom by Idan Ben-Barak

Man vs. Weather: Be Your Own Weatherman by Dennis DiClaudio

MySpace/Our Planet: Change is Possible by the MySpace Community with Jeca Taudte

A Natural History of the Antarctic: Life in the Freezer by Alastair Fothergil

A Natural History of the Unnatural World by Carroll and Brown Limited

Ocean: The World's Last Wilderness Revealed by Robert Dinwiddie, Sue Scott, and Fabian Cousteau

Out of the Blue: A 24-Hour Skywatcher's Guide by John Naylor

Restless Skies: The Ultimate Weather Book by Paul Douglas

SOS: Stories of Survival: True Tales of Disaster, Tragedy and Courage by Ed Butts

Volcano: The Eruption and Healing of Mount St. Helens by Patricia Lauber

Volcano Weather: The Story of 1816, the Year Without a Summer by Elizabeth Stommel and Henry Stommel

Within Reach: My Everest Story by Mark Pfetzer and Jack Galvin

12

Knowing Your World

Consumerism, going green, labor and unions, diversity, cultures, teens around the planet, and how the world got this way. These are books to make teens think about their world and how they can make a difference.

This topic spans quite a few subjects—current events, country studies, social studies, the environment and earth science, consumerism and economics. We've grouped these books together under this topic because they all do the same thing—encourage teens to think about their community, neighborhood, nation and world. When you were a child, did you ever list your geography location pushing out past the world and into space? Jill, Clarksville, Tennessee, United States, Planet Earth, the Solar System, the Milky Way Galaxy, the Universe. We play this game because it gives us a place. We may belong to a small community, but we also belong to the universe. Small and large, close and far, we are both here and out there. We are a part of something bigger. These books show teens just how much we are all interconnected, how we are jointly responsible for our home whether that home is our local neighborhood or our galaxy. These books show teens how we are alike, how we are different and how we can't always sit back and let others change the world for us. From being aware of unchecked consumerism to rampant pollution to learning to ask questions and being curious, the books in this chapter will help teens connect with their communities and learn more about the world—from their neighborhoods to their hemisphere.

Book Ideas with Booktalks, Discussion Questions, and Project Ideas

Chew On This
by Eric Schlosser and Charles Wilson

How many of you have ever had a McDonald's strawberry milkshake? McDonald's strawberry milkshakes contain a color additive to give it that pretty pink color. Do you know what that color additive is made of? It is made of cochineal extract, which is made from the dead bodies of small bugs harvested in Peru and the Canary Islands. There are bugs in your milkshake. These bugs are also in Dannon yogurt and Ocean Spray pink grapefruit juice. Cochineal extract (those bugs) are used to turn food pink, red and purple.

Let's talk about those McDonald's hamburgers. When's the last time you had one? In Greeley, Colorado, there's the Swift & Co slaughterhouse where two feedlots hold over 100,000 cattle each with the cows so close together that they poop in each other's food. Each cow produces over 50 pounds of urine and manure every day. Do you know how much manure 100,000 cows can produce in one day? Now, E. coli, which is a disease that affects your digestive system and often kills smaller children, is spread through this manure. So, take one cow infected with E. coli that poops in another cow's food. The second cow gets it and spreads it on. Before you know, the feedlot is infected. The infected cow goes to slaughter; the E. coli gets on the meat grinders. Other cows are ground up and that meat gets infected and so on and so on and so on. And your hamburger wasn't made from just one cow. It was made from hundreds of cows when all the meat gets mixed together so your chances of getting an infected hamburger increase a whole bunch. Yummy!

Discussion Questions

1. Do you think schools should offer fast food in their cafeterias? How would you feel if part of your school day consisted of gardening food that would be eaten in your cafeteria?
2. Why do schools provide lunch and breakfast?
3. Read the "Beef Trust" section of the "Meat" chapter. Why would the meatpacking companies refuse to set a fair price on beef? Besides the meat companies and supermarkets, who else benefits from the low cost of meat? Who suffers? Do you think the meatpacking companies should pay ranchers more for their beef? What would happen if they did?
4. Read the "Storming KFC" section in the "Your Way" chapter. Why are oversees American fast food restaurants the most likely targets of demonstrations against the United States?
5. Read the "Threatening Nag" section in "The Youngster Business" chapter. Why do ads try to get kids to nag their parents? Do you think this marketing tactic works?
6. Why do fast food restaurants hire teenagers?

Project: Daily Nutrition Chart

Ask teens to create a chart that depicts how many calories, total fat, cholesterol, sodium, protein and fiber each teen should be consuming on a daily basis. Visit http://www.bcm.edu/cnrc/consumer/archives/percentDV.htm for a quick guide. Next, ask teens to create a chart that records calories, total fat, cholesterol, sodium, protein and fiber for lunch and dinner over a period of a week, Monday through Friday. Visit the "Interactive Fast Food Menu" at http://www.extension.org/pages/Interactive_Fast_Food_Menu and ask your teens to choose meals and enter the totals into their chart. For each day, add up all of the nutritional information for lunch and dinner and compare that total to the daily recommended total. Record the difference between the two totals. Did the teen consume more or less than the daily recommendation?

Some rules to follow include:

- Teens should choose two meal items and one drink for each lunch and each dinner.
- Items must be a meal choice and not a condiment, such as a sauce or salad dressing.
- Teens may not choose the same meal twice.
- If choosing a salad, teens must also choose a salad dressing.

MySpace/Our Planet
by the MySpace Community with Jeca Taudte

MySpace/Our Planet makes you an expert on going green. Learn how to go from green to greenest, to never be fooled by greenwashing again and to do your part for the health of the world. Here's a small quiz to test your expertise now:

- True or False: Bottled water is purer and healthier than the water you get out of your tap. False: Aquafina is tap water from the cities of Detroit and Fresno.
- True or False: Green energy is way too expensive to be a viable alternative. False: Green energy would only cost about $3.50 more a month.
- True or False: Sleep mode on your computer saves energy. True: But make your computer go into standby mode or hibernate if you really want to save energy.
- True or False: Hybrid cars are the answer to our dependence on fossil fuels. False: If our non–hybrid cars gave us 45 mpg instead of 25 mpg, we would eliminate our dependency on foreign oil.
- True or False: Plastic makes up most of our waste. False: Paper makes up most of our waste
- True or False: Paper bags are better than plastic bags. Actually both are horrid; use reusable canvas instead.

To learn more about how you can go green or go greener, read *My Space/Our Planet* and see what My Space suggests for helping the environment.

DISCUSSION QUESTIONS

1. What is your community doing for the environment? What are they not doing that you would like to see happen?
2. Are there any eco suggestions that are impossible for you right now? Why?

Books straight from the teen culture, like *My Space/Our Planet: Change is Possible*, make your topics feel more relevant and timely.

3. What suggestions are you already doing? Which do you want to try? Are there any that you don't want to try?
4. After reading through MySpace users comments, what comments or suggestions would you add?
5. Does your mayor participate in the U.S. Mayors Climate Protection Agreement? Find out at usmayors.org.

Project: Swap Meet!

In the "Money — The Original Green" chapter, read the real-life story of Wendy Treymane. Now, get your group to organize their own Swap-O-Rama-Rama! Have your teens bring in clothes, CDs and other items they no longer want and let them swap out for items or clothes that are new to them. It's free and it recycles!

The Explainer
by the writers of *Slate Magazine*

Answers to questions you never thought to ask:

For instance, What happens to recalled meat? Meat that is suspected to be bad can sometimes be recalled. The factories ask you to take it back to the supermarket and not to use it because it could be contaminated. Once you've taken it back to the supermarket, the meat is shipped back to the factory that produced it. From there, the meat either goes to a landfill, gets tossed into an incinerator or is set aside to make pet and livestock food.

Do you own the movie rights to your life? Nope. We do NOT own movie rights to our lives. Facts are not owned by anyone, not even facts about particular people. As long as the moviemakers tell the truth and stick to the facts, they can do whatever they want with your life story.

Who do you call when you find a ticking nuclear bomb? You call the police. The police calls NEST — the Nuclear Emergency Search Team made up of thousands of scientists, engineers and computer programmers from the Energy Department. Between 1974 and 1998, NEST was deployed 110 times.

Who can lie to Congress? Members of Congress can lie to Congress. According to the "Speech and Debate Clause" in Article 1, Section six of the U. S. Constitution, when in session, members of the House and Senate have an absolute privilege to lie without consequences. This only applies when Congress is in session and not outside.

Discussion Questions

1. *The Explainer* asks a lot of questions. Do you think these questions are important or a waste of our time?
2. Are there any questions that really concern you?
3. Are the any questions that have surprising answers? What surprised you about the answer?
4. What other questions should have been included in this book?

5. What is the purpose of asking these questions? Of asking any question?
6. Have any of these questions or answers changed how you see your world?

PROJECT: RAISING CURIOSITY

Ask your teens to write their favorite questions on large pieces of poster board or colored paper and then post these questions around the library or school. There are a few options to help other teens, teachers, or library patrons find the answers.

- Post the answers within easy reach of the questions, either behind the questions or beside them.
- Let your students be the answers. Make sure your posters instruct others to find one of your teens to get the answer (e.g., look for someone wearing *The Explainer* button for the answer). Make sure your teens have a distinctive identifier so others will know who to ask.
- A third option is to offer the answers at a designated time and place. If anyone wants to know the answers, they must attend your next discussion group meeting or a special event in the school library. How your teens present the answers is up to you.

The Girlo Travel Survival Kit
by Anthea Paul

When you decide to travel somewhere, there are some important things to consider such as: why do you want to travel, how are you going to get there, and what are you going to do while you're there? If you could visit any place in the whole world, where would it be and why? *Call on 2–3 students to share their thoughts.*

What kinds of things should you do to get ready for an international trip? *Call on various students to help come up with a list of good ideas.*

The *Girlo Travel Survival Kit* answers your burning travel questions, such as:

- Where should I go?
- What is a visa and how do I get one?
- What should I pack?
- I can only sleep on my pillow, what should I do?
- What on earth is travel insurance?
- What do I do when I meet the man of my dreams?

DISCUSSION QUESTIONS

1. Where would you want to travel and why?
2. What is the difference between a tourist and a traveler?
3. Explain how you would plan for a trip.
4. What should you wear when traveling?
5. List two safety tips.
6. How can you lower the likelihood of getting lost?

PROJECT: TRAVEL PLANNING

This is a great project for a geography or social studies class. Instruct each student to decide on a location they would like to visit outside of their home country. After deciding, they need to do research on the following: terrain and weather, current political situations and general safety of the country, languages spoken in the country and acceptable clothing and other cultural norms.

At this point each student must create a travel plan on posterboard. Using the Internet and any other resources, they must plan a mock itinerary including when they will go, where they will stay, how they will get from location to location, total cost, and what they will pack. The plans will be presented to the class.

Three Cups of Tea
by Greg Mortenson and David Oliver Relin

When Greg Mortenson's sister died, he vowed to tackle one of the most difficult summits on Earth to place his sister's necklace at the top. Unfortunately, Mortenson almost died trying to climb it and spent time in an isolated mountain town in Pakistan recuperating. After receiving the most hospitable care, Greg Mortenson made a promise. *Open to the last page of the "Progress and Perfection" chapter and read the last paragraph or have a student read it.*

This promise changed not only his life but the lives of the students of 55 schools in some of the most volatile locations on the planet.

Note to educator: Depending on your age group, you may want to consider Three Cups of Tea: One Man's Journey to Change the World ... One Child at a Time (The Young Reader's Edition) *by Sarah Thomson, Greg Mortenson, David Oliver Relin, and Jane Godall.*

DISCUSSION QUESTIONS

1. What was the name of the mountain Mortenson tries to climb at the beginning of the book?
2. At the beginning of chapter 5, how much money was Mortenson trying to raise? What was he doing to raise the money?
3. Why is tea a central idea in the book?
4. How did Mortenson decide where to build other schools?
5. List some of the barriers Mortenson confronted when building schools. How did he overcome them?

For more great discussion questions, visit: www.threecupsoftea.com.

PROJECT: HUMANITARIAN WORK FOR TEENS

After reading a book like *Three Cups of Tea*, it is an excellent opportunity to research what humanitarian work teens are doing on a national and international level. Split your class into groups and, with access to the Internet, have each group come up with at least two existing humanitarian groups that allow teens. They must find:

- What is the group's mission?
- How does a teen become a member?
- What are the responsibilities of the teen member?

This information will be presented to the class. To go one step further, invite a local humanitarian worker to speak to the class on the day of presentations.

Girl, 13
by Starla Griffin

Have you ever wondered what your life would be like if you lived in another country? Would you like different food, have a different religion, wear different clothes or speak a different language? Would you study the same subjects in school? This book is filled with the biographies of 13-year-old girls from all over the world. They talk about their friends, their best days ever, their schools, talents, dreams and families. Do they have cell phones? Do they use the Internet? Do they have pets?

At this point tell the teens some interesting facts from the featured biographies. Some of the facts we like to use include:

- Lavanya in India has 8 dogs and 2 cows for pets and no one will let her do any house chores.
- Lynsey from Scotland loves the word "teapot" and calls herself a strawberry.
- Franzi from Germany's favorite book is *Witch Child* by Celia Rees.
- Kate from Russia takes horseback riding lessons in gym class.
- Meera from the United Arab Emirates does NOT want to travel in space, be the leader of her country, be a pop star or movie star or win an Olympic medal.
- Louise in Uganda starts school at 8 a.m. and it doesn't end until 6 p.m. that evening!

Discussion Questions

1. Starla asks each of the girls, "What comes to mind when you think of the United States?" The girls provide a wide variety of answers such as "terrorists," "racism," "McDonalds," "Disneyland," "the Statue of Liberty," "the FBI," and "cactuses along desert highways." Pick three biographies from the book and list the first word that come to mind when you think of their countries.
2. Do you think their perceptions of the United States are true?
3. How are all of these girls similar?
4. Are there any aspects of these girls' lives that you wish you could have?
5. Which of these girls would you most like to meet? Why?
6. Can you find any similarities between girls living in the same regions?

Project: Group Snapshot

Each biography in *Girl, 13* begins with a list of questions and short answers. Let your teens answer each of these questions for themselves. Have your teens list the questions and their answers on a large posterboard. Once the posterboards are completed, hang the posters around the room so that your teens can walk around and compare their answers.

Made You Look
by Shari Graydon and Warren Clarke

How would you define advertising? A: "anything someone does to grab your attention and hold onto it long enough to tell you how cool, fast, cheap, tasty, fun, rockin' or rad whatever they're selling is," or B: "trickery used to shut down your brain just long enough to convince you to open your wallet."

Either way you look at advertising, can you imagine life without it? What would the world look like if no one advertised their products? Would this be a good thing or a bad thing? OK, name all of the ways companies advertise their products to you. *Let the teens list all of the ads they can think of. These might include TV commercials, billboards, magazine ads, ads on the Internet. Try to get them to think of other advertisement methods as well such as branding on clothes, word of mouth advertising and product placement in movies.* If you want to know more about the sneaky, dirty world of advertising, try *Made You Look* and you'll see the world in a whole new light, as one giant spinning billboard.

DISCUSSION QUESTIONS

1. What is the "nag factor"?
2. How do we as consumers take the role of the product?
3. What is the the "third-person effect"? Do you think this effect applies to you?
4. Why do advertisers use stereotypes?
5. What is persuasive language? What are some examples of persuasive language?
6. What is "branding"? Where did the term come from? How do advertisers use this strategy?
7. What is a food stylist? What do they do to food in advertisements? Why?
8. What are some of the rules governing what advertisers can and cannot do in an advertisement? Why do we have these rules? Do you think advertisers always follow these rules?

PROJECT: HOW MANY ADVERTISEMENTS?

Made You Look offers several activity ideas under sections called "Try This at Home!" One activity suggests that readers count every advertisement they see during a single day. To complete this activity, ask your teens to keep a notepad and pencil handy for one entire day from the time they wake up until they go to sleep that night. Ask your teens to record every advertisement they see that day, from ads on cereal boxes, signs on local stores, billboards, branding on clothing, bumper stickers, posters in school hallways, ads on Internet sites, ads in magazines, and commercials on television. Teens may not have time to write down what the advertisement is, but they should at least try to count them in categories. For example, rather than specifying each poster they see in a school hallway, count the number of school posters they see. Or instead of listing each shirt they see with a logo, list the number of clothes they see with logos and other branding on them.

Amazing Stories of Survival
by the editors of *People Magazine*

What is a hero? *Allow a couple of students to answer.* Webster's defines a hero as "one that shows great courage." Can you think of examples of heroes? *Again, allow a few students to answer with their stories.*

Our world is full of all sorts of heroes of every shape and size. And most heroes don't know they are such until after they become a hero—as was the case with Amanda, now known as the gator girl. *Read the short article, "Gator Girl to the Rescue!" in the first chapter. Before the story reveals that Amanda rescues her friend, stop reading and poll the class asking how they would respond.*

DISCUSSION QUESTIONS

1. What does it mean to be a hero?
2. List different kinds of heroes.
3. What heroes do you know?
4. In what ways have you been a hero?
5. When it seemed like all hope was lost, like in the "Choosing the Live" story, what do you think causes a person to keep on trying to live?
6. Do you think trying to live despite dire circumstances makes someone a hero? Why?
7. Have you ever been in a natural disaster? What was it like?
8. When bad things happen, what helps you get through them?
9. What story impacted you the most? Why?

PROJECT: HERO STORY

Using a personal story, instruct the teens to write their own hero story in which they were a hero or someone was their hero. Encourage them that these stories don't have to be as dràmatic as a plane crash or a rescue from the jaws of an alligator—it can be small, perhaps unseen to most people, but with a profound effect. After the hero stories are written and graded (or approved by the educator), students will read them aloud in class or within a smaller group.

This is the perfect opportunity to discuss the importance of our impact on others in ways we cannot see or quantify. Also, consider going through the discussion questions after this project, allowing the students to use the time writing their stories to reflect on this subject.

Generation Green
by Linda Sivertsen and Tosh Sivertsen

Show of hands: How many of you have been preached to about protecting the environment? What are some things you've heard? *Allow a few students to share.* This book,

Green Generation, is full of not just reasons why you should care but ways to care that are natural for you. For example, who has heard of the three Rs when it comes to protecting the environment — reduce, reuse, and recycle? *If you're working with younger students, explain the meaning behind those words.* The authors of this book added two extra — one is RETHINK; they are encouraging you to reevaluate (or rethink) whether you should buy something. The other R is REFUSE; they explain this as when you decide to refuse to buy something you don't need or when the packaging isn't recyclable. Can anyone tell me all of the five Rs? *Reduce, Reuse, Recycle, Rethink, and Refuse.*

This book is filled with some cool ideas that you can use now or even when you're an adult. I mean, did you know you can buy vegan shoes?

DISCUSSION QUESTIONS

1. List and describe the five Rs.
2. What is contaminating human food?
3. List three things you can realistically change today.
4. What are VOCs? How are you affected by them?
5. What is technotrash?
6. What are some rules to remember when camping?
7. What did you think of the section "A Day in a Green Life"? What parts are you going to try to integrate into your life?

PROJECT: GREEN TIPS

The book has its own Web site: generationgreenthebook.com. Head over there and click on the link titled "Green Tips." With your class, review some of the tips and decide which one the class wants to do. If there are some discrepancies, have a private vote to decide; if you have a big enough class and plenty of resources, you may even want to split your class into groups and have each group choose a different tip. Allow students to lead (vote on a leader, if necessary) and reinforce this responsibility to students. When your class succeeds, submit your plan and the outcome to the Web site — you may even be a featured story! Even better, make this a yearly tradition and younger students will look forward to the project.

Classroom Integration

The books featured in this chapter were written to show teens just how important a part they play in their own communities and just how much the world affects them everyday. So often in school students do not see that the lessons they are learning have real world applications. Use the books featured in this chapter to tie your classroom lessons to your students' worldviews.

If you are doing a lesson on country studies, for example, ask your teens to read *Girl, 13* or *The Girlo Travel Survival Guide* for a new perspective on different countries.

In addition to learning about various countries' mineral supplies, population size, languages, traditions and cultures, teens can also view "A Day in the Life of..." for international teens their own age, allowing your students to see the personal side of these countries rather than just statistics and faceless facts. If you are teaching an economics course or lesson, let your students read *Chew on This* for a different point of view of supply and demand and the teenage workforce. If you are teaching a social studies or science class that is covering a section on environmentalism, read *MySpace/Our Planet* and *Generation Green* with your teens. These books gives teens ideas for being more environmentally mindful without preaching the subject to them. The ideas in *Myspace/Our Planet* come from other teens and from the MySpace community and *Generation Green* was cowritten by a teen. They are real world ideas with practical results that are easy to follow and put into practice. Your teens will be able to see themselves practicing these suggestions.

Whether you are teaching a lesson on consumerism (*Made You Look*) or government (*The Explainer*) or even if you are preparing your students to do their senior project or reminding them of their volunteer requirements (*Three Cups of Tea*), the books in this chapter will help your teens understand that they are an integral part of their communities and the lessons you are teaching them really do apply to their own lives.

More Great Books

Amazing Stories of Survival: Tales of Hope, Heroism, and Astounding Luck by the editors of *People Magazine*

Be the Change: Your Guide to Freeing Slaves and Changing the World by Zach Hunter

Chew on This: Everything You Don't Want to Know About Fast Food by Eric Schlosser and Charles Wilson

Declare Yourself: Speak, Connect, Act, Vote: More Than 50 Celebrated Americans Tell You Why by Declare Yourself

Do Hard Things: A Teenage Rebellion Against Low Expectations by Alex Harris

Earth from Above by Yann Arthus-Bertrand

The Explainer by the writers of *Slate Magazine*

Generation Change: Roll Up Your Sleeves and Change the World by Zach Hunter

Generation Green: The Ultimate Teen Guide to Living an Eco-Friendly Life by Linda Sivertsen and Tosh Sivertsen

Girl, 13: A Global Snapshot of Generation E by Starla Griffin

The Girlo Travel Survival Kit by Anthea Paul

Green Volunteers: The World Guide to Voluntary Work in Nature Education by Fabio Ausenda, ed.

How to Hold a Crocodile by the Diagram Group

It's Your World — If You Don't Like It, Change It: Activism for Teenagers by Mikki Halpin

Lose Your Cool: Discovering a Passion that Changes You and the World by Zach Hunter

Made You Look: How Advertising Works and Why You Should Know by Shari Graydon and Warren Clarke

My So-Called Digital Life: 2,000 Teenagers, 300 Cameras, and 30 Days to Document Their World by Bob Pletka, ed.

MySpace/Our Planet: Change is Possible by the MySpace Community with Jeca Taudte

The Rights of Students by Eve Cary, Alan H. Levine and Janet Price

Skateboard Roadmap by James Davis

Teen Power Politics: Make Yourself Heard by Sara Jane Boyers

Three Cups of Tea: One Man's Mission to Promote Peace ... One School at a Time by Greg Mortenson and David Oliver Relin

War is...: Soldiers, Survivors and Storytellers Talk About War by Marc Aronson and Patty Campbell

13

Life Skills

Life skills books used to be embarrassing; no teen would pick up a book about this topic within view of any of his friends. Today life skills books are written with humor, wit, and a delicate understanding of this age-old embarrassment. Booktalking these books with openness and light banter is key!

It's embarrassing. It's mortifying. It's boring. And it's too often assumed that teens know this stuff. It's a necessary topic that covers a wide range of skill sets every teen should have, from money management to social networking, health and body issues to setting goals and working toward them.

Life Skills like banking, setting goals, using deodorant or shaving correctly (so we don't get that annoying razor burn), or wearing a bra or undershirt may seem so natural to us as adults, but we've got experience on our side. We've been there, done that and made those mistakes or at least watched some other poor sap make the mistake while we learned from his embarrassment.

Do you remember the very first time you learned about the menstrual cycle — not the first time your parents or teachers told you (because by then you already knew) but the VERY first time you learned what happened every month? When your friends told you or you read your older sibling's health book? Do you remember the first time you kissed or wanted to be kissed? The first time you were told you needed to start wearing deodorant or start shaving? Do you remember how embarrassing NOT knowing these essential skills could be?

When teens have questions about their bodies, they are not likely to pick up a book with a stiff title and a picture of a girl with a side ponytail on the cover. And the majority of teens are not going to ask an adult. But there are plenty of books out there that are not so embarrassing to pick up with smart covers and witty titles; they speak to teens with humor and maturity in an upfront manner without preaching. We just need to let teens know that these books exist and actually contain information that might interest them. And if you can get teens interested in a few of these books, they might even learn the answers to questions they never thought to ask.

Book Ideas with Booktalks, Discussion Questions, and Project Ideas

101 Things to Do Before You're Old and Boring
by Richard Horne and Helene Szirtes

How many of you think your parents are boring? Well, they weren't always this way but some things in life are just inevitable. You *are* going to get old. You *will* become boring, probably without even realizing it. One day, you're up all night, staying out with friends, and then you'll start a full-time job and when a friend calls you up to go out, you'll say, "OK, but I need to get home early: I have to work tomorrow." Or you'll realize that you just can't play basketball like you used to because your knees hurt too much, or you'll watch some teens running up the down escalator and you'll yell at them. It WILL happen — just you wait. But, this book, *101 Things to Do Before You're Old and Boring*, helps you create 101 memories NOW, before its too late; because if you don't do them now, chances are you never will.

Here are some of the challenges you'll find in this book:

- Run up the down escalator.
- Learn to tell when someone likes you and when they don't. For example: do they tease you a lot? How often do you catch them looking at you? Does anyone else think this person likes you? Are they nervous when you're alone together?
- This book also challenges you to have an embarrassing moment and then get over it. Embarrassing moments could include farting loudly, throwing up, peeing your pants, falling down some stairs, walking into a pole, getting caught on the toilet, sporting a wide-open fly, or realizing your skirt is tucked into your under-wear. The trick, however, is to then get over it, and laugh it off. Good luck with that.
- Another challenge is to fart in public. Public places could include: in a school assembly, a crowded elevator, while taking a test, at the movies, while you're kissing or in a swimming pool. Please note that you could easily kill two birds with one stone here as farting in public could also fulfill challenge #10, the Embarrassing Moment, or challenge #69, Make a Scene in Public.

DISCUSSION QUESTIONS

1. Out of all of these challenges, which do you most want to do and why?
2. Which challenge do you think you'll never do and why?
3. Are there any challenges that you think do not really fit into this book? Why do you think they were included?
4. Which of these challenges have you already done?
5. Are there any challenges that you found in this book that you had never thought to do until now?
6. Are there any challenges that you want to accomplish that are not in this book?

PROJECT: CHALLENGE JOURNAL

Expanding on the last discussion question for this book, have teens make their own challenges and put them into their own book. This is a great project to combine with an altered books program. Supplies needed: blank paper, scissors, string, yarn or book binding materials, hole punch, discarded books, glue, cardboard, pens or pencils and decorating supplies such as glitter, stickers, paint, and sequins.

Ask teens to think of several challenges they would like to try or experiences they would like to have. Teens can make their challenges be either things to do while they are still teenagers or even things to do in their lifetime. The teens should put each challenge on a separate page with an explanation for each (so they remember what they are talking about when they try to complete the challenge years from now), as well as a chart or area to note when they completed the challenge and a space to write down how they did it. Once the pages are finished, let the teen rip apart the old, discarded books and recreate new book covers or even use a whole cover from an old book if they want to disguise their creation. Bind the new books using either the string or yarn or with your book binding materials.

The Teenage Guy's Survival Guide
by Jeremy Daldry

Guys, this book is mostly about girls. Also, dumping, zits, girls, being stinky, money, failure, girls, confidence, depression, girls, clothes, and friends. Oh, and did I mention girls?

Here are a few tips from the *Survival Guide*.

Fighting: No one who gets into a fight really wants to be there. No matter how tough you might like to think you are, no one wants to go to school on Monday morning with a black eye. You can't flirt with a black eye and girls aren't impressed.

Bullying: What's the difference between bullying someone and teasing him? Absolutely nothing if every time you see someone you tease him.

Pimples: Fess up! How many of you have popped a pimple? What can you do about these pesky, red, pus-filled monsters? Not much. But NEVER scratch, pick or pop them!

The #1 basic asking-out rule: It's not the best idea to go up to a girl when she is surrounded by her friends. Even if she is desperate for you to ask her out, she's going to be embarrassed if you ask and all her friends can overhear. And even more important, you will feel even worse if she says NO.

Kissing: When you want to kiss a girl, DON'T lunge at her as if you are trying to tackle her.

DISCUSSION QUESTIONS

1. How often do you see bullying in your school or in the community? How do you define bullying? What do you think about Daldry's suggestions to stop bullying from happening to you? Do you think his suggestions are effective? Explain.
2. Daldry states, "Sexuality isn't a switch that is either on or off, gay or straight. It's

more like a slide that will eventually nestle somewhere between gay and straight but may be closer to one than the other." What do you think about that statement?

3. According to Daldry, when guys get together to hang out they can be "kind of stupid," meaning that guys often do things to impress girls or look tough that could potentially be harmful to themselves or to others. Do you think this is true?

4. How often do you feel peer pressure? How successful do you think you are at making the smart choice? How often do you see others making the stupid choices because of peer pressure?

5. Masturbation: okay or wrong? What do you think?

6. Without naming names, what is the worst break up you have ever seen? What made it so bad? How could it have been less hurtful? What could the couple involved have done differently to make the breakup less painful?

PROJECT: VERIFYING HEALTH WEB SITES

Jeremy Daldry provides a list of resources for additional information on the topics covered in *The Teenage Guy's Survival Guide*. This project is a great way to teach teens to verify any health information they are gleaning from the Internet. With this project you can show your students why choosing authoritative, trustworthy resources is even more important for topics like health and other life skills. Getting information about your body from a false resource doesn't just get you a bad grade on your research paper, it could be detrimental to your health.

For this project have students pick a Web site from the list of resources at the back of *The Teenage Guy's Survival Guide*. Then, to analyze the Web site, have them answer the following questions: 1. Who created this Web site? 2. What do you learn about the site on the "About Us," "Biography," "Home," or "Credits" page? 3. Why was this site created? To inform? To entertain? To advertise? To promote a single point of view or belief? How does this affect the credibility of the site? 4. How clear is the Web site? Are the menus easy to find? Is the site clear of clutter and advertisements? 5. How informative is the Web site? 6. How does the Web site cite where they found the information? 7. Can you name five new facts about your topic that you learned from this Web site? What are these facts? 8. How often is this Web site updated?

Once the students have evaluated a Web site from the resource list, ask them to find a different Web site on the same topic and ask them to evaluate that Web site using the same questions listed above. As an additional task, have your students verify the facts they have listed with at least two other resources. Are the facts the same? Are any facts contradictory? How do you know which fact is true and which is false?

Guys Are Waffles, Girls Are Spaghetti
by Chad Eastham and Bill and Pam Farrel

Raise your hand and name something you think is better about your gender. *Remind the teens to keep it appropriate for the classroom!* If you wouldn't say it to your kindergarten sister or your grandma, you shouldn't say it in here.

Raise your hand if you've heard of ways guys think different than girls. This book covers the differences between guys and girls and some extra stuff, like how to get rid of creepy guys and an explanation as to why you become dumb when you kiss. I'm always seeing advice in magazines and relationship books on how to win a certain boy or a certain gal you've got your eye on. In this book I found a different list; first, the list for guys.

How to fail in relationships—for guys:

- Pressure people to do what you want, especially girls.
- Don't just tease a girl you like, embarrass her.
- Whine.
- Flex your muscles all the time and act super macho.
- Call, text, and IM the girl you like. All. The. Time.
- Have you seen a yappy dog running around in circles, begging for attention? Do that.
- Constantly evaluate how much better you are than everyone else. And then tell everyone your thoughts.
- Objectify women. They love that.

How to fail in relationships—for gals:

- Make guys the most important thing in your life. Seriously. More important than brushing your teeth.
- Find a guy, any guy, and try to change him. Guys love that!
- Do everything possible to make a guy love you.
- Forget the word "no." Just forget it. Only say "yes."
- Trust everybody. So what if the 40-year-old creepy guy in the van just asked if you wanted some candy? It's free candy!
- Start dating as young as possible.
- Never be single. Uhmm … hello?
- Talk about how stupid you think guys are. All the time.

Discussion Questions

1. What do you love most about being your gender?
2. What is frustrating?
3. What frustrates you about the opposite gender?
4. Do you think it's important for male and females to understand how differently we think?
5. What new piece of information did you learn about guys?
6. What new piece of information did you learn about gals?
7. List three things you like about yourself.

Project: Comparing Notes

Have each person write down three ways they think their gender is misunderstood. If you have a co-ed class, split them into groups of 2–3 females and 2–3 males and have them compare notes. Afterward, open up the floor for teens to share something they learned from their groups.

Indie Girl
by Arne Johnson and Karen Macklin

For each of the questions, call on a couple of students to share their ideas or experiences. Make sure to be affirming and, if necessary, remind them to keep their ideas appropriate.

- Does anyone have an idea for a cool band?
- Are you tired of the lame styles you see EVERYONE else wearing?
- Is there a zine you wish existed but you've never seen before?
- Is anyone in here an artist that wants to get discovered?
- Are you sick of lame poetry? Do you or your friends know how to write good poetry?
- Is anyone an actress who wants to direct her own play?

Ladies (and dudes, but this book is more for the gals), you don't need to sit around and wait for opportunity to present itself! This book will teach you how to start a band, put on a play, create a not-lame parade (yes, the kind with people walking down the street), launch a fashion company, and a ton of other things. It goes through idea by idea and even gives you outside sources.

DISCUSSION QUESTIONS

1. If you could do any one of these projects, which one would it be?
2. Why is it important to do what you're passionate about?
3. Should you change your art for the people you're expecting at your art exhibit? Why or why not?
4. If you're in a band, why is it important to play what you love?
5. What is "the hook"? Is it important in other areas of performance besides television?
6. If you are a writer, which chapters would apply to you?
7. List some ways you could make a parade cool!

PROJECT: MAKE-BELIEVE — BUT NOT REALLY

Even though this book is for girls, you can do this project with guys. Split your class into groups of 3–5. Instruct each group to choose a topic chapter and complete the following:

1. Construct a goal: What do you want to do?
2. Create a plan of action: What steps need to be taken to meet your goal?
3. Schedule in the plan of action: This helps teens learn how to make a theoretical idea a reality. They need to think of things like "Who do I need to contact to be able to have my parade walk down Main Street?" "Who is going to call that person?" "What is the deadline for the phone call?"

4. Wrap-Up: This section should contain either a clean-up plan if it's a one-time event (like a concert) or a plan to keep things running smoothly after the goal has been launched (for instance, a fashion line).

After the projects have been completed, provide 10-minute time slots for the students to present their projects to the class.

What's That Smell? (Oh, It's Me)
by Tucker Shaw

What do you do when you do a number two at your boyfriend's house and the toilet overflows? What do you do when you burp up a little bit of your dinner while making out? What do you do when you throw up in class? What do you do when your online diary has been hacked and is posted on a school bulletin board? Or you catch your little brother posing as you online and IMing inappropriate things to your crush? What do you do if while playing around online you come across an anti–you webpage? What do you do if you accidentally hit send when you had already come to your senses and meant to hit delete? What do you do when your best friend gets arrested and needs bail? Or you get caught "accidentally" shoplifting? What do you do when you are at the drugstore with tampons and foot odor powder in your arms and you run into your crush or worse, your nemesis? Or worst of all, you fall for your best friend and ask him out only to have him act disgusted, laugh or stop hanging out with you?

Tucker Shaw offers advice for getting out of life's most sticky and embarrassing situations with a little bit of dignity and grace. Embarrassing moments happen to EVERYONE, it's just that some people seem to be able to navigate those moments more smoothly than others. This book can help you go from blushing and blabbering to suave smiles.

Discussion Questions

1. Without naming names, think about a situation in which you saw someone else as the butt of an embarrassing moment. How did they react? How did their reaction determine how everyone else responded?
2. When you find yourself in an embarrassing situation where lots of people are looking and laughing at you, what do you think is the best way to diffuse the situation and take attention off of yourself? On the flipside, what is the worst thing you could do?
3. When you find yourself in trouble, whether with your parents, teachers or with the law, what do you think is the best way to get past that situation with minimal damage? What is the quickest way to make these situations go away? How should you react in these situations?
4. Are there any situations in this book that you don't think would be embarrassing despite the author's claim that they would be?
5. Do you think Tucker Shaw offers good advice in these situations? If not, why not? What would you do differently?

PROJECT: SURVEY TIME!

Popular teen magazines are full of surveys about health, beauty, dealing with relationships and embarrassing situations. Teens (especially teen girls) love taking these surveys with their friends. Harness that interest and have your students create their own survey of how to deal with embarrassing moments. This is a great project for students to do either in groups or all together in class (or discussion group).

First, have your students brainstorm a series of embarrassing situations and then pick the most popular 10–15 to use in the survey. Be sure to let the teens pick the final list. Next, using a calm-to-freak-out scale, have the teens come up with three solutions to each situation making sure that each solution sits at a different position on the scale. You don't want all three solutions to be of the freak-out variety, right? Here's the intricate part, have the students create a grading scale. Based on which solution they think is best and which is worst, assign points to each solution. But before you begin, make sure you decide if a lower total score is better or if a higher total score is better and make sure you mark each solution appropriately. Make sure that the grading scale and grading instructions are included with the survey. Now, since your students created the survey, they can't very well complete the survey themselves (they'll all get the best scores), so instead, have your students distribute the surveys to other teens. It is up to you if you want to get the surveys back or if just handing them out is enough.

The Rights of Students
by Eve Cary, Alan H. Levine, and Janet Price

For this booktalk we take some of the questions from The Rights of Students *and let the teens see if they know the answer. Most of the time our teens have had very mixed guesses. Here are some of the questions that we have asked.*

Can school officials remove books from school libraries because they disagree with their content? *Let your teens answer.* No. School officials often remove books from school libraries because they disapprove of the books' contents, but this practice is unconstitutional.

Can students be forced to recite the Pledge of Allegiance? *Let your teens answer.* No. The First Amendment not only prohibits the government from punishing you for expressing your views, it also prohibits the government from forcing you to express views that you do not hold.

Can students form religious clubs and organizations at school? *Let your teens answer.* Yes. If student groups and clubs are permitted to hold meetings on school property, the students must also be permitted to hold meetings for religious purposes.

Can schools control the way students dress and wear their hair? *Let your teens answer.* Yes and No. In most cases schools can control only what doesn't affect students outside of school. For example, students can change their clothes as soon as they get home so schools can dictate what they wear to school. However, students can't change their haircut as soon as they get home or change their hair color, so schools often are not allowed to dictate how students wear their hair. So, if your school tries to make you look a certain way that will affect what you look like outside of school, you don't have to follow those rules. Well, you can at least fight those rules. It's best to get your parents involved rather than just rebelling.

Can schools punish students for expressing their views off campus? *Let your teens answer.* Courts have consistently overruled schools that have punished students for out-of-school activities protected by the First Amendment. For example, one school tried to prohibit a student from handing out an underground newspaper off of school property. Another student who criticized his high school principal on a radio program went to court when he found that a report of his comments had been placed in his school record. The report had to be removed from his school record.

Does a school have to tell students what the punishment is for breaking a rule before that rule is broken? *Let your teens answer.* Yes. Courts have held that school rules must not only be very specific about the conduct they prohibit, but also must spell out the punishments for each violation. And that's before a student breaks the rule, not after. Your teachers and principal can't just go making up punishments for you.

Discussion Questions

1. Are there rules in this book that you don't agree with? Why? What should be changed about the rule?
2. Do you think schools follow these rights for students all of the time? What are some of the reasons for not following them?
3. Have you ever seen or heard of a school not respecting the rights of their students? What happened?
4. Which rights do you think are not respected most often? Why?
5. Why are many of these rights so unclear? Why are they sometimes upheld and sometimes not?

Project: Discussion

Teens like talking about topics that directly affect them. For this project we suggest picking one of the topics discussed in *The Rights of Students* and letting your teens discuss their views and feelings. Some topics to consider: 1. Should your school require uniforms? What are the pros of having uniforms? What are the cons? 2. Is it possible to list every single one of the rules and punishments in a school? 3. *The Rights of Students* asks the question, "Can students be suspended because of their parents' behavior?" What about getting into trouble for being tardy if your parents' drive you to school? Should you be punished if they are the cause of the tardiness?

The Worst-Case Scenario Survival Handbook
by Joshua Piven and David Borgenicht

How many of you have ever thought about what you would do if you were in an elevator and it started to free fall? *As students raise their hands, select a couple to explain how they would try to survive.*

Today, with the help of this book, I'm going to show you what to do to increase your chances of survival. Can I get a volunteer? *Select a student and set up the scene, speaking directly to the student.* Pretend you are standing in an elevator and you feel it begin to plummet. Now lay down on your stomach in the middle of the pretend elevator. Make sure your legs are out straight and your toes aren't pointed. Turn your head sideways and cover your face and hands to prevent pieces of the elevator falling and hitting you when you impact the ground. If you are in a hydraulic elevator (*if necessary, explain what that is*), your chances of falling increase but your chances of surviving also increase because these can be no taller than 70 feet.

According to the authors, more than 50 percent of travelers run into problems while sight-seeing. That means your chances of running into some sort of problem on your next vacation is above average. In this book you'll learn how to survive a volcanic eruption, control a runaway camel, escape when you're tied up and so many more things.

Sometimes even librarians can be surprised by the honesty found in current personal health books.

DISCUSSION QUESTIONS

1. Explain two things you learned how to do.
2. Why do you think the author mixes legitimate how-to segments with really weird ones (like "How to Foil a UFO Abduction")?
3. Have you ever had any emergencies or weird things happen while you were on vacation?
4. What is the number one rule to surviving when lost in the jungle?
5. What is a "mugger's wallet"?
6. What was the most important thing you learned?

PROJECT: SURVIVAL TRAINING

Even though some of the topics covered in this book are non–essential, others are very helpful. After students have read the book, split them into groups of two and instruct each to come up with a team name. Structure the Survival Training game much like a spelling bee, each team will have an opportunity to respond to a scenario. If they respond correctly, they will be allowed to stay up; if incorrect, they must return to their seats and the next team will get a chance. This is a great game to play before a big break when everyone is restless—it's just as fun as it is informational. Also, completing the tasks in front of the class will help the students remember the proper techniques!

Classroom Integration

Unless your class is boys only or girls only, many topics within this subject will be a challenge. In fact, if you have the opportunity to split them up, even for a day, take advantage of it. Even then there will still be lots of giggling and red cheeks, but you will have the freedom to discuss more in detail and the students will, in turn, be more likely to ask and answer questions. If this is not possible, it is so important to remember how humiliating some of these topics are and to be very careful to not put students on the spot by overtly or inadvertently calling on them to answer questions. The sensitivity you show your students when covering these personal issues will gauge how comfortable they are coming to you at a later date for advice.

Also, when you read through some of the discussion questions, you'll notice they cover issues that many groups of people deem moral issues. Choose which questions to cover based on your audience—some questions are more gender-only questions, others may be less appropriate for a public school setting. Be sure to allow all students to express their opinions, and the moment the situation becomes more about the conflict than the discussion, move on. With this topic, more so than the others, a safe place to learn is the most crucial factor.

More Great Books

All the Wrong People have Self-Esteem: An Inappropriate Book for Young Ladies by Laurie Rosenwald
Body Drama: Real Girls, Real Bodies, Real Issues, Real Answers by Nancy Amanda Redd
The Book of Lists for Teens by Sandra and Harry Choron
Chill: Stress-Reducing Techniques for a More Balanced, Peaceful You by Deborah Reber
Do Hard Things: A Teenage Rebellion Against Low Expectations by Alex Harris
Extraordinary Jobs for Adventurers by Alecia T. Devantier and Carol Ann Turkington
Flirtology: 100 Ways to Release Your Inner Flirt by Anita Naik
For Boys Only: The Biggest, Baddest Book Ever by Marc Aronson and HP Newquist
Girl, 13: A Global Snapshot of Generation E by Starla Griffin
The Girlo Travel Survival Kit by Anthea Paul
Guys Are Waffles, Girls Are Spaghetti by Chad Eastham and Bill and Pam Farrel
Indie Girl by Arne Johnson and Karen Macklin
Is It Still Cheating If I Don't Get Caught? by Bruce Weinstein
Jon and Jayne's Guide to Throwing, Going To, And Surviving Parties by Jon Doe
Letters to a Bullied Girl: Messages of Healing and Hope by Olivia Gardner
My So-Called Digital Life: 2,000 Teenagers, 300 Cameras, and 30 Days to Document Their World by Bob Pletka, ed.
The Naked Roommate: And 107 Other Issues You Might Run Into at College by Harlan Cohen

101 Things to Do Before You're Old and Boring by Richard Horne and Helen Szirtes
Privacy Please! Gaining Independence from Your Parents by Odile Amblard
Punk Rock Aerobics: 75 Killer Moves, 50 Punk Classics, and 25 Reasons to Get Off Your Ass and Exercise
   by Maura Jasper and Hilken Mancini
The Rights of Students by Eve Cary, Alan H. Levine and Janet Price
The Teenage Guy's Survival Guide by Jeremy Daldry
Teen Manners: From Malls to Meals to Messaging and Beyond by Cindy Post Senning
Three Little Words by Ashley Rhodes-Courter
What Are My Rights?: 95 Questions and Answers about Teens and the Law by Jacob Law
What's That Smell? (Oh, It's Me): 50 Mortifying Situations and How to Deal by Tucker Shaw
Who Do You Think You Are? 15 Methods for Analyzing the True You by Tucker Shaw
The Worst-Case Scenario Survival Handbook: TRAVEL by Joshua Piven and David Borgenicht

14

Pairing

Sometimes a novel will spark a teen's interest in a certain topic and will open a gateway to learning about a whole new subject. Sometimes learning about a trendy, dangerous or just plain cool topic will encourage a teen to read a topic-related novel. Either way, pairing fiction and nonfiction together is an opportunity for reading and learning.

There are a lot of great nonfiction books out there but some of them don't have the flashy appeal of *Bat Boy Lives* (who can resist excerpts from the *Weekly World News*?). Flip through the latest edition of *School Library Journal* or *VOYA* and you will find titles such as *Outbreak: Plagues That Changed History* by Bryn Barnard. While these books are excellent choices to put into your public or school library, they will most likely sit on those library shelves unless you do something about it. And let's face it, these nonfiction books written specifically to appeal to teens are so much more interesting than textbooks! To booktalk these, simply pair them with a fiction book of the same topic. Just as the popular television show CSI raised interest in forensic science, we can use the drama, mystery, and excitement of fiction to inspire curiosity in issues such as weather, history, or physics. By exposing your students to imagination-inspiring fiction, there is a simple transition to the truth (nonfiction) behind it all; all it takes is a little bit of research into the compelling world around them to discover their own chimera of a book. Use the fiction book to inspire their imaginations while showing them the fascinating reality. Below are four specific ideas to engage your students by using nonfiction and fiction book pairs.

Book Ideas with Booktalks, Discussion Questions, and Project Ideas

The Forensics Pair

When Objects Talk
by Mark Friedlander and Terry Phillips

The snoopy old lady next door noticed that her neighbors, the Marlboros, had been unusually quiet lately. She called the police and they suggested the Marlboros were just out of town. She reassured them that wasn't likely since they usually asked her to take in the newspapers, which were piling up in the front yard. The police responded.

Searching the house, they discover the bloody body of Ann Marlboro on the floor of the master bedroom. There's no sign of her husband or 9-year-old son.

Has anyone in here seen CSI? *Allow students time to raise hands.* This book follows the murder mystery through all of the steps in a murder investigation. From the police photographer, blood testing, document examination, autopsy, particle analysis, and more.

Data is gathered and assembled; probable cause is considered. Once the detectives determine whether they have enough evidence to put together a case against the suspect, they request a search warrant and make an arrest.

Angel of Death
by Alane Ferguson

She walked into the eerie bedroom. Far in the corner was an oak sleigh bed; the middle of bed held the remains of someone she knew. Under the cotton sheet, she could see the peaks and valleys that were his knees and elbows. As she drew closer to the bed, she could see the tip of his tongue — no longer pink but a weird dark grey color. His skin was withered like a dead leaf and his teeth were stained with blood. Dark holes were all that was left of his eyes. She tried to push the thoughts out of her mind but they plagued her — this man was her English teacher.

Sometimes I stop the booktalk here; however, depending on my audience, I may go onto explain the premise of the series.

Imagine that you were a crime scene investigator — that is exactly what this series of books is about. Sixteen-year-old Cameryn is the assistant coroner and in *The Angel of Death* (the second book in the series), she must determine how her teacher died and who killed him.

DISCUSSION QUESTIONS

1. What is forensic science?
2. Cameryn's dream job is to work in forensic science. If you could do your dream job right now, what would it be?
3. Do you agree with Cameryn's grandmother? Do you think working with dead people would affect Cameryn in a negative way? Why or why not?
4. What do you think of the fact that Cameryn's mother disappeared?
5. Do you think Cameryn should've told her father about her mother's return?
6. Alane Ferguson writes in her blog, "It takes me quite a long time and a lot of research to complete a book." List three facts you learned reading this book.
7. Compare and contrast Kyle and Justin. How are they alike? How are they different?
8. If you were a crime scene investigator, what do you think would be the most difficult part of the job?

PROJECT: DIORAMA BOOK REPORT

This activity is perfect for a history or science class. While covering a specific topic in class, World War II for example, assign the students to bring in a fiction book that has something to do with World War II. Allow the students 1–2 weeks to read their independently selected novels and create a diorama that incorporates World War II and their World War II influenced novel. What did they learn from their fiction book about World War II?

The Phobia Pair

Phobias
by Judy Monroe

Note for booktalkers: The nonfiction part of this pair could be done by any current nonfiction book about phobias. We've just found that although over ten years old, Judy Monroe's book still has teen appeal.

For this booktalk we name the phobia and then give the teens a few seconds to guess. If they can't guess the phobia, we give them a hint. Once the teens have guessed what the phobia refers to, we give them a few facts about the phobia.

Pop quiz! I'll name the phobia and you tell me the fear. Ready?

Anemophobia —*Let students guess for a few seconds.* Here's a hint: If you have this phobia you are afraid kite flying. Yes! It is the fear of air, wind or strong drafts. Can you imagine being afraid of the stuff you breathe in?

Give not-so-flashy nonfiction books a boost by pairing them with popular novels of the same topic.

- Apiphobia — Hint: you probably wear shoes outside and stay away from trees. And you despise the sound of buzzing. Correct! Apiphobia is the fear of bees.
- Bibliophobia — Hint: you're probably hyperventilating RIGHT NOW. It's the fear of books! oohhh! booooooooks!
- Nephophobia — Hint: spending the day finding shapes in these would not be considered your ideal day. Yep, it's the fear of clouds.
- Sitophobia — Hint: with this fear you'll have a hard time during lunch period. Yes! It's the fear of food.
- Selenophobia — Hint: you probably don't like the night time. You got it! It's the fear of the moon as opposed to nyctophobia, which is the fear of the night.
- Numerophobia — Hint: You most definitely hate math. It's the fear of numbers.

- Scolionophobia — Hint: You probably wouldn't be here right now if you had this phobia. Exactly, it's the fear of school. Who here is scolionophobic?
- Phronemophobia — Hint: your brain can't stop doing this so I have no idea how people are afaid of this. Right, it's the fear of thinking!

From the fear of air to the fear of spiders, snakes, cats and people, this book is going to tell you all the things that you never even thought were fearful.

What Are You Afraid Of?
by Donald R. Gallo

What are you afraid of? Everyone is afraid of something — some are just more afraid than others. How would you feel if you were too terrified to step out your front door? And your parents decide to take a month long vacation? Everything is fine until your refrigerator starts to run out of food.

Or what if you are terrified of strings? — any and all strings? Your father comes home with new dish rags with tassles or a string comes loose from your jacket during the day? Your response: scream, run upstairs and hyperventilate. Or just throw up. Doesn't sound like a terrible phobia to have, at least until you discover your crush is teaching a summer class in the park. You join, eager to please and be noticed. You arrive only to discover that it's a weaving class. Throwing up in front of your crush — not so hot.

What if you are terrified of knives; terrified that if you pick one up you're going to stab whoever is closest to you?

What if you are terrified of clowns? And girls just go out with you to torture you with clown trivia? You're at a party and heading to a girl's bedroom to make out; dear heavens, she's decorated her room with clowns.

What if you weren't afraid of anything? You made fun of everyone else's fears? You taunted and teased until you were kicked out of school and sent away to a boarding school, where you discover that every student there has an extreme phobia. What if whenever one of those students touched you, they were freed from their phobia but you caught it? What if the plan was to have every student touch you, giving you their fear, healing themselves? What if you were being given panphobia, the fear of everything? These are just some of the short stories in *What Are You Afraid of?* edited by Donald Gallo.

DISCUSSION QUESTIONS

1. What is the difference between a fear and a phobia?
2. How do you think the authors of the short stories in *What are You Afraid Of* know enough about these phobias to write about them?
3. Recalling the short story "Thin," do you know anyone who is obsessed with being thin? Have you ever thought of that obsession as a phobia?
4. In the short story, "Rutabaga," the main character's fear of knives is cured when she confronts her mother. What do you think caused her fear?

5. In some of the stories it is clear what started the phobias and in other stories it isn't so clear. Do you think there is always a reason or something that triggers phobias?
6. Out of all the phobias listed in *Phobias* by Judy Monroe, which makes the most sense to you? Which phobias do you have slight fears of as well?
7. Have you ever seen anyone react irrationally from fear? What happened?
8. How do you work through your fear and conquer it so that you can continue with the task at hand? How is that different from a phobia?
9. Which phobia seems ridiculous to you?

PROJECT: RESEARCHING FOR YOUR OWN SHORT STORY

This activity shows students how research is vital to every story. As an introduction to the topic, have your students read a novel or short story as well as a nonfiction book on the same topic (*Angel of Death* by Alane Ferguson or *What Are You Afraid Of?* edited by Donald R. Gallo are good choices). Lead a discussion with your students about how much research the authors needed to do in order to write these stories. Do the students think that research is important in writing fiction?

For the assignment students will choose a topic of their choice. Locate and browse through three nonfiction books on that topic. Write a short story (length of your choosing) that includes at least six facts derived from the nonfiction books.

The Author Pair

Sledding Hill
by Chris Crutcher

"My name is Billy Bartholomew and I was arguably the smartest kid in class. My best friend is Eddie Proffit, whom according to the IQ test was the dumbest kid in class. Eddie scored a 65. And then my dad (the school janitor) found out that Eddie started seeing what a neat pattern filling in the ovals made and started making neater and neater patterns without even reading the questions. His answer sheet looked "way cool" according to Eddie. My dad retested Eddie's IQ and Eddie scored a 165. Eddie's problem is that his mind jumps from one thought to another and very rarely stays on one thought for very long. In class Eddie always asks too many questions—questions the teachers don't want to answer, especially when Eddie doesn't believe what the teacher is saying. Eddie used to get in trouble all the time for asking too many questions so Eddie and I came up with a plan. We got an electric dog collar and put it around his ankle. And whenever I noticed that Eddie was going to ask one too many questions and get himself sent to the principal's office, I would hit the button on the remote control I was holding, sending a shocking jolt right up Eddie's leg. Eddie stayed in class a lot more after that.

Anyway, the summer before we started high school, Eddie's dad was fixing tires at his Chevron station and got distracted. Big mistake. It's Eddie who finds his dad lying next to an exploded truck tire, deader than a doornail.

Three weeks later, as Eddie is starting to learn to deal with his dad's death, I kick a stack of sheetrock that is leaning precariously against a wall and turn my back on it to leave. The sheetrock falls forward and the upper edge catches me at the base of the skull snapping my spine. Guess who finds me? Yep, Eddie. Eddie is now one seriously messed up dude. Who wouldn't be after find both your dad and your best friend dead in one summer? It will be awhile before Eddie talks again. And I think I'll stick around for awhile — just to help him out a little."

King of the Mild Frontier
by Chris Crutcher

As a child, Chris Crutcher was a bad-tempered crybaby, prone to coonskin caps and too many candy bars. One of his family's favorite stories told at every get-together was about how Chris's temper was cured at the age of 2. It went something like, "Chris was very difficult to deal with. He would throw these temper-tantrums where he would throw himself into the air, kick out his legs and land hard on the floor. I called the doctor for advice and he said to put an alphabet block under him the next time he does it. Sure enough, he never did it again. But then he started storming into the bathroom and slamming his head into the bathtub. So I called the doctor again and he said to just help Chris by pushing his head a little bit harder than he intended."

Chris Crutcher's autobiography tells the story of one of today's most popular teen novelists — about his childhood, growing up a crybaby, being a sucker for doing whatever his older brother told him too and then always getting into trouble for it, never getting a date with a girl, thinking that coonskin caps were cool, deciding to walk to work for the exercise and eating 2–3 candy bars each way to keep up his strength. Chris's autobiography also gives us a glimpse of the inspiration for his novel, *Sledding Hill*, as he tells the true side of the story of 7-year-old Eddie who kicks over a large piece of sheetrock, which falls over and snaps his neck. And about how Eddie starts appearing in his dreams as they go sledding together and discussing whether or not Chris's grandpa is in heaven. Throughout the book you'll find pieces of stories that have found their way into Chris's novels. But even if you have never read one of Crutcher's books, his autobiography, *King of the Mild Frontier,* will not only make you wonder, "how did this man ever become an award-winning author?," but you'll also be wondering, "how did this man ever survive childhood?"

DISCUSSION QUESTIONS

1. *King of the Mild Frontier* tells the story of seven-year-old Eddie who is killed by sheetrock. This story is also featured in *Sledding Hill* but with some alterations. What are the differences in the two stories? Why do you think the author changed the true story to the story in the novel?
2. Where else in *King of the Mild Frontier* do you see inspiration for Crutcher's novels?
3. In *King of the Mild Frontier* when a student asks him why someone always dies in his books, Crutcher states that "without death there is no story." What do you think he means by that? How does death affect the story in *Sledding Hill*? How does death affect the story in *King of the Mild Frontier*?

4. In *Sledding Hill* the author puts himself into the story. Does this enrich the story or does it seem like a gimic to get your attention? Why? How would the story have been different if Crutcher had written another author into the story rather than himself?

5. In *King of the Mild Frontier* Crutcher paints his younger self as a goofy crybaby. Why does he do this? How would you write about yourself when you were five years old; eight years old?

6. In *Sledding Hill* Eddie stops talking. Why? Does this help Eddie or make his life more difficult? Why would anyone make such a decision?

7. In *Sledding Hill*, what roles do the two fathers play in Eddie's life? How do they make an impact on Eddie? Compare the two fathers in *Sledding Hill* to the author's father in *King of the Mild Frontier*. How are they different? How are they alike?

PROJECT: MEMORY TO STORY

Have your students keep a daily journal for an amount of time specified by you. (If you are doing this project in conjunction with your discussion group, for example, have your students keep a journal every day between two meetings.) Stress that this journal should contain all of the facts about their day not just the interesting bits. After your teens have enough days recorded in their journals, ask them to use two or three facts or situations or incidents from their journals to write a fictional short story. As an additional discussion, have the students report which facts they used as inspiration and if they made any changes to the true story. Ask the students why they made the changes that they did.

The Science Group

Ninjas, Piranhas, and Galileo
by Greg Leitich Smith

For this booktalk, you will pretend to be three different characters in the book. To indicate you're taking on different personas, face a different direction for each one; try to make eye contact with the people in the room for the direction you're facing.

Elias (face right): Hi, my name is Elias and people think that I'm an overachiever but I'm really not, I'm just from a family that requires I do everything "just so." My father is literally obsessed with Johann Sebastian Bach (*ask students if they recognize the name*). Anyway, so it was science fair time and I decided to do the same project my genius older brother did—in the name of "experimental confirmation." However, suddenly things went horribly awry and I was stuck in front of the judge, the jury, and my crazy, controlling science teacher.

Honoria (face front): Hello. My name is Honoria. People think that Eli and I are overachievers; however, what they do not know is I am and he is not. Do not get me wrong, I like Eli and he does get good grades but I am the ultimate overachiever. Everything has a place, I am perpetually right, and I was determined to win this year's science fair. Unfortunately, due to Eli's rambunctiousness, I am defending him in front of the judge, the jury, and my crazy, controlling science teacher.

Shohei (face left): Hey, what's up? My name is Shohei and I'm a Japanese American adopted into an Irish American family, and my parents are super crazy about me understanding my Japanese heritage — it's outta control. I think you already met Elias and Honoria, my two best friends — they are super overachievers, which is kinda funny because I like getting good grades and all, but it's not like I live for it. Anyway, I was supposed to help Elias with the science fair project but I kinda slacked off so, now I'm admitting guilt and plagiarism in front of the judge, the jury, and my crazy, controlling science teacher.

Light, Sound, and Waves Science Fair Projects
by Robert Gardner

What better way to booktalk a science fair book than to do a small project in front of the class! You'll need a couple supplies that you can inevitably find in the teacher's lounge: 1 large bowl, plastic wrap, salt, wooden or plastic cooking spoon, and cooking pan. This project can be found in the chapter "Some Properties of Sound and Waves." This would be a great project to get different students to come up and help with different portions.

Did you know your eardrum actually moves when it picks up sound waves? Sound waves are bombarding your body like ripples in the water, and while, most of the time, sound waves do not move your body, they do move your eardrums. First, we need to make a membrane, which we'll do by stretching this plastic wrap tightly over the top of a bowl. Then we'll sprinkle some salt over the top. *Call up a volunteer.* Gently tap the membrane (the plastic wrap) with your finger and tell the class what happens to the salt. *Call up a different volunteer.* Clap your hands together near the membrane. Report what happens to the salt. *Call up a third volunteer.* Bang this pan with the spoon and observe what happens with the salt crystals. Does anyone in here like to sing? *Call up a student that volunteers.* Sing one note, do the crystals move? Sing a higher note and then a lower note. Does the pitch make the crystals move?

Guinea Pig Scientists
by Leslie Dendy, Mel Boring, and C. B. Mordan

Another great option to accompany either science book above is Guinea Pig Scientists.
After attending a college run by priests, Lazzaro Spallanzani thought he may want to join them. Unfortunately, his father wanted him to study law. After taking classes he discovered that while he definitely was not interested in law, he loved science and math. He soon became a professor of natural history and was particularly interested in the digestive system. Now, keep in mind, this was in 1776 — the same year the United States of America became a nation; there were no x-rays or internal cameras, so Spallanzani began his work on birds, then frogs and snakes, and eventually horses and dogs. He learned that a chicken could swallow a solid glass ball and its gizzard would turn it to sand; a turkey could swallow metal and its gizzard would break it into small pieces. Snakes bit him, dogs tried to, and falcons attempted to attack him. Experiments on the digestive tract were not easy. After Spallanzani had done extensive work on various members of the animal kingdom, he needed to know more about the human species. He knew he

could not ask a human to endure the potential pain and other side effects, so he began experimenting on himself.

The first experiment was done with a piece of bread. He put a bite of bread in his mouth, chewed it, spit it out, and weighed it. He then put the already chewed bite into a linen bag and sewed the bag's opening shut. Then he swallowed the bag! Twenty-three hours later the bag came out — empty. The bread was gone. His experiments did not end there — he swallowed whole grapes, a beef membrane, bones, and tried to set his gastric juices on fire.

This book is filled with bravery in science — men and women who have used themselves as guinea pigs to try out experiments to further our knowledge of the human body.

DISCUSSION QUESTIONS

1. What is plagiarism?
2. Talk about a science fair project you've done.
3. What did you think of the trial and punishment system at Elias' school? How is your school like that? How is it different?
4. Do your parents want you to know about your ancestors like Shohei's parents? Do you know any interesting facts about your heritage?
5. Why do you think people get upset when they learn new information that doesn't agree with what they thought was true?
6. How are questions important in science?
7. What are two facts we learned from Lazzaro Spallanzani?
8. If you had to be one of guinea pig scientists, which one would you be?
9. What have we learned from Marie and Pierre Curie?
10 What honor was Marie Curie given after death?
11. What did you think of Stefania Follini's experiment? Would you ever try something like that? What would be the most difficult part of it?

PROJECT: FACTS INTO FICTION

This project is great for a science class or an English class. Split the class into groups and have them do a simple experiment, one that can be completed within 1–2 class periods. After getting the results and the answers, instruct them to type up a report of their experiment using each step of the scientific method as a heading for each section.

After their report is typed up, they will then need to collaborate with their group members to create a fictional story that communicates the results they reached in their original experiment. For example, if they do an experiment about the digestive tract, their fictional story may be about a piece of apple with a personality and the twists and turns on its trip from the mouth and through the body.

Classroom Integration

Pairing is not only a way to inspire students to read nonfiction books but to incite their curiosity about school subjects. Teachers are encouraged to use historical fiction in the classroom to teach history — why not use this tool with every subject? For every subject you teach, we assure you there is a novel that has the potential to light the fire of curiosity within the minds of your students. For example, what if your high school students read the World War II novel *The Book Thief* by Markus Zusak in your history class or your book discussion group and then followed it up with *i never saw another butterfly*, poems by the children of the Terezen Concentration Camp? Once your students read the poignant *Book Thief*, the chances of keeping their interest and empathy for the nonfiction poetry book of *i never saw another butterfly* will be much greater. And your high school students will get a powerful look at some riveting primary sources from the Holocaust beyond Ann Frank's, *The Diary of a Young Girl*.

Or perhaps the students could read the *da Vinci Code* by Dan Brown in their English class while reading *Amazing Leonardo da Vinci Inventions You Can Build Yourself* in physics class. Or as a library program teens could read or watch the *Da Vinci Code* and then experiment with building some of the inventions in *Amazing Leonoardo da Vinci Inventions*. Booktalking both of the books at the same time will tie the two books together for your students and help them realize that science, history, literature, and mathematics all play a part in their world. Literature isn't created in a vacuum and our school subjects do not exist as islands unto themselves. In our suggested pairs for booktalking, we have listed many books with their intriguing pair; however, we encourage you to do your own searches at your local library or bookstore to find novels that appeal to your demographic.

More Great Books

Typically we pair nonfiction books with a riveting novel; however, there are some instances when it's applicable to pair a nonfiction book with another nonfiction book. For example, *Freaks of the Storm* is a collection of true stories involving extreme weather. This nonfiction book has independent appeal and would be a great addition to another nonfiction book about meteorology, such as *Restless Skies: The Ultimate Weather Book*. Here's a list of some of our favorite books to pair up!

Amazing Leonardo da Vinci Inventions You Can Build Yourself by Maxine Anderson and *Da Vinci Code* by Dan Brown
A Big Little Life: A Memoir of a Joyful Dog by Dean Koontz and *The World According to Dog: Poems and Teen Voices* by Joyce Sidman
Comedy Improvisation: Exercises & Techniques for Young Actors by Delton Horn and *My Nights at the Improv* by Jan Siebold
Dangerous Planet: Natural Disasters That Changed History by Bryn Barnard and *Life as We Knew It* by Susan Pfeffer
Dark Dreams: The Story of Stephen King by Nancy Whitelaw and *Cell* by Stephen King
The Explainer by the writers of *Slate Magazine* and *Canned* by Alex Shearer
Fact, Fiction, and Folklore in Harry Potter's World by George Beahm and *Harry Potter* (any) by J. K. Rowling
Geekspeak by Dr. Graham Tattersall and *An Abundance of Katherines* by John Green
The Grand Tour: A Traveler's Guide to the Solar System by Ron Miller and William Hartmann and *Double Cross* by Sigmund Brouwer

Guinea Pig Scientists: Bold Self-Experimenters in Science and Medicine by Leslie Dendy, Mel Boring, and C. B. Mordan or *Light, Sound, and Waves Science Fair Projects: Using Sunglasses, Guitars, CDs, and Other Stuff* by Robert Gardner and *Ninjas, Piranhas, and Galileo* by Greg Leitich Smith

I'll Tell What I Saw: Select Translations and Illustrations from the Divine Comedy by Michael Mazur and *Divine Comedy* by Dante Alighieri

Island of Hope: The Story of Ellis Island and the Journey to America by Martin Sandler and *The Arrival* by Shaun Tan

i never saw another butterfly by Hana Volavkova, ed. and *The Book Thief* by Markus Zusak

The Invisible Kingdom by Idan Ben-Barak and *Peeps* by Scott Westerfeld

King of the Mild Frontier by Chris Crutcher and *Sledding Hill* by Chris Crutcher

Lewis & Clark Revisited: A Photographer's Trail by Greg MacGregor and *Sacagawea Speaks: Beyond the Shining Mountains with Lewis & Clark* by Joyce Badgley Hunsaker

Mysteries Unwrapped: The Secrets of Alcatraz by Susan Sloate and *Al Capone Does My Shirts* by Gennifer Choldenko

Phobias: Everything You Wanted to Know but Were Afraid to Ask by Judy Monroe and *What are You Afraid of?: Stories About Phobias* by Donald R. Gallo, ed.

Restless Skies: The Ultimate Weather Book by Paul Douglas and *Freaks of the Storm: From Flying Cows to Stealing Thunder: The World's Strangest True Weather Stories* by Randy Cerveny

Spyology by Spencer Blake and Dugald A. Steer and *I'd Tell You I Love You But Then I'd Have to Kill You* by Ally Carter

When Objects Talk by Mark P. Friedlander Jr. and Terry M. Phillips and *Angel of Death* by Alane Ferguson

15

Interactives

Sometimes you may find it more difficult than usual to get your teens interested in your booktalking session. Either you are talking to sleepy teens at 7:30 in the morning or they've just eaten lunch and are ready for their midday nap. Whatever the reason for their lack of enthusiasm, there are surefire ways to energize your booktalks. Let them show off their trivia knowledge, give them an improvisational challenge or make them do the bunny hop, punk style. By getting the teens involved, this style of booktalk will get your sessions motivated!

Instead of a genre, this chapter is more about booktalking style. Writing and performing booktalks that are interactive is one of the greatest joys in booktalking. An interactive booktalk involves anything from students acting things out to a quiz show setup. Interactive booktalks are a lifesaver for any dead booktalking session and will bring to life even the most serious teens. They break up the monotony and are best done either in the middle or at the end; we typically pull them out the moment we start seeing yawns. By interspersing interactive booktalks among the serious or longer talks, it will be easier to maintain attention and the diversity will compliment the different books. Also, ending your booktalking session with an interactive booktalk leaves students laughing and with an overall good impression of the books. If you haven't had your caffeine before taking on the interactives, go grab some. They require energy and the willingness to be silly.

Book Ideas with Booktalks, Discussion Questions, and Project Ideas

Maria Shaw's Book of Love
by Maria Shaw

This book is a great introduction if you are doing a set of booktalks for a group of teens. The Book of Love *gets teens interested in your talk and gives them hope that you aren't going to bore them to tears for the next 45 minutes. The majority of this book consists of compatibility charts for zodiac signs. To begin, we usually do not let teens know what this book is or even what it is about. We even go so far as to hide it behind our backs. Ask for two volunteers and once you have two teens standing up front with you, ask them if they know their zodiac sign. Many teens will not know their signs so we generally put a quick Post-it note guide on the back of the book in order to figure out their sign from their birthday.*

Once we have their signs and have found our place in the book we often start out with something like "Now we're going to see how these two would do together if they were a couple." The group of teens will react with "oohs" and "aaahs" and laughter. The teens up front will be embarrassed and will either mimic running away from each other or running to each other. So far we've found that teens are very good-natured about the task at hand. After all, we did ask for volunteers. Read aloud the section of the book that pairs these two signs together in front of the whole group. Be sure to pause when your teens laugh at a particular point or when your volunteers need to react to what they've just heard. It is impossible to listen to the couple's romance horoscope without reacting in some fashion. At the end of each compatibility paragraph is a chart rating the couple from one to five stars on attraction, compatibility, communication, friendship and marriage material. One is the least compatible and five is the most compatible. Be sure to read off the ratings from this chart as well. You'll be amazed at how many teens raise their hand to be the next volunteer after you read through the first potential couple's section.

Discussion Questions

1. Read the introductory paragraph for your sign's chapter. Do you think the horoscope is correct? Do you think you are like the person described in these paragraphs?
2. Have you read any couple's horoscopes for either you and your boyfriend or girlfriend or for you and your crush? Do you think the horoscope holds any truth?
3. Are you happy or disappointed with your horoscope?
4. Do you think these horoscopes are vague enough to hold true for anyone, or do you think they are specific enough for you to want to follow their advice?
5. Have you ever considered what colors mean when giving flowers or jewelry?
6. Do you think the instructions for palm reading in this book are easy or difficult to follow? Why?
7. Would you suggest this book to anyone else?

Project: Valentine's Day Fund Raiser

Does your group or class need an idea for a fund raiser? Use *Maria Shaw's Book of Love* to create a small intimate fund raiser on or near Valentine's Day. Set up a booth at your school's spirit fair or your library's book sale and let your teens tell couples' horoscopes to customers. The only supplies needed are this book and birthdates from the couples. You could also let your teens try their hand at palm reading using the instructions in the book or they could sell flowers to customers based on the meaning of their colors.

Encyclopedia Horrifica
by Joshua Gee

To make this booktalk interactive, we use the "Ghost or Hoax" section of the book. We let the teens take a look at the photos of supposed ghosts and ask them if each photo is of a real ghost or simply a hoax. After the teens respond with their thoughts, we give them information about each photograph. The answers to the "Ghost or Hoax" quiz are found in the back of the book.

Number 1: "Old Nanna's Here!" Is this photo a hoax? *Let the teens look at the photo and respond.* The kid in this photo used to point to the air and say, "Old Nanna's here!" When his parents took this photo there was no fog or mist in the room but the mist showed up in this picture. This picture is real and not a hoax!

Number 2: "The Mourning Matron of Arkham House." What about this photo of a lady with no reflection in the mirror? *Let the teens look at the photo and respond.* This is a hoax! The lady in the picture is actually a costumed tour guide.

Number 3: "The Ghost of Freddy Jackson." Some claim that the man circled in this photo was dead at the time the photo was taken. Do you believe them? *Let the teens look at the photo and respond.* This picture is supposedly real! According to several eyewitnesses, the man in the back of this group photo died two days before this photo was taken.

Number 4: "The Backseat Driver." What about the person in the backseat of this car? Ghost or hoax? *Let the teens look at the photo and respond.* This is a real ghost! According to the man in the front seat and the lady taking the picture, the person in the backseat is the man's mother-in-law. The picture was taken at the cemetery just after visiting her grave!

Number 5: "An Ectoplasmic Spiral in Gorey-Edward Gardens." Are the lights in this photo a ghost or just a hoax? *Let the teens look at the photo and respond.* Hoax! Sometimes an image will blur if the camera is moved while the picture is being taken. This happened to this photo. It is actually just a light that has been blurred across the page.

Number 6: "The Ghost Girl in the Burning Building." What about this picture? Real ghost or just a hoax? *Let the teens look at the photo and respond.* Supposedly, the image of this girl was taken while the village's town hall was on fire. The door in which she is standing is engulfed in flames so no human could possibly be standing there unharmed. She's a real ghost caught on film.

Discussion Questions

1. Who was Vlad Dracula? How is he different from the vampires seen in movies and read about in books? Why is he the basis for these movies and books? What are the similarities?
2. What are the seven types of close encounters with aliens? Do you think you've ever seen a UFO? Do you think it was actually an alien spaceship? If not, what do you think it was?
3. What was the Beast of Gevaudan? What myth did it inspire?
4. Who was the Bell Witch? Do you think the witch was really supernatural? What other explanations are there for these occurrences?
5. Read the paragraph about the Ghost Cat in the section "Permanent Pets." Do you think this photograph is real? What other explanations are there?
6. Do you believe in superstitions? Do you follow them? Why or why not?
7. What is a zombi jardin and a zombi gate?

Project: Local Haunts

Every town has a local ghost story. Let your teens investigate! Begin with a group discussion of what they have heard about the ghost, haunting, alien, monster or legend. Are the teens' stories different? Where did they first hear these stories? After ensuring that everyone is familiar with the subject, ask your teens to research the truth behind the legend. Some questions they should consider are:

- Who are the people discussed in the stories? Are there any records of these people such as obituaries, news articles or genealogy records?
- How did this story become a supernatural tale? What were the first supernatural occurrences? Are there records of these happenings?
- Do the supernatural events still occur today? If not, when did they stop and why?

You may want to ask your local special collections librarian for assistance and to help you gather local resources for your teens. This is a great project to do in groups or individually and your teens can report their findings in any format you prefer. The important aspect of this project is to get your teens to delve into the local records and local history of your community.

How to Survive a Horror Movie
by Seth Grahame-Smith

Many booktalks can become interactive by using a quiz show format. How to Survive a Horror Movie *offers plenty of fodder to create a quiz that lets teens show off their horror movie knowledge or just their natural sense of survival.*

You're running through the woods with a crazed maniac close behind you You see a toolshed up ahead and run straight in. Which tool should you not grab to defend yourself?
     A. chainsaw
     B. hatchet
     C. rake
     D. sickle
Let the teens choose their answer.
Answer: Never grab a rake. What are you going to do, scratch them to death?

Which item should you never, ever, ever put into a child's room?
     A. any representation of a clown.
     B. windows
     C. ouija boards
     D. closets
Let the teens choose their answer
Trick Question! Don't put any of these items into a child's bedroom. Clowns and

ouija boards are just plain evil. Windows are what kids get snatched out of and closets are where the monsters live.

> Which of these actions should you take if there are snakes on your plane?
> A. panic
> B. unleash a suitcase full of mongooses
> C. pretend nothing is wrong
> D. sacrifice the pilots to the snakes
> *Let the teens choose their answer*

Answer: You're allowed two carryons. Fill one with mothballs and the other with hungry mongooses. What? You've never read *Rikki Tikki Tavi*? A snake doesn't stand a chance against a mongoose!

DISCUSSION QUESTIONS

1. Read "An Apology from Wes Craven." What is he apologizing for? What does he mean when he says, "Death finds a way"?
2. Grahame-Smith writes his manual as if the reader has been placed inside of a horror movie. How does his writing style reflect this?
3. What are the six methods for surviving a haunted high school? Are these tips useful for real life?
4. What are the types of slasher characters? Do you think there are slasher villains missing from this list?
5. How do you survive a night of babysitting? Why does the author consider babysitting such a dangerous profession in horror movies?
6. Why are horror movies so popular? Why do we enjoy watching something that makes us afraid? Do you enjoy horror movies or avoid them?

PROJECT: HOMEGROWN HORROR MOVIE

After reading this survival manual for horror movies, ask your teens to write a 3-page horror movie based on the rules discussed in the book. Who are the characters in the book? Which characters break which rules and meet their untimely deaths? Who is the villain? What type of horror movie is it? There are so many rules to break in horror movies your teens should have plenty of opportunity to create disastrous accidents for each of their characters.

The Zombie Survival Guide
by Max Brooks

This booktalk catches the attention of every teen boy and some teen girls. To make this booktalk interactive we just let the teens tell us as much about zombies as they think they know.

What is a zombie? *Let the teens tell you what they think zombies are. You'll probably get answers ranging from the walking dead to voodoo zombies. Let your teens know that they are all correct! Zombies cover a wide range of seemingly dead people!* Answer: A zombie can be (1) an animated corpse that feeds on human flesh, (2) a voodoo spell that raises the dead, (3) a voodoo snake-god, or (4) one who moves or acts in a daze.

How do you become a zombie? *Again let the teens tell you all the gruesome ways one can become a zombie!* Answer: Direct fluidic contact — which means most commonly a zombie bite. Also by brushing an open wound against a zombie or by being splattered by its remains after an explosion.

What happens once you become infected? How long does it take to turn into a zombie?

- Hour 1: pain and discoloration of the infected area, immediate clotting of the wound
- Hour 5: fever, chills, slight dementia, vomiting, acute pain in the joints
- Hour 8: numbing of extremities and infected area, increased fever, increased dementia, loss of muscular coordination
- Hour 11: paralysis of the lower body, overall numbness, slowed heart rate
- Hour 16: coma
- Hour 20: heart stoppage; zero brain activity
- Hour 23: reanimation

What is the treatment for a zombie bite? Trick question! There is no cure once you've been bitten.

There are four classes of zombie outbreaks. *For this part of the talk, we don't ask a question but just let their imaginations run wild while we are talking.*

- Class 1: 1–20 zombies; 20-mile radius. Response to the outbreak is almost completely civilian. Which means you are out there bashing in zombie heads with your baseball bat!
- Class 2: 20–100 zombies; 100-mile radius. Response to the outbreak can be local, state or even federal law enforcement.
- Class 3: 1000s of zombies; 1000s of victims; 1000s of miles included. Expect rioting, rationed supplies, martial law and widespread panic.
- Class 4: You are living in an undead world. Expect burned-out buildings, silent roads, crumbling homes, abandoned ships, gnawed and bleached bones scattered over a world now ruled by machines of walking dead flesh. You are on your own.

What is the best weapon against a zombie? *The teens will give you all kinds of answers here ranging from fire to guns to axes and chainsaws!* Answer: a hatchet or axe is the best weapon. While a gun works well at a distance, if you have a hatchet or axe you can keep lobbing off zombie heads indefinitely! And you can use it to chop down your staircase if zombies are invading your house. Fortunately for you, there is the *Zombie Survival Guide*, which will teach you how to zombie proof your house, teach you what weapons to use and how to survive indefinitely.

Discussion Questions

1. *The Zombie Survival Guide* is considered nonfiction. Why is a book about something imaginary considered nonfiction?
2. Why are zombies so fascinating to us? Why are they so scary?
3. Brooks spends a large part of the book discussing various weaponry. Is this thorough discussion necessary? Why or why not?
4. Where is the safest place to go during a zombie attack? Why? Would you be able to get to this location?
5. Do you think you would survive a zombie attack?
6. Do you believe the true accounts of zombie encounters discussed at the end of the *Survival Guide?*

Project: Z-Day Emergency Preparedness Plan

Are you prepared for Z-Day? Every good home, school, library and business has an emergency preparedness plan that provides instructions on what to do in case of fire, biohazards, earthquakes, tornadoes and other large-scale natural disasters but do those plans include the inevitable Z-Day? Ask your teens to create this plan. Questions to consider include:

- What is your first line of defense?
- What supplies do you need to have stored and ready?
- What supplies do you need in case you have to vacate your home?
- What weapons will you use? Are they nearby, and in good working condition?
- How will your family and friends meet up? Where is the rendezvous point?
- What is the backup rendezvous point?
- Where will you head for safety?
- What are your longterm goals for survival?
- How will you protect yourself from disease, cold, hunger and other humans?
- How will you protect yourself from the zombie horde at your safety location?

The Vampire Is Just Not That into You
by Vlad Mezrich

This book is a humorous take on popular vampire series like Twilight. *It assumes that all of the teen girls in your group are in love with vampires and desperately want to date one; they want their own Edward. There are several surveys in this book, so pick your favorite and let your teens discover their own vampire type. We suggest that you use the survey "Is He Tired of You?" as it is a good sample of the types of quizzes found in the book. For the survey ask your teens to write down their answers on a scrap sheet of paper so they can remember at the end of the short quiz. Once the survey is complete ask them to add up the number of a's, b's, c's and d's they have and pick the letter they answered the most. If they answered mostly a's, the vampire is getting tired of them. If they answered mostly b's, the vampire is getting REALLY tired of them. If they answered mostly c's, the vampire hates them and if they answered mostly d's the vampire still loves them!*

Discussion Questions

1. Who is your favorite vampire? What is your favorite vampire book or series?
2. Why do you think vampires are now considered so desirable when originally they were terrifying monsters?
3. When do you think vampires stopped being terrifying monsters and started being romantic conquests?
4. There are many vampire myths such as vampires being able to fly or turning into bats. Vampires are allergic to garlic, sunlight, holy water, and bells ringing. Vampires prefer specific blood types. Which vampire myths do you prefer? Are there any myths that you do not like?
5. Who are the different experts that appear in Vlad Mezrich's book? Why do you think the author uses several different expert voices in this book?

Project: Sexiest Vampire of the Year Award

Vampire myths abound. Each book, movie or television series creates its own rules for their vampires. Let your teens research five different vampires of their choosing. What are the different rules for these vampires? For each vampire ask the following questions:

- Can they handle sunlight?
- Is it mandatory for them to sleep during the day?
- Must they rejuvenate inside of a coffin?
- Can they eat, smell or be around garlic?
- Will holy water or crosses hurt them?
- Can they stand the sound of bells?
- Must they be invited into your home in order to enter?
- Do they have any tolerance for humans? Have they ever dated a human?
- What is their favorite pastime? Hobbies?
- Do they kill for fun or do they avoid killing at all?

Once your teens have answered these questions for their five vampires, ask them to make a chart to display the results.

Next ask your teens to choose their favorite of the five vampires and ask them to explain why they like that particular vampire or vampire myth the most.

The Encyclopedia of Immaturity: Volume 2
by the editors of *Klutz*

We're going to play a game called "Show Your Proboscis." Rule number 1: everybody needs to stand up without talking. Rule number 2: I'm going to say the name of a body part and you need to point to it. And just for the record, none of these are inappropriate.

- Epiglottis: Students should point to the throat. It is the flap that covers the windpipe while swallowing.

- Umbilicus: Students should point to their belly button.
- Philtrum: Students should point to the place above their top lip. It is the verticle groove between your nose and top lip.
- Hallux: Students should point to their big toe.
- Humerus: Students should point to the bone that runs from their shoulder to their elbow.
- Proboscis: Students should point to their noses.

Variation: If you have a lot of students in your session, it might be more feasible to have a couple volunteers come up to the front of the room and try to point to the various parts (this may also be funnier).

For discussion questions for The Encyclopedia of Immaturity: Volume 2, *please refer to the "Introduction to Performing" project below.*

Project: Introduction to Performing

This book is a great tool to get students comfortable with getting up in front of people. First, split them up into groups of 2–3 students. Instruct them to choose an activity from the book. Provide them 5–10 minutes to quickly create a skit around the activity — their lines should be improvised to achieve the outcome they intended. Grading will be based on the completed activity they chose and the ability to fill lulls in an improv skit.

After project discussion is crucial in this option. Discussion questions may include:

1. What was the most difficult part about this project?
2. When you noticed a lull, what types of thoughts did you focus on to get out of it?
3. Were different activities easier than others? Why or why not?
4. Now that you have the opportunity to reflect on your performance, what could you have done in the planning portion to make it easier?

Acting Games
by Marsh Cassady

Raise your hand if you'd like to be an actor or actress someday. We're going to do a few acting games to test your acting abilities. Even if you don't want to be an actor, play along for fun — you may be better than the people around you. Before we get started we're going to do a few exercises. I'm going to tell you a certain emotion and you need to make the facial expression that goes with it.

Coming up with a comedy skit is oftentimes more fun than actually performing it!

- surprise
- anger
- disappointment

- really, really sad
- bored out of your mind

During this section, draw attention to teens who are doing particularly well.

Great job! Now, this next one is a little more challenging. First, I'll need two volunteers. *Get their names and use them instead of saying student A or student B.* Student A, you will say, "I was trying to *blank* but..."—for the blank part make up something you were trying to do for example, brush your iguana's teeth or jog backwards on a treadmill. Student B, you will complete the sentence. In other words, if Student A says, "I was trying brush my iguana's teeth but...," you have to come up with a solution to the what she was trying to do. *This is a great opportunity to get multiple teens involved; call other groups of two up if you have time.* More weird and totally cool acting games can be found in the book, *Acting Games* by Marsh Cassady.

Discussion Questions

1. What is the purpose of acting games?
2. Were there any games that you thought were pointless? Were there any games you thought were really helpful or made you think about things differently?
3. Why do you think it can be so embarrassing to do these in front of others?
4. The author talks about the importance of space; describe how you view space after reading it.
5. The author stresses the importance of being sensitive; why should an actor be sensitive?

Project: Learning and Teaching

The most obvious project idea for this book is doing the games listed in the book. A great twist on this is, after practicing them together, split your class into groups of at least two teens and assign each group a game from the book. Then partner with a class from a younger grade and have your older teens teach the younger teens the acting skills they learned. If you have time perform them for each other at the end of class.

This project can also be easily integrated into a library setting by hosting an acting class for teens and then empowering them to host one for the tween library patrons. If it is particularly successful, you may have a teen and tween population to start a drama club!

The Big Book of Gross Stuff
by Bart King

Some books seem to provide booktalks for you! This book has a lot of amazing ideas but one we particularly enjoy is called "Magical Spit-Swallowing Activity." The only thing you'll need to prepare for this talk is a glass, preferably one that is transparent. Go ahead and do the first three steps listed in the activity. While the student volunteer is spitting into the glass, go ahead and do one or two different booktalks to take up 3–5 minutes. After you have com-

pleted the talks, have the student come up to the front of the room and complete the remaining steps. Be sure remember that asking the student to drink their saliva is a joke and not something they actually have to do. Follow this activity up with the following facts found in the book:

When Neil Armstrong landed on the moon, he didn't just leave behind the American flag; he also left his defecation collection devices. In other words, Armstrong left behind astronaut doody. Whales vomit and apparently it is worth a lot of money to the fragrance industry. Has anyone in here ever heard of shrunken heads? If you've ever wondered how they came to be, here are the steps. *Read aloud the section called "Shrinking Heads" in the chapter "It's a Gross Job."*

DISCUSSION QUESTIONS

1. Fill in the blank: Skunks have the most well-developed _____. (*In the chapter "Animals!"*)
2. What are some different words for flatus?
3. What is ambergris and why is worth $4,000 per pound?
4. Where does 90 percent of human sewage get dumped?
5. What was the most interesting thing you read?
6. What was the grossest thing you read?

PROJECT: DISGUSTINGLY FUNNY LIMERICKS OR HAIKU

It seems that talking about gross things and talking to teens go together! Give into their endless efforts to discuss all things disgusting and allow them to write either a limerick or a haiku that tells a story about something truly gross, fact or fiction. This is a great opportunity to discuss different forms of poetry, and it promotes poetry in a way that appeals to them! Also, it's quite difficult to tell a story with just a few lines— this will require some brain storming and, possibly, some help. Encourage students to work together but assure them that they will have to each turn in their own poem.

Time Travelers' Handbook
by Lottie Stride

Let's say you are taking a walk through a field and stumble across a box with blinking lights. You walk over and, feeling brave, you push the button that says GO. Suddenly you're standing in a lush forest and you spot a Tyrannosaurus rex. Just moments after you spot him, he makes eye contact with you and begins running toward you. What should you do? *Allow about three students to try and answer the question but be sure not to give an opinion on their ideas.*

I'm going to list some options of what to do if you want to survive a charging T. rex. For each one, I will give you the opportunity to raise your hand and we'll see if you would survive. *In the chapter called "How to Tackle a Tyrannosaurus Rex" there are a list of do's and dont's. Go through each one without reading the do or don't but allow students to decide if it's a good idea. After you've polled the class for each suggestion, tell them the logic behind the correct answer.*

DISCUSSION QUESTIONS

1. Why do you need to know how to tie knots to beat the Spanish Armada?
2. Name at least two tips you must remember if you ever hunt a mammoth.
3. This question is for the girls: What are some tips for ladies who are competing in the Ancient Olympiad? *Trick question, females were not permitted to compete!*
4. What is the keep of the castle?
5. How would you leap a Minoan bull?

PROJECT: HIEROGLYPHIC WRITING!

There are so many fun projects to choose from! Our favorite: Make a cartouche. If you have the supplies, do it as a class. If not, choose another from the book! Whatever project you choose will give you the opportunity to discuss the historical event or time period at even greater length. Bonus for the educator!

The Government Manual for New Superheroes
by Matthew David Brozik and Jacob Sager Weinstein

According to the authors, this book is official, written by the government, just like "The Government Manual for New Homeowners." It gives you tips on how to pick out a superhero name, how do design your super outfit, how to make enemies, and finding a secret hideout. One section in particular describes the ten things that you, as a superhero, need to have on you at all times. Between the guys and the gals, I'm going to see who can guess the most. *Allow students to answer based on the amount of extra time you have, three minutes or eight minutes. To find the correct list of items, find the section called "Survival of the Outfittest" in chapter 3. Also, if you have a fellow booktalker, have them calculate the score to keep the booktalk moving. Give each gender the opportunity to answer equal number of times. After you have provided the allotted amount of time, read the list and the short explanations.*

Another option for this book (though not interactive) is to simply read the memorandum at the very beginning of the book in your most official voice. It's short and clever—your students will love it!

DISCUSSION QUESTIONS

1. What is your superhero name?
2. Besides a costume, what other things do you need to be a superhero?
3. What are some ways listed in the book to keep this superhero business a secret?
4. Who can you trust?
5. How do you know if you should get a superhero sidekick?
6. According to the authors, what makes a person go bad?

PROJECT: CREATE YOUR SUPERHERO

It's time for your students to reveal their superhero identities. Using the tips in the book, have your students come up their superhero identity. They must come up with a name, costume, superpower, location and layout for a secret hideout, sidekick's name (if they have one) and a list of three enemies.

With these in hand, each student will get up in front of the class, dressed as their superhero, and reveal their identity. It may be embarrassing for students to get up in front of the class dressed up; to help, you should do it first!

This project is a great option to do for a bookclub — simply have your attendees show up in their costumes and describe their identities.

More Great Books

Acting Games: Improvisations and Exercises by Marsh Cassady

The Alien Invasion Survival Handbook by W. H. Mumfrey

Almanac of the Gross, Disgusting & Totally Repulsive: A Compendium of Fulsome Facts by Eric Elfman

Art Fraud Detective: Spot the Difference, Solve the Crime by Anna Nilsen

Bat Boy Lives! The WEEKLY WORLD NEWS Guide to Politics, Culture, Celebrities, Alien Abductions, and the Mutant Freaks that Shape Our World by editors of *Weekly World News* and David Perell

The Big Book of Gross Stuff by Bart King

Can You Drill a Hole Through Your Head and Survive?: 180 Fascinating Questions and Amazing Answers About Science, Health, and Nature by Simon Rogers, ed.

Chew on This: Everything You Didn't Want to Know About Fast Food by Eric Schlosser and Charles Wilson

Comedy improvisation: Exercises & Techniques for Young Actors by Delton Horn

Encyclopedia Horrifica: The Terrifying Truth About Vampires, Ghosts, Monsters and More by Joshua Gee

Encyclopedia of Immaturity: Volume 2 by the editors of *Klutz*

Essential Cat by Caroline Davis

The Explainer by the writers of *Slate Magazine*

For Boys Only: The Biggest, Baddest Book Ever by Marc Aronson and H. P. Newquist

The Government Manual For New Superheroes by Matthew David Brozik and Jacob Sager Weinstein

How to Be a Villain: Evil Laughs, Secret Lairs, Master Plans, and More!! by Neil Zawacki

How to Hold a Crocodile by the Diagram Group

How To Survive a Horror Movie: All the Skills to Dodge the Kills by Seth Grahame-Smith

King George: What Was His Problem? by Steve Sheinkin

Maria Shaw's Book of Love by Maria Shaw

MySpace/Our Planet: Change is Possible by the MySpaceCommunity with Jeca Taudte

Mythbusters: Don't Try This at Home by Discovery Channel and Mary Packard

The Ninja Handbook: This Book Looks Forward to Killing You Soon by Douglas Sarine and Kent Nichols

Oh Yikes! History's Grossest Moments by Joy Masoff and Terry Sirrell

101 Things You Wish You'd Invented and Some You Wish No One Had by Richard Horne and Tracey Turner

The Other Book of Perfectly Useless Information by Mitchell Symons

Phobias: Everything You Wanted to Know but Were Afraid to Ask by Judy Monroe

Punk Rock Aerobics: 75 Killer Moves, 50 Punk Classics, and 25 Reasons to Get Off Your Ass and Exercise by Maura Jasper and Hilkin Mancini

The Rights of Students by Eve Cary, Alan H. Levine and Janet Price

Ripley's Believe It or Not by Ripley Entertainment, Inc.

The Stunning Science of Everything: Science with the Squishy Bits Left In! by Nick Arnold and Tony De Saulles

The Stupid Crook Book by Leland Gregory

That Book of Perfectly Useless Information by Mitchell Symons

They Broke the Law — You Be the Judge: True Cases of Teen Crime by Thomas A. Jacobs

Time Travelers' Handbook: A Wild, Wacky and Wooly Adventure Through History! by Lottie Stride

The Vampire Is Just Not That into You by Vlad Mezrich

Vile Verses by Roald Dahl

Wearing of This Garment Does Not Enable You to Fly: 101 Real Dumb Warning Labels by Jeff Koon, Andy Powell, and Tim Carroll

Weird U.S. by Mark Moran and Mark Sceurman

The Wicked History of the World: History with the Nasty Bits Left In! by Terry Deary and Martin Brown

The Zombie Survival Guide: Complete Protection from the Living Dead by Max Brooks

Booktalking Resources

SUGGESTED BOOKS WITH BOOKTALKS

Acting Games: Improvisations and Exercises by Marsh Cassaidy

Alex & Me by Irene M. Pepperberg

The Alien Invasion Survival Handbook: A Defense Manual for the Coming Extraterrestrial Apocalypse by W. H. Mumfrey

Amazing Leonardo da Vinci Inventions You Can Build Yourself by Maxine Anderson

Amazing Stories of Survival: Tales of Hope, Heroism & Astounding Luck by the editors of *People Magazine*

American Born Chinese by Gene Luen Yang

Andy Warhol: Pop Art Painter by Susan Goldman Rubin

Angel of Death by Alane Ferguson (fiction title, perfect to pair with *When Objects Talk*)

The Animal Dialogues: Uncommon Encounters in the Wild by Craig Childs

Backyard and Beyond: A Guide for Discovering the Outdoors by Edward Duensing and A. B. Millmoss

Be Afraid, Be Very Afraid: The Book of Scary Urban Legends by Jan Harold Brunvand

Beowolf by Gareth Hinds

Between a Rock and a Hard Place by Aron Ralston

The Big Book of Gross Stuff by Bart King

Bitten: True Medical Stories of Bites and Stings by Pamela Nagami, M.D.

Blizzard! by Jim Murphy

Blue Lipstick by John Grandits

Boards: The Art + Design of the Skateboard by Jacob Hoye, ed.

Brain: The Complete Mind by Michael S. Sweeney

The Burn Journals by Brent Runyon

Can You Drill a Hole Through Your Head and Survive?: 180 Fascinating Questions and Amazing Answers About Science, Health, and Nature by Simon Rogers, ed.

Change Your Room by Jane Bull

Chew On This: Everything You Don't Want to Know About Fast Food by Eric Schlosser and Charles Wilson

Chow: From China to Canada: Memories of Food and Family by Janice Wong

Clueless in the Kitchen: A Cookbook for Teens by Evelyn Raab

Cooking Up a Storm: The Teen Survival Cookbook by Sam Stern and Susan Stern

The Craft Queen's Guide to Hip Knits by Catherine Tough

Crime Scene: The Ultimate Guide to Forensic Science by Richard Platt

Custom Kicks by Kim Smits

The Dangerous Book for Dogs: A Parody by Rex & Sparky by Joe Garden, Janet Ginsburg, Chris Pauls, Anita Serwacki, and Scott Sherman

The Diary of Ma Yan by Ma Yan

Dangerous Planet: Natural Disasters That Changed History by Bryn Barnard

Earth from Above by Yann Arthus-Bertrand

Encyclopedia Horrifica: The Terrifying Truth! About Vampires, Ghosts, Monsters, and More by Joshua Gee

Encyclopedia of Immaturity: Volume 2 by the editors of *Klutz*

Essential Cat by Caroline Davis

Ethel & Ernest: A True Story by Raymond Briggs

Every Creeping Thing: True Tales of Faintly Repulsive Wildlife by Richard Conniff

The Explainer by the writers of *Slate Magazine*

The Fatal Bullet: The Assassination of President James A. Garfield by Rick Geary

Focus: Love: Your World, Your Images by Lark Books

Fortune's Bones: The Manumission Requiem by Marilyn Nelson

Freaks of the Storm: From Flying Cows to Stealing Thunder, The World's Strangest True Weather Stories by Randy Cerveny

Generation Green: The Ultimate Teen Guide to Living an Eco-Friendly Life by Linda Sivertsen and Tosh Sivertsen

Girl, 13: A Global Snapshot of Generation E by Starla Griffin

The Girlo Travel Survival Kit by Anthea Paul

The Government Manual for New Superheroes by Matthew David Brozik and Jacob Sager Weinstein

Graffiti L.A.: Street Styles and Art by Steve Grody

Graffiti World: Street Art from Five Continents by Nicholas Ganz

Graphic Storytelling and Visual Narrative by Will Eisner

The Guerilla Art Kit: Everything You Need to Put Your Message Out into the World by Keri Smith

Guinea Pig Scientists: Bold Self-Experimenters in Science and Medicine by Leslie Dendy, Mel Boring, and C. B. Mordan

Gut-Eating Bugs: Maggots Reveal the Time of Death! by Danielle Denega

Guys Are Waffles, Girls Are Spaghetti by Chad Eastham and Bill and Pam Farrel

History's Greatest Lies by William Weir

Hole in My Life by Jack Gantos

Houdini: The Handcuff King by Jason Lutes and Nick Bertozzi

How to Survive a Horror Movie: All the Skills to Dodge the Kills by Seth Grahame-Smith

How to Survive a Robot Uprising: Tips on Defending Yourself Against the Coming Rebellion by Daniel H. Wilson

I never saw another butterfly by Hana Volavkova, ed.

I'll Tell What I Saw: Select Translations and Illustrations from the Divine Comedy by Michael Mazur

In Defiance of Hitler: The Secret Mission of Varian Fry by Carla Killough McClafferty

Indie Girl by Arne Johnson and Karen Macklin

The Inner City Mother Goose by Eve Merriam

Invasion of the Road Weenies and Other Warped and Creepy Tales by David Lubar

Island of Hope: The Story of Ellis Island and the Journey to America by Martin W. Sandler

King of the Mild Frontier by Chris Crutcher

Lewis & Clark Revisited: A Photographer's Trail by Greg MacGregor

Light, Sound, and Waves Science Fair Projects: Using Sunglasses, Guitars, CDs, and Other Stuff by Robert Gardner

a long way gone: Memories of a Boy Soldier by Ishmael Beah

Made You Look: How Advertising Works and Why You Should Know by Shari Graydon and Warren Clarke

Make It You: Sew Hip by Shannon Mullen

ManCrafts: Leather Tooling, Fly Tying, Ax Whittling, and Other Cool Things to Do by the editors of *Popular Mechanics*

The Manga Cookbook by The Manga University Culinary Institute

Maria Shaw's Book of Love by Maria Shaw

Meerkat Manor: Flower of the Kalahari by Tim Clutton-Brock

Monster Hunt: The Guide to Cryptozoology by Rory Storm

MySpace/Our Planet: Change is Possible by the Myspace Community with Jeca Taudte

Mysteries Unwrapped: The Secrets of Alcatraz by Susan Sloate

The Naked Roommate: And 107 Other Issues You Might Run Into at College by Harlan Cohen

Nature's Art Box by Laura C. Martin

99 Ways to Cut, Sew, Trim & Tie Your T-Shirt Into Something Special by Faith and Justina Blakeney, Anka Livakovic, and Ellen Schultz

Ninjas, Piranhas, and Galileo by Greg Leitich Smith (fiction title, perfect to pair with *Guinea Pig Scientists*)

Ocean: The World's Last Wilderness Revealed by Robert Dinwiddie, Sue Scott, and Fabian Cousteau

101 Things to Do Before You're Old and Boring by Richard Horne and Helen Szirtes

2000 Questions and Answers About the Civil War: Unusual and Unique Facts About the War Between States by Webb Garrison

Outbreak: Plagues That Changed History by Bryn Barnard

Outlaws, Mobsters, and Murderers: The Villains — The Deeds by Diana Claitor

Out of the Blue: A 24-Hour Skywatcher's Guide by John Naylor

Phineas Gage: A Gruesome but True Story About Brain Science by John Fleischman

Phobias: Everything You Wanted to Know but Were Afraid to Ask by Judy Monroe

Pitch Black by Youme Landowne and Anthony Horton

Play with Your Food by Joost Elffers

The Radioactive Boy Scout: The True Story of a Boy and His Backyard Nuclear Reactor by Ken Silverstein

Real Food Real Fast: Quick & Healthy Eating from the British Teen Cooking Sensation by Sam and Susan Stern

Red Scared! The Commie Menace in Propaganda and Popular Culture by Michael Barson and Steven Heler

The Restless Dead: Ten Original Stories of the Supernatural by Deborah Noyes

The Rights of Students by Eve Cary, Alan H. Levine and Janet Price

R.I.P.: Here Lie the Last Words, Morbid Musings, Epitaphs & Fond Farewells of the Famous and Not-So-Famous by Susan K. Hom

Robo sapiens: Evolution of a New Species by Peter Menzel and Faith D'Aluisio

Sacagawea Speaks: Beyond the Shining Mountains with Lewis & Clark by Joyce Badgley Hunsaker

Satchel Paige: Striking Out Jim Crow by James Sturm and Rich Tommaso

Shark Life: True Stories of Sharks & the Sea by Peter Benchley

Shelf Life: Stories By the Book by Gary Paulsen, ed.
Sledding Hill by Chris Crutcher (fiction title, perfect to pair with *King of the Mild Frontier*)
Stiff: The Curious Lives of Human Cadavers by Mary Roach
The Stupid Crook Book by Leland Gregory
Sweet! The Delicious Story of Candy by Ann Love and Jane Drake
Technically, It's Not My Fault by John Grandits
The Teenage Guy's Survival Guide by Jeremy Daldry
10 Sure Signs a Movie Character is Doomed and Other Surprising Movie Lists by Richard Roeper
They Broke the Law — You Be the Judge: True Cases of Teen Crime by Thomas A. Jacobs
Thoreau at Walden by John Porcellino
Three Cups of Tea: One Man's Mission to Promote Peace...One School at a Time by Greg
    Mortenson and David Oliver Relin
Time Travelers' Handbook: A Wild, Wacky and Wooly Adventure Through History! by Lottie
    Stride
Toe-Tagged: True Stories From the Morgue by Jaime Joyce
Troll's Eye View: A Book of Villainous Tales by Ellen Datlow and Terri Windling, eds.
True Notebooks: A Writer's Year at Juvenile Hall by Mark Salzman
The Underdog: How I Survived the World's Most Outlandish Competitions by Joshua Davis
The Vampire Is Just Not That into You by Vlad Mezrich
Vile Verses by Roald Dahl
Voices from the Streets: Young Former Gang Members Tell Their Stories by S. Beth Atkin
The Wall: Growing Up Behind the Iron Curtain by Peter Sis
Weird U.S. by Mark Moran and Mark Sceurman
What Are You Afraid Of?: Stories About Phobias by Donald R. Gallo, ed. (Short story col-
    lection, perfect to pair with *Phobias*)
What's that Smell? (Oh, It's Me): 50 Mortifying Situations and How to Deal by Tucker Shaw
When Objects Talk by Mark P. Friedlander Jr. and Terry M. Phillips
The Wicked History of the World: History with the Nasty Bits Left In! by Terry Deary and
    Martin Brown
The World According to Dog: Poems and Teen Voices by Joyce Sidman
The World of the Spider by Adrienne Mason
Worlds Afire by Paul B. Janeczko
The Worst-Case Scenario Survival Handbook: TRAVEL by Joshua Piven and David Bor-
    genicht
Written in Bone by Sally M. Walker
Zero-G: Life and Survival in Space by Peter Bond
The Zombie Survival Guide: Complete Protection from the Living Dead by Max Brooks

OTHER SUGGESTED TITLES

An Abundance of Katherines by John Green (fiction title, perfect to pair with *Geekspeak*)
Action Philosophers!: Volume 1 by Fred Van Lente and Ryan Dunlavey
Action Philosophers!: Volume 2 by Fred Van Lente and Ryan Dunlavey
Adventures in Tornado Alley by Mike Hollingshead and Eric Nguyen
Al Capone Does My Shirts by Gennifer Choldenko (fiction title, perfect to pair with *Mysteries
    Unwrapped: The Secrets of Alcatraz*)
All the Wrong People have Self-Esteem: An Inappropriate Book for Young Ladies by Laurie
    Rosenwald

Almanac of the Gross, Disgusting & Totally Repulsive: a Compendium of Fulsome Facts by Eric Elfman

Always Faithful: A Memoir of the Marine Dogs of WWII by William Putney

Angel Girl by Laurie Friedman

Angels of Mercy: Army Nurses of World War II by Betsy Kuhn

Angry Management by Chris Crutcher

The Arrival by Shaun Tan (fiction title, perfect to pair with *Island of Hope*)

Art Attack: A Short Cultural History of the Avant-Garde by Marc Aronson

Art Fraud Detective: Spot the Difference, Solve the Crime by Anna Nilsen

The Art of Marvel by Lee Stan

The Art of the Catapult: Build Greek Ballistae, Roman Onagers, English Trebuchets, and More Ancient Artillery by William Gurstelle

Ask the Bones: Scary Stories from Around the World by Arielle North Olson and Howard Schwartz

Backyard Ballistics by William Gurstelk

Bat Boy Lives! The WEEKLY WORLD NEWS Guide to Politics, Culture, Celebrities, Alien Abductions, and the Mutant Freaks that Shape Our World by the editors of *Weekly World News* and David Perell

The Beast of Chicago: An Account of the Life and Crimes of Herman W. Mudgett by Rick Geary

Before Midnight by Cameron Dokey (fiction title, perfect to pair with *Chinese Cinderella*)

Behind the Wheel: Poems About Driving by Janet S. Wong

Being Dead by Vivian Vande Velde

Be the Change: Your Guide to Freeing Slaves and Changing the World by Zach Hunter

A Big Little Life: A Memoir of a Joyful Dog by Dean Koontz

Black Potatoes: The Story of the Great Irish Famine by Susan Campbell Bartoletti

Bling: The Hip-Hop Jewelry Book by Reggie Osse and Gabriel Tolliver

Body Drama: Real Girls, Real Bodies, Real Issues, Real Answers by Nancy Amanda Redd

The Book of General Ignorance by John Mitchinson and John Lloyd

The Book of Lists for Teens by Sandra Choron and Harry Choron

The Book of Perfectly Useless Information by Mitchell Symons

The Book Thief by Markus Zusak (fiction title, perfect to pair with *i never saw another butterfly*)

The Brimstone Journals by Ron Koertge

Brush Up Your Shakespeare: An Infectious Tour from the Most Quotable and Famous Words and Phrases from the Bard by Michael Macrone and Tom Lulevitch

Bury the Dead: Corpses, Skeletons, Mummies, Skeletons, & Rituals by Christopher Sloan

Canned by Alex Shearer (fiction title, perfect to pair with *The Explainer*)

Causing a Scene by Charlie Tood and Alex Scordels

Cell by Stephen King (fiction title, perfect to pair with *Dark Dreams*)

Chased by Sea Monsters: Prehistoric Predators of the Deep by Nigel Marven and Jasper James

Che: A Graphic Biography by Spain Rodriguez

The Children We Remember by Chana Byers Abells

Chill: Stress-Reducing Techniques for a More Balanced, Peaceful You by Deborah Reber

Chinese Cinderella: The True Story of an Unwanted Daughter by Adeline Yen Mah

Comedy Improvisation: Exercises & Techniques for Young Actors by Delton Horn

Creatures of the Deep by Erich Hoyt

Dancing with Cats by Burton Silver and Heather Busch

Dark Dreams: The Story of Stephen King by Nancy Whitelaw

The Darwin Awards: Intelligent Design by Wendy Northcutt

Dave Barry's Book of Bad Songs by Dave Barry

Da Vinci Code by Dan Brown (fiction title, perfect to pair with *Amazing Leonard da Vinci Inventions You Can Build Yourself*)

Declare Yourself: Speak, Connect, Act, Vote: More Than 50 Celebrated Americans Tell You Why

Decorate Yourself by Tom Andrich

Divine Comedy by Dante Alighieri (perfect to pair with *I'll Tell What I* Saw)

Do *Hard Things: A Teenage Rebellion Against Low Expectations* by Alex Harris

Double Cross by Sigmund Brouwer (fiction title, perfect to pair with *The Grand Tour*)

The Duel: The Parallel Lives of Alexander Hamilton & Aaron Burr by Judith St. George

Earth Shock: Hurricanes, Volcanoes, Earthquakes, Tornadoes and Other Forces of Nature by Andrew Robinson

E=Einstein: His Life, His Thought, and His Influence on Our Culture by Donald Goldsmith and Marcia Bartusiak

Einstein: Visionary Scientist by John B. Severance

Entertaining Edibles: 50 Fun Food Sculptures for All Occasions by Sidney Escowitz

The Eternal Kiss: 13 Vampire Stories of Blood and Desire by Trisha Telep, ed.

Every Man for Himself: Ten Short Stories About Being a Guy by Nancy E. Mercado, ed.

Everything I Ate: A Year in the Life of My Mouth by Tucker Shaw

Exploding Ants: Amazing Facts About How Animals Adapt by Joanne Settel

The Exploding Toilet: Modern Urban Legends by David Holt

Extraordinary Jobs for Adventurers by Alecia T. Devantier and Carol Ann Turkington

Fact, Fiction and Folklore in Harry Potter's World by George Beahm

Falling Hard: 100 Love Poems by Teenagers by Betsy Franco, ed.

Famous Players: The Mysterious Death of William Desmond Taylor by Rick Geary

Firefighterette Gillete: A Firefighter Who Crashed & Burned: A Success Story by Kathy Gillete

First Kids: The True Stories of All the Presidents' Children by Noah McCullough

Flirtology: 100 Ways to Release Your Inner Flirt by Anita Naik

For Boys Only: The Biggest, Baddest Book Ever by Marc Aronson and H.P. Newquist

Fueling the Teen Machine by Ellen L. Shanley and Colleen A. Thompson

Gastroanomalies: Questionable Culinary Creations from the Golden Age of American Cookery by James Lileks

Geekspeak by Dr. Graham Tattersall

Geektastic: Stories from the Nerd Herd by Holly Black and Cecil Castellucci, ed.

Generation Change: Roll Up Your Sleeves and Change the World by Zach Hunter

Getting Away with Murder: The True Story of the Emmett Till Case by Chris Crowe

Ghoulish Goodies by Sharon Bowers

Girlosophy: Real Girls Eat by Anthea Paul

Gorgeous Gifts: Use Recycled Materials to Make Cool Crafts by Rebecca Craig

The Grand Tour: A Traveler's Guide to the Solar System by Ron Miller and William Hartmann

Graphic Classics: H. P. Lovecraft by Richard Corren, Matt Howarth, Mason Crumb, and Gahan Wilson

Grayson by Lynne Cox

Green Volunteers: The World Guide to Voluntary Work in Nature Education by Fabio Ausenda, ed.

Grossology by Sylvia Branzei and Jack Keely

Gross-out Cakes: The Kitty Litter Cake and Other Classics by Kathleen Barlow and Britney Schetselaar

Half-human by Bruce Coville, ed.

Harry Potter series by J. K. Rowling (fiction series, perfect to pair with *Fact, Fiction and Folklore*)

Hey Ranger 2: More True Tales of Humor and Misadventure from the Great Outdoors by Jim Burnett

Hidden on the Mountain: Stories of Children Sheltered from the Nazis in Le Chambon by Deborah Durland DeSaiz and Karen Gray Ruelle

Hippo Eats Dwarf: A Field Guide to Hoaxes and Other B.S. by Alex Boese

How It Feels to be Attacked by a Shark by Michelle Hamer

How to Be a Villain: Evil Laughs, Secret Lairs, Master Plans, and More!! by Neil Zawacki

How to Fossilize Your Hamster and Other Amazing Experiments for the Armchair Scientist by Mich O'Hare

How to Hold a Crocodile by the Diagram Group

How to Speak Dog by Sarah Whitehead

I See the Rhythm by Toyomi Igus

I'd Tell You I Love You But Then I'd Have to Kill You (fiction title, perfect to pair with *Spyology*) by Ally Carter

Imaginary Museum: Poems on Art by Joseph Stanton

Immigrant Kids by Russell Freedman

In My Hands: Memories of a Holocaust Rescuer by Irene Gut Opdyke with Jennifer Armstrong

Insatiable: The Compelling Story of Four Teens, Food and Its Power by Eve Eliot

Investigating Fakes & Hoaxes by Alex Woolf

The Invisible Kingdom by Idan Ben-Barak

Is It Still Cheating If I Don't Get Caught? by Bruce Weinstein

Isadora Duncan: a Graphic Biography by Sabrina Jones

It's Your World — If You Don't Like It, Change It: Activism for Teenagers by Mikki Halpin

J. Edgar Hoover: A Graphic Biography by Rick Geary

Jack the Ripper by Rick Geary

Jon and Jayne's Guide to Throwing, Going To, And Surviving Parties by Jon Doe

Keesha's House by Helen Frost

Kids on Strike! by Susan Campbell Bartoletti

Killer at Large: Criminal Profilers and the Cases They Solve! by D. B. Beres

Killer Wallpaper: True Cases of Deadly Poisonings by Anna Prokos

King George: What Was His Problem? by Steve Sheinkin

Letters to a Bullied Girl: Messages of Healing and Hope by Olivia Gardner

Life as We Knew It by Susan Pfeffer (fiction title, perfect to pair with *Dangerous Planet*)

The Lindbergh Child by Rick Geary

Little Black Book for Guys: Guys Talk about Sex by St. Stephen's Community House

Logicomix: An Epic Search For Truth by Apostolos Doxiadis and Christos H. Papadimitriou

Lose Your Cool: Discovering a Passion that Changes You and the World by Zach Hunter

Louis Braille: A Touch of Genius by C. Michael Mellor

Love, Football and Other Contact Sports by Alden Carter

The Lovely Bones by Alice Seabold (fiction title, perfect to pair with *Lucky*)

Lucky by Alice Seabold

MAD: Cover to Cover: 48 Years, 6 Months, & 3 Days of MAD Magazine Covers by Frank Jacobs

Man vs. Weather: Be Your Own Weatherman by Dennis DiClaudio

March of the Penguins: Companion to the Major Motion Picture by Luc Jacquet, Jerome Maison, and Donnali Fifield

Maus: A Survivor's Tale by Art Spiegelman

Mechanika: Creating the Art of Science Fiction by Doug Chiang

Mini Weapons of Mass Destruction: Build Implements of Spitball Warfare by John Austin

Monsterology: Fabulous Lives of the Creepy, the Revolting, and the Undead by Arthur Slade and Derek Mah

More Bones: Scary Stories from Around the World by Arielle North Olson and Howard Schwartz

The Murder of Abraham Lincoln by Rick Geary

My Nights at the Improv by Jan Siebold (fiction title, perfect to pair with *Comedy Improvisation*)

My Season with Penguins: An Antarctic Journal by Sophie Webb

My So-Called Digital Life: 2,000 Teenagers, 300 Cameras, and 30 Days to Document Their World by Bob Pletka, ed.

The Mystery of Mary Rogers by Rick Geary

MythBusters: Don't Try This at Home by Discovery Channel and Mary Packard

Nat Turner by Kyle Baker

A Natural History of the Antarctic: Life in the Freezer by Alastair Fothergil

A Natural History of the Unnatural World by Carroll and Brown Limited

Necessary Noise: Stories About Our Families As They Really Are by Michael Cart, ed.

Nevermore: A Graphic Adaptation of Edgar Allan Poe's Short Stories by Dan Whitehead, ed.

The Ninja Handbook: This Book Looks Forward to Killing You Soon by Douglas Sarine and Kent Nichols

Oh Yikes! History's Grossest Moments by Joy Masoff and Terry Sirrell

Oh, Yuck: The Encyclopedia of Everything Nasty by Joy Masoff

101 Things You Wish You'd Invented and Some You Wish No One Had by Richard Horne and Tracey Turner

Origami with Dollar Bills by Duy Nguyen

The Other Book of Perfectly Useless Information by Mitchell Symons

Partly Cloudy: Poems of Love and Longing by Gary Soto

Peeps by Scott Westerfeld (fiction title, perfect to pair with *The Invisible Kingdom*)

People's History: Locked Up: A History of the U. S. Prison System by Laura B. Edge

A People's History of the American Empire by Howard Zinn

Perfect Example by John Porcellino

The Perilous Journey of the Donner Party by Marian Calabro

Persepolis: The Story of a Childhood by Marjane Satrapi

Planet Yumthing: Do-It-Yourself by Ela Jaynes and Darren Greenblatt

Poems from Homeroom: A Writer's Place to Start by Kathi Appelt

Primate Behavior by Sarah Lindsay

Privacy Please! Gaining Independence from Your Parents by Odile Amblard

Prom Nights from Hell by Meg Cabot, et al.

Punk Rock Aerobics: 75 Killer Moves, 50 Punk Classics, and 25 Reasons to Get Off Your Ass and Exercise by Maura Jasper and Hilken Mancini

Pyongyang: A Journey in North Korea by Guy Delisle

Rats: Observations on the History and Habitat of the City's Most Unwanted Inhabitants by Robert Sullivan

Really Useful Things: The Origins of Everyday Things by Joel Levy

Red Hot Salsa: Bilingual Poems on Being Young and Latino in the United States by Lori Marie Carlson

The Restless Dead: More Strange Real-Life Mysteries by Jim Razzi

Restless Skies: The Ultimate Weather Book by Paul Douglas

Revolting Rhymes by Roald Dahl

Ripley's Believe It or Not! by Ripley Entertainment, Inc.

The Saga of the Bloody Benders by Rick Geary

Show Off: How To Do Absolutely Everything One Step at a Time by Sarah Hines Stephens and Bethany Mann

Skateboard Roadmap by James Davis

Slumber Parties: Things to Make and Do by Jennifer Traig

SOS: Stories of Survival: True Tales of Disaster, Tragedy and Courage by Ed Butts

Spies: The Undercover World of Secrets, Gadgets and Lies by David Owen

Spyology by Spencer Blake and Dugald A. Steer

Still I Rise by Lairel Bey

Street Scene: How to Draw Graffiti-Style by John Lee

Street World by Roger Gastman

Student's Go Vegan Cookbook by Carole Raymond

The Stunning Science of Everything: Science with the Squishy Bits Left In! by Nick Arnold and Tony De Saulles

The Surrender Tree: Poems of Cuba's Struggle for Freedom by Margarita Engle

Tales of the Cryptids: Myserious Creatures That May or May Not Exist by Kelly Milner Halls, Rick Spears, and Roxyanne Young

The Tarantula Scientist by Sy Montgomery and Nic Bishop

Teen Manners: From Malls to Meals to Messaging and Beyond by Cindy Post Senning

Teen Power Politics: Make Yourself Heard by Sara Jane Boyers

Teens Cook Dessert by Megan, Jill, and Judi Carle

Teens Cook: How to Cook What You Want to Eat by Megan, Jill, and Judi Carle

Teens Take It To Court: Young People Who Challenged the Law and Changed Your Life by Thomas A. Jacobs

The Teen's Vegetarian Cookbook by Judy Krizmanic

That Book of Perfectly Useless Information by Mitchell Symons

That Gunk On Your Car: A Unique Guide to Insects of North America by Mark Hostetler

That's Not My Science Book by Kate Kelly

Theatre Games for Young Performers by Maria Novelly

There's a Hair in My Dirt! A Worm's Story by Gary Larson

Thieves! Ten Stories of Surprising Heists, Comical Capers and Daring Escapades by Andreas Schroeder

Things I Have to Tell You: Poems and Writings by Teenage Girls by Betsy Franco

13: Thirteen Stories that Capture the Agony and Ecstasy of Being Thirteen by James Howe, ed.

Three Little Words by Ashley Rhodes-Courter

Toilets, Bathtubs, Sinks, and Sewers: A History of the Bathroom by Penny Colman

Tough Boy Sonatas by Curtis Crisler

Travels with the Fossil Hunters by Peter J. Whybrow, ed.

Triangle Fire by Leon Stein

The Truth About Poop by Susan E. Goodman

The Ultimate Improv Book: A Complete Guide to Comedy Improvisation by Edward Nevraumont and Nicholas Hanson

The United States Constitution: A Graphic Adaptation by Jonathan Hennessey

Volcano: The Eruption and Healing of Mount St. Helens by Patricia Lauber

Volcano Weather: The Story of 1816, the Year Without a Summer by Elizabeth Stommel and Henry Stommel

Wake Up Our Souls: A Celebration of Black American Artists by Tonya Bolden

War is...: Soldiers, Survivors and Storytellers Talk About War by Marc Aronson and Patty Campbell

Wearing of This Garment Does Not Enable You to Fly: 101 Real Dumb Warning Labels by Jeff Koon, Andy Powell, and Tim Carroll

Weird and Wonderful Words by Erin McKean, Roz Chast, and Simon Winchester

Whale by Joe Roman

What Are My Rights?: 95 Questions and Answers about Teens and the Law by Jacob Law

Whatcha Mean, What's a Zine?: The Art of Making Zines and Minicomics by Mark Todd

What the World Eats by Faith D'Aluisio and Peter Menzel

The What to Expect Baby-Sitter's Handbook by Heidi Murkoff and Sharon Mazel

While You're Waiting for the Food to Come by Eric Muller

Who Do You Think You Are? 15 Methods for Analyzing the True You by Tucker Shaw

Within Reach: My Everest Story by Mark Pfetzer and Jack Galvin

Words with Wings: A Treasury of African-American Poetry and Art by Belinda Rochelle

Write Your Own Graphic Novel by Natalie Rosinsky

YM's Best of Say Anything by Tucker Shaw

You Hear Me?: Poems and Writing by Teenage Boys by Betsy Franco

Young Oxford Book of Nasty Endings by Dennis Pepper

You Remind Me of You: A Poetry Memoir by Eireann Corrigan

You Want Women to Vote, Lizzie Stanton? by Jean Fritz

BOOKTALKING RESOURCES

Anderson, Sheila B. *Serving Older Teens*. Libraries Unlimited, 2003.

Baxtar, Kathleen A. and Marcia Agness Kochel. *Gotcha!: Nonfiction Booktalks to Get Kids Excited About Reading*. Libraries Unlimited, 1999.

Gotcha Again!: More Nonfiction Booktalks to Get Kids Excited About Reading. Libraries Unlimited, 2002.

Bodart, Joni Richards. *Booktalk 2: Booktalks for All Ages and Audiences*. H. W. Wilson, 1985

_____. *Radical Reads: 101 Young Adult Novels on the Edge*. Scarecrow Press, 2002

Fraser, Elizabeth. *Reality Rules: a Guide to Teen Nonfiction Reading Interests*. Libraries Unlimited, 2008.

Langemack, Chapple. *The Booktalker's Bible: How To Talk About the Books You Love To Any Audience*. Libraries Unlimited, 2003.

Schall, Lucy. *Booktalks and Beyond: Promoting Great Genre Reads to Teens*. Libraries Unlimited, 2007.

_____. *Booktalks and More: Motivating Teens To Read*. Libraries Unlimited, 2003

_____. *Genre Talks for Teens: Booktalks and More for Every Teen Reading Interest*. Libraries Unlimited, 2009.

Index

À la Recherche du Shoe Perdu 66
Act I: Scene: Bugs! 105
acting 86, 105, 116, 167, 168
Acting Games: Improvisation and Exercises 167–168
activism 31, 134, 138
advertising 132
Affleck, Ben 11
Africa 99
Aksum 115, 116
Alcatraz 47–48
Alcatraz Headline Timeline 48
Alex & Me 105–106
alien abduction 8, 9
alien invasion 8–9
The Alien Invasion Survival Handbook: A Defense Manual for the Coming Extraterrestrial Apocalypse 8–9
aliens 8, 9
All About the Brain — You Be the Teacher 100
allegories 88
Allen, Ethan 17
Alternative Worlds 116
Amazing Leonardo da Vinci Inventions You Can Build Yourself 92–93, 157
Amazing Stories of Survival: Tales of Hope, Heroism and Astounding Luck 133
American Born Chinese 87–88
American Civil War Quiz Show 24
The American Slave 36
amputation 37, 38
Anderson, Maxine 92
Andy Warhol: Pop Art Painter 66
Angel of Death 149–150
Angels of Mercy 38
The Animal Dialogues: Uncommon Encounters in the Wild 112
Animal Planet 111
animalcules 22
animals 104–113, 121
anthropomorphism 53
archeologists 19
Archimboldo, Guiseppe 53
Armstrong, Neil 169

art 13, 20, 21, 53–54, 61–69, 73–77, 82–85, 87, 91, 98, 99, 116, 119
Arthus-Bertrand, Yann 114
Artistic Interpretation of Classical Literature 68
Asia 57
astronauts 101–102
Atkin, S. Beth 44
Auschwitz 73
Australian Museum 96
authors 152–154
autobiography 32, 37, 75, 87, 153
Autobiography and Altered Book 87
autopsy 96

Backyard and Beyond: A Guide for Discovering the Outdoors 120–121
bank robbers 40
Barnard, Bryn 93, 115
barnstorming 88
Barson, Michael 22
baseball 48, 88
basketball 29
Bass, Franta 73
Bastille 26
Bat Boy Lives! 5, 15, 148
BBQ 10
Be Afraid, Be Very Afraid: The Book of Scary Urban Legends 15, 71–72
Beagle, Peter S. 76
Beah, Ishmael 29, 30
Beast of Chicago 2
Beast of Gevaudan 161
Bell Witch 161
Benchley, Peter 109
Beowulf 84–85
Berlese funnel 105
Berlin Wall 21
Berlin Wall Art 21
Bermuda 109
Bertozzi, Nick 83
Between a Rock and a Hard Place 36–38
Bible 18

The Big Book of Gross Stuff 168–169
The Big Clown 48
Billy the Kid 40
biographies 29–39, 37, 82, 83, 84, 131
bioluminescence 123
biominetics 98
Birdman of Alcatraz 47
Bitten: True Medical Stories of Bites and Stings 117–118
Black Death 93
Blakeney, Faith 58
Blakeney, Justina 58
blizzard 119–120
Blizzard! 119–120
block printing 55
Bloody Mary 71
Blue Lipstick 72–73
Boards: The Art + Design of the Skateboard 62–63
Bond, Peter 101
Bonnie and Clyde 40
Booger Beast 8
book binding 8, 85, 87, 111, 138
The Book Thief 157
Borden, Lizzie 40
Borgenicht, David 144
Boring, Mel 155
Boston Red Dragons 44
boy soldiers 30
brain 22, 99–100
Brain: The Complete Mind 99–100
Briggs, Raymond 86
Bristowe, W.S. 106
Brooks, Max 163
Brown, Dan 157
Brown, Martin 17
Brozik, Matthew David 170
Brunvand, Jan Harold 71, 72
Bull, Jane 50
bullying 138
bunyip 99
burglary 6, 41
The Burn Journals 32–33, 38

cadaver 96–97
Caesar, Julius 45
California 47

Campbell's soup 66
Can You Drill a Hole Through Your Head and Survive? 9–11
Canada 56
Canary Islands 125
candy 50, 57–58
Candy from Around the World 57–58
Canyonlands National Park 36
Capone, Al 40, 47
Cary, Eve 143
"Casket Cascade" 8
Cassady, Marsh 167, 168
cats 107–108
Cerveny, Randall 2, 116
Challenge Journal 138
Challenger space shuttle 101
Change Your Room 50–51
Charles River 83
Chew on This: Everything You Don't Want to Know About Fast Food 2, 125–126, 135
Chicago Defender 88
Childs, Craig 112
Chile 102
China 31, 93, 115
Chinese Exclusion Act 56
Chow: From China to Canada: Memories of Food and Family 56
Cinderella 76
Civil War 23, 26, 47
civilization 115–116
Claitor, Diana 48
Clark, William 35, 65–66
Clarke, Warren 132
Clarkson, Sarah May 30
Classic Literature Adaptation 85
climbing 37
Cliver, Sean 63
cloning 10
Clueless in the Kitchen 51–52
Clutton-Brock, Tim 111
cochineal extract 125
Cold War 23, 26, 27
color 50, 74, 122, 125
Colorado Front Range 1
Colorado Springs, Colorado 1
Columbia University 94
The Comedy Shtick 12
Comedy Writing Secrets 12
Communism 20, 22
Compare and Contrast 89
Comparing Notes 140–141
competition 33, 34
computer equipment 13
computer forensics 46
Concrete Poems 73
Confederacy 23
Congress 86, 128
Conniff, Richard 118
consumerism 132–133
cookbook 50, 51–52, 56
Cooking Up a Storm: The Teen Survival Cookbook 51–52
coping saw 55

cormorant 118
Cousteau, Fabien 122
The Craft Queen's Guide to Hip Knits 58–59
crafts 50–51, 54–56, 58–59, 87, 93, 94
Craven, Wes 163
Create Your Own Custom Kicks 64
Create Your Own Focus Book 68
Create Your Superhero 170–171
Creative Animal Writing 112
Creative Essay 44
Creative Writing 111
creative writing 9, 13, 14, 15, 26, 31, 43, 44, 46, 88, 97, 111, 112
Creative Writing: Allegories 88
A Creatively Altered History 26
creativity 9, 19, 26, 43, 58, 76, 118
crime 7
Crime Scene: The Ultimate Guide to Forensic Science 45–46
crimes 40–49, 61, 104–105
criminal justice system 40
criminals 6, 7, 40, 42, 46, 48
The Crips 44
critical thinking 32, 48, 61
Crutcher, Chris 152–154
Cryptid Discovery Presentations 99
cryptids 98–99
cryptozoology 98–99
Cuba 82
Curie, Marie 156
Curie, Pierre 156
curiosity 10, 129, 148, 157
Custom Kicks 63–64
Czechoslovakia 20

D'Aluisio, Faith 97
Dahl, Roald 70, 79
Daily Nutrition Chart 126–127
Daldry, Jeremy 138
Damn! That's Funny!
The Dangerous Book for Boys 111
The Dangerous Book for Dogs: A Parody 110–111
The Dangerous Book for Girls 111
Dangerous Planet: Natural Disasters That Changed History 115–116
Dante 68
databases 26, 48, 62, 74
dating 138
Datlow, Ellen 76
Da Vinci Code 157
Davis, Caroline 107
Davis, Joshua 33, 38
Dear Diary 110
Deary, Terry 17
Debate 30
debate 30, 45, 62, 144
Debate: Parental Fault or Teen Responsibility? 45
Dendy, Leslie 155
Denega, Danielle 104
de Rodellec du Porzic 43
Design a Friend 98

Design Your Own 63
Detroit, Michigan 100
diaries *see* journals
Diary of a Young Girl 157
The Diary of Ma Yan 31–32, 38
Dicker-Brandeis, Friedl 73–74
digestive system 155–156
dinosaurs 115, 116
Dinwiddie, Robert 122
diorama 116, 149–150
Diorama Book Report 149–150
Discovering the Teen Brain 22
Discussion 144
discussion 3, 7, 10, 12, 22, 31, 36, 48, 51, 61, 63, 65, 75, 78, 79, 101, 107, 121, 140, 144, 152, 154, 162, 167
Discussion Groups 78
Disgustingly Funny Limericks or Haiku 169
Divine Comedy 68
Do It Yourself (Sailboats) 66
dogs 110–111
Downs, Diane 48
Dracula 161
Drake, Jane 57
Duensing, Edward 120
Dynamic Brain 97

E. Coli 126
Earth 9, 115–116, 118
Earth from Above 114–115
East Coast 119
Eastham, Chad 139
Egypt 115
Eisner, Will 90
electroparalysis 9
elephant 10
Elffers, Joost 53
Ellis Island 24, 25
embarrassment 142–143
Encyclopedia Horrifica: The Terrifying Truth About Vampires, Ghosts, Monsters, and More 160–162
The Encyclopedia of Immaturity: Volume 2 166–167
energy 101, 127
England 17, 86
environment 114–115, 127–128, 133–134
epitaph 14
Essential Cat 107–109
Ethel & Ernest: A True Story 86–87
etymology 15
Europe 93, 94
European settlements 19
Every Creeping Thing: True Tales of Faintly Repulsive Wildlife 118–119
Expedition Supply List 35
The Explainer 128–129, 135

Facebook 33
Facts Into Fiction 156

Farrel, Bill 139
Farrel, Pam 139
The Fatal Bullet 85–86
Federal Environmental Protection
    Agency 100
Ferguson, Alane 149
fiction 148–158
field trips 14–15, 21, 65, 68, 123
fighting 138
Firefighterette Gillete 38
First Nation 44
First Person Witness Letters 18–19
5boro 63
Fleischman, John 21
Focus: Love: Your World, Your
    Images 67–68
folklore 119
food 50, 51–54, 56–58, 128
Food as Art 53–54
Food Web 107
forensic science 45, 46, 95–96,
    104–105, 148–150
Forensic Science Career Analysis 46
Fortune's Bones: The Manumission
    Requiem 35–36, 38
fossil fuels 115
France 18, 41, 42, 85
Frank, Ann 157
Freaks of the Storm: From Flying
    Cows to Stealing Thunder: The
    World's Strangest True Weather
    Stories 22, 116–117
freedom 18, 20, 30, 36, 43
Friedlander, Mark 148
Friedmann, Paul 73
Friesema, Jessica 114
Frog People 8
Fry, Varian 41, 42, 43
fund raiser 160

Gage, Phineas 21
Galileo 26
Gallo, Donald R. 151
game shows 24, 145–146
gangs 44, 45, 61
Gantos, Jack 46, 47
Ganz, Nicholas 61
Garden, Joe 110
Gardner, Robert 155
Garfield, James A. 85, 86
Garrison, Webb 23
Geary, Rick 2, 85
Gee, Joshua 160
gender 139–140
genealogy 26, 156
Genealogy! 26
Generation Green: The Ultimate
    Teen Guide to Living an Eco-
    Friendly Life 133–135
Geneva Convention 18
geography 15, 35, 57, 130
Germany 87
"The Ghost of Ethyl Work" 8
ghosts 160–162
Gillete, Kathy 38
Ginsburg, Janet 110

Girl, 13: A Global Snapshot of
    Generation E 131–132
The Girlo Travel Survival Kit
    129–130
goals 141–142
gold rush 47
Gondwana 12
Goodall, Jane 130
Goths 26
government 20, 24, 48, 101, 170–
    171
The Government Manual for New
    Superheroes 170–171
graffiti 61–62
Graffiti as Art Debate 62
Graffiti L.A.: Street Styles and Art
    61–62
Graffiti World: Street Art from
    Five Continents 61–62
Grahame-Smith, Seth 162, 163
Grandits, John 72
The Grapes of Wrath 80
Graphic Biography: Historical
    Adaptation 83, 84
graphic novels 2, 82–91
Graphic Storytelling and Visual
    Narrative 90–91
graves 8, 14, 19
Graydon, Shari 132
Great Britain 87
Greatest Show on Earth 70
Greeley, Colorado
Green Tips 134
Gregory, Leland 5, 6
Grendel 85
Griffin, Starla 131
Grody, Steve 61
group projects 22, 23, 24, 35, 41,
    46, 48, 84, 85, 98, 100, 102, 105,
    106, 107, 118, 119, 122, 130, 140,
    141–142, 145–146, 167
Group Snapshot 131–132
guerilla art 64–65
The Guerilla Art Kit: Everything
    You Need to Put Your Message
    Out Into the World 64–65
guest speakers 38, 131
Guinea Pig Scientists: Bold Self-
    Experimenters in Science and
    Medicine 155–156
Guiteau, Charles 85, 86
Gut-Eating Bugs: Maggots Reveal
    the Time of Death! 104–105
Guys Are Waffles, Girls Are
    Spaghetti 139–141

Haddix, Margaret Peterson 78
Hahn, David 100
Haiti 82
hallucination 10
Hammurabi's code 18
Hansel and Gretel 76
Harris, Janet 44
Hartford, Connecticut, circus fire
    70–71
Harvard 41

Harvard Bridge 83
health 139
Hegel, Georg
heist 7
Helizter, Melvin 12
Heller, Steven 22
Henry VIII 17
Heorot 85
Hero Story 133
heroes 29, 36, 40, 43, 84, 86, 133
Hidden Title Story 78
Hieroglyphic Writing! 170
hiking 36, 37, 38
Hiking Safety 38
Hinds, Gareth 84
Hiroshima 87
Historical Poetry 71
history 15, 17–28, 37, 38, 43, 48,
    65, 71, 73, 82, 84, 90, 95, 114–
    115, 149–150, 170; local 8, 14–
    15, 26, 71, 162
History's Greatest Lies 26, 27
Hitler, Adolf 23, 41
hoax 160–161
Hole in My Life 46–47
Hom, Susan K. 13
Home economics 50
Homegrown Horror Movie 163
homicide 45
Hood, Robin 26
Horne, Richard 2, 137
"Hornet Spook Light" 8
horoscope 160
Horton, Anthony 82
hot tube lung 10
Houdini 83–84
Houdini, Harry 83–84
Houdini: The Handcuff King 83–
    84
How Many Advertisements? 132–
    133
How-To Graphic Story 91
How to Survive a Horror Movie:
    All the Skills to Dodge the Kills
    162–163
How to Survive a Robot Uprising:
    Tips on Defending Yourself
    Against the Coming Rebellion
    12–13
Hoye, Jacob 62
HUAC 23
Huang Di
Human Rights Watch 30
Humanitarian Work for Teens
    130–131
humanitarianism 130–131
humor 5, 11, 12, 13, 14, 70, 136,
    169; potty humor 5, 12, 169
Hunsacker, Joyce Badgley 34

I Never Saw Another Butterfly
    73–74, 157
ichijyuusansai 52
I'll Tell What I Saw: Select Trans-
    lations and Illustrations from
    the Divine Comedy 68

Illustrating the Creepy 77
immigrants 24, 25, 27
improvisation 167–168
In Defiance of Hitler: The Secret Mission of Varian Fly 41–43
indentured servant 19
India 17, 18, 34
Indian Ocean 115
Indie Girl 141–142
The Inner City Mother Goose 74–75, 80
insects 10, 12, 104–105, 117
Instruction Manual and Speech 59
An Interactive Autopsy 96
An Interactive Autopsy Short Story 97
Introduction to Performing 167
Invasion of the Road Weenies and Other Warped and Creepy Tales 76–77
inventions 92–93
iPod 10
Iron Curtain 20
Island of Hope 24–26, 27

Jack the Ripper 48
Jacobs, Thomas A. 40, 41
James, Jesse 26, 40, 48
James Fort 19
Jamestown 19
Janeczko, Paul B. 70
Japan 47, 82, 93
Jericho 17
Jews 41, 43, 73–74
Jim Crow South 36, 88
Johnson, Arne 141
Johnson, Clayton 96
Johnson, Janice 96
Johnson, Marc 63
Jordan, Michael 29
The Journal Experiment 32
journals 31, 32, 65, 73, 90, 110, 115, 137, 138, 154
Joyce, Jaime 95
Juaniata College 30
juvenile delinquents 40, 43
juvenile hall 43, 44

Kenya 82
kidnapping 40
King, Bart 168
King of the Mild Frontier 153–154
kissing 138
Klutz 166
Komodo dragon 118
Korean War 86
Kublai Khan 116
Kuhn, Betsy 38

Landowne, Youme 82
Laos 82
Lark Books 67
Latin Queens 44
Lavender Sam 66
lawn of 2093 milk jugs 8
laws 7, 40, 48, 62, 143–144

Learning and Teaching 168
Leonardo da Vinci 92–93
Letter to the Author 47
letters 18, 19, 20, 47
Levine, Alan H. 143
Lewis, Meriwether 35, 65–66
Lewis & Clark Revisited: A Photographer's Trail 65–66
libraries 1, 2, 13, 26, 27, 29, 50, 61, 67, 82, 94, 102, 120, 129, 143, 148, 157, 162
Light, Sound and Waves Science Fair Projects: Using Sunglasses, Guitars, CDs and Other Stuff 155–156
Lincoln, Abraham 82
lists 12, 35, 56, 88, 131, 143
Livakovic, Anka 58
Lizard Man 8
Local Haunts 162
Loch Ness, Great Glen, Scotland 98
A Long Way Gone 29–31, 38
Love, Ann 57
Lubar, David 76, 77
Lutes, Jason 83

Ma Barker 48
MacGregor, Greg 65
Machine Gun Kelly 47
Macklin, Karen 141
MacPherson, Duncan 96
Made You Look: How Advertising Works and Why You Should Know 132–133, 135
Maguire, Gregory 78
Make-Believe — But Not Really 141–142
Make It You: Sew Hip 58–59
ManCrafts: Leather Tooling, Fly Tying, Ax Whittling, and Other Cool Things to Do 55–56
manga 2, 50, 52, 82, 83, 85
The Manga Cookbook 51–52
The Manga University Culinary Institute 52
Manson, Charles 40, 48
manure 126
Maria Shaw's Book of Love 159–160
Mars 78
Martin, Laura C. 54
Mason, Adrienne 106
mass communications 15
masturbation 139
Mazur, Michael 68
McClafferty, Carla Killough 41
McDonald's 125–126
meat 128
Meerkat Manor 111
Meerkat Manor: Flower of the Kalahari 111
Meerkat Manor Series 111
meerkats 111
melodrama 86
Melodrama Adaptation 86

memoirs *see* biographies
Memory Cookbook 56
Memory to Story 154
Menzel, Peter 97
Merriam, Eve 74
meteorite 10
Mexico 57
Mezrich, Vlad 165
mice 118
Middle Ages 18, 95
milkshake 125
Millmoss, A.B. 120
Minnetarees 34
Minoans 115, 116
Molaison, Henry Gustav 99
Monroe, Judy 150
Monster Hunt: The Guide to Cryptozoology 98–99
Montreal 17
morality 40
Moran, Mark 7
Mordan, C.B. 155
Mortenson, Greg 130
Mothman 99
Mount Tambora 116
movies 11, 12, 162–163
mp3 player 9
Mullen, Shannon 58
Mumfrey, W.H. 8
murder 19, 30, 40, 43, 44, 46, 48, 72, 95, 104, 148–149
Murphy, Jim 119
Murray, Mary 30
MySpace 127–128, 135
MySpace/Our Planet: Change Is Possible 127–128, 135
Mysteries Unwrapped: The Secrets of Alcatraz 47–48
MyYearbook 33

Nagami, Pamela 117
Native American 20, 35, 47, 65
natural disaster 114
naturalist 120–121
nature 50, 54–55, 114–124
Nature's Art Box 54–55
Naylor, John 121
Nazis 41, 43, 73–74
Nelson, Baby Face 40
Nelson, Marilyn 35
Neu, Harold
New York City 25, 30, 46, 82, 83, 119–120
Newark, New Jersey 6
News Report: A Survivor's Tale 118
Nicaragua 33
99 Ways to Cut, Sew, Trim & Tie Your T-Shirt Into Something Special 58–59
Ninjas, Piranhas, and Galileo 154–156
North America 19
Nuclear Emergency Search Team 128
Nuclear Energy Studies 101
nuclear reactor 100

nursery rhymes 74–75
Nursery Rhymes Revisited 75
nutrition 126

Ocean: The World's Last Wilderness Revealed 122–123
Olaudah 18
100 Cans 66
101 Things to Do Before You're Old and Boring 2, 137–138
online 19–20, 23, 30, 34, 36, 38, 57, 90, 96, 97, 120, 126, 130, 134, 139
Online Interactives 19–20
Opposing Viewpoints 62
oral report 34
Our Sky in a Day 122
Out of the Blue: A 24-Hour Skywatcher's Guide 121–122
Outbreak: Plagues That Changed History 93–95, 148
Outlaws, Mobsters and Murderers: The Villains...The Deeds 48

Pacific Ocean 18
Pakistan 130
Pangea 123
panoramas 20
papier-mâché 94–95
Papier-Mâché Doctor's Mask 94–95
park ranger 38
Past Folklore, Present Fact 119
Paul, Anthea 129
Pauls, Chris 110
Paulsen, Gary 78
Pease, Dotti 100
peer pressure 139
People magazine 133
Pepperberg, Irene M. 105
Perel, David 5
Perret, Gene 12
Personalized Reader Story 78–79
personification 53
Peru 125
pet care 108
Pet Poetry or Prose 75
Phillips, Terry 148
Phineas Gage: A Gruesome but True Story About Brain Science 21–22
Phobias: Everything You Wanted to Know but Were Afraid to Ask 150–152
Photo Journals 115
Photograph Your Adventure 65
photography 8, 14–15, 59, 61, 65–66, 67–68, 114–115, 122, 123
phrenology 100
Pick a Craft! (The Manly Approach) 54–56
picture books 61
A Picture Is Worth a Thousand Words 74
Pigza, Joey 46

Pikes Peak Library District 1, 29
pimples 138
Pitch Black 82–83
Pittsburgh Courier 88
Piven, Joshua 144
plagiarism 156
Platt, Richard 45
Play with Your Food 53–54
Pledge of Allegiance 143
Poe, Edgar Allan 82
poetry 36, 70–71, 72–75, 79–80, 82, 85, 169; concrete 72–73
Poetry Presentations 79
Pompey's Pillar 35
Pop Art 66
popular culture 13
Popular Mechanics 55
Porcellino, John 89
portable toilets 5
Porter, Preserved 35
Potential Robots Become Art 13
Potluck Snacks 52
Practice Creative Writing — The Alien Edition 9
Prague 73
prehistory 18
presentations 12, 22, 23, 34, 35, 43, 46, 52, 59, 68, 79, 99, 106, 116, 130, 141–142, 170, 171
presidents 17, 85
Price, Janet 143
Primary and Secondary Resources 117
primary resources 8, 117
prison 43, 46, 47
Project Idea Index
project planning 7, 141–142, 165
Project Planning with Crime 7
propaganda 22, 23
Propaganda 23
prose 75
public speaking 34
Public Speaking (If Joshua Can Arm Wrestle...) 34
puns 5

questioning 10
Questioning the Norm 10–11
quiz show 24

Raab, Evelyn 51
rabies 118
Rabinowitz, Stefanie 95
radio 20
The Radioactive Boy Scout: The True Story of a Boy and His Backyard Nuclear Reactor 100–101
railroad 21
Raising Curiosity 129
Ralston, Aron 36
Rapunzel 76
Rawick, George P. 36
Ray, James Earl 48
Read Aloud 31

read aloud 31, 36, 75, 86, 87, 97, 112, 133
reader retention 91
reading 1, 2, 5, 29, 31, 45, 61, 79, 80, 123
Red Hand Day 31
Red Scared! The Commie Menace in Propaganda and Popular Culture 22–23, 27
Rees, Celia 131
relationships 140, 159–160
Relin, David Oliver 130
reluctant readers 1, 6, 70, 80, 82
Renaissance 93
Republican convention 85
research 8, 10, 19, 23, 26, 34, 35, 71, 84, 99, 101, 108, 109, 112, 117, 119, 123, 130, 139, 152, 162, 166
Researching a New Pet 108–109
Researching for Your Own Short Story 152
Revere, Paul 26, 45
Revolutionary War 17
rhyme 75
rhythm 75
Righteous Criminal 43
The Rights of Students 143–144
rigor mortis 96
R.I.P.: Here Lie the Last Words, Morbid Musings, Epitaphs & Fond Farewells of the Famous and Not-So-Famous 13–15
Roach, Mary 96
Robo Sapiens: Evolution of a New Species 97–98
robots 12, 97–98
Roche, Jenny 12
Rock and Roll 20
Roeper, Richard 11
Rogers, Simon 9
Rokitansky method 96
role-play 41
Role-Playing 41
Rome 17, 19, 115
Romeo and Juliet 102
Room Decorations 51
Roswell, New Mexico 6
Route 666 8
Rubin, Susan Goldman 66
Runyon, Brent 32
Russia 47

Sacagawea 34, 65–66
Sacagawea Speaks: Beyond the Shining Mountains with Lewis and Clark 34–35, 65
Salzman, Mark 42, 43
San Diego 33
Sandler, Martin W. 24
Sanghi Island 18
Satchel Paige: Striking Out Jim Crow 88–89
Sceurman, Mark 7
Schlosser, Eric 125

School Library Journal 148
Schultz, Ellen 58
science 15, 22, 36, 50, 82, 92–103, 106, 154–156
scientific method 105, 106
The Scientific Method and Beyond 106
Scott, Sue 122
secondary resources 8, 117
Secret Service 86
Serwacki, Anita 110
Sesame Street 9
Sexiest Vampire of the Year Award 166
Shark Life: True Stories of Sharks and the Sea 109–110
sharks 109–110, 118, 123
Shats, Mark 12
Shaw, Maria 159
Shaw, Tucker 142
Shelf Life: Stories by the Book 78–79
Sherman, Scott 110
shoes 63–64
show and tell 63
Show and Tell 63
Sidman, Joyce 75
Sierra Leone 31
Silverstein, Ken 100
Silvinova, Nely 73
Simon, Rogers 9
Sioux 47
Sis, Peter 20
Siversten, Linda 133
Siversten, Tosh 133
skateboards 61, 62–63
skipper caterpillar 5
skull 17, 19, 22
sky 122
Slate Magazine 128
slave narratives 36
Slave Narratives 36
slaves 35, 36
Sledding Hill 152–154
Sleeping Beauty 76
sleeping sickness 118
Sloate, Susan 47
sloth 118
smallpox 93
Smith, Greg Leitich 154
Smith, Hye-Yon 105
Smith, John 20
Smith, Keri 64
Smits, Kim 63
Snow White and the Seven Dwarfs 76
social networks 33
social studies 15, 38, 73, 125, 129
songs 36
Soviet Union 20
Space Settlement 102
Spain 34
Spallanzani, Lazzaro 155
Spectrograph Game 30
spiders 106–107, 117
sports 34, 37

Stalin 23
Status Update 33
stereotypes 90
Stern, Sam 51
Stiff: The Curious Lives of Human Cadavers 96–97
stories 5, 6, 8, 15, 17, 19, 26, 29, 36, 38, 44, 70, 71–72, 75, 76–80, 82, 90, 112, 117, 118, 133, 151–152, 154, 162
Storm, Rory 98
storytelling 1, 30, 72, 73, 85
Storytelling 72
"The Strange, Ax-wielding, Child Killing Bunny Man" 8
Stride, Lottie 169
student teaching 100, 168
The Stupid Crook Book 5–7
stupidity 6, 10, 11, 139
Sturm, James 88
suicide 32, 45
sumo wrestling 34
Sun, Wei-Chen 87
sunscreen 10
superheroes 170–171
supernatural 8
Survey Time! 143
surveys 143
survival 144–146
Survival Training 145–146
sustainable development 115
swap meet 128
Swap Meet! 128
Sweeney, Michael S. 99
Sweet! The Delicious Story of Candy 57–58
Szirtes, Helene 137

T-shirts 58
tagging 62
Taiwan 87
tamping iron 21
Taudte, Jeca 127
teachers 5, 17, 26, 50, 75, 76, 78
Technically, It's Not My Fault 72–73
technology 13, 14, 98
Teen Bureau of Investigation 7
The Teenage Guy's Survival Guide 138–139
telephone 20
television 111
Temple, Shirley 66
10 Sure Signs a Movie Character Is Doomed and Other Surprising Movie Lists 11–12
Terezin 73
text messages 10
theft 40, 41
They Broke the Law — You Be the Judge: True Cases of Teen Crime 40–41
This Day in Thoreau's Journal 90
Thomson, Sarah 130
Thoreau, Henry David 89–90
Thoreau at Walden 89–90

Three Cups of Tea: One Man's Mission to Promote Peace...One School at a Time 130–131, 135
3-D Ocean Research 123
time travel 169–170
Time Traveler's Handbook: A Wild, Wacky and Wooly Adventure Through History 169–170
timeline 33, 48
TNS 44
To Kill a Mockingbird 80
Toe-Tagged: True Stories from the Morgue 95–96
Tombstone Observation and Creative Writing 14–15
Tommaso, Rich 88
Tough, Catherine 58
toxoplasmosis 94
tracking 112, 120–121
Transcendentalism 89
travel 129–130
Travel Planning 130
Troll's Eye View: A Book of Villainous Tales 76
True Crime 40
True Notebooks: A Writer's Year at Juvenile Hall 43–44
The Truth About Poop 5
tuberculosis 93–94
2000 Questions and Answers About the Civil War: Unusual and Unique Facts About the War Between States 23–24

UFO 161
The Underdog: How I Survived the World's Most Outlandish Competitions 33–34, 38
United Nations 30, 31
United States 8, 15, 18, 21, 22, 23, 31, 47, 65, 82, 85, 87, 118, 131
U.S. Constitution 128
U.S. Mayors Climate Protection Agreement 128
U.S. National Arm Wrestling Championship 33
U.S. Signal Corps 119
U.S. Weather Service 119
urban legends 5, 8, 71–72
USSR 23
Utah 36

Valentine's Day 160
Valentine's Day Fund Raiser 160
The Vampire Is Just Not That Into You 165–166
vampires 165–166
The Vegetable Gardener 53
Venn diagram 89
Vermont 21
Vertemus (Emperor Rudolf II) 53
video project 118
vigilante 43
Vile Verses 70, 79, 80
villains 40, 76, 86, 163
Virgin Islands 46

Virtual Alcatraz Museum 48
Visit the Berlin Wall 21
Voices from the Streets: Former Gang Members Tell Their Stories 44–45
volcano 18, 115
Volvkova, Hana 73
VOYA 148

Waldsteinova, Sonja 73
Walker, Sally M. 19
The Wall: Growing Up Being the Iron Curtain 20–21, 27
Wang, Jin 87–88
Warhol, Andy 66
Washington, D.C. 35
Washington, George 36
water 122–123
Waterbury, Connecticut 35
weather 117, 119–120
Weather on Your Birthday 120
Weekend Naturalist 121
Weekly World News 148
Weinstein, Jacob Sager 170
Weir, William 26
Weird and Wonderful Words 15
Weird U.S. 7–8, 15

Weiss, Ehrich 83
Weissova, Helga 73
What Are You Afraid Of? 151–152
What's That Smell? (Oh, It's Me): 50 Mortifying Situations and How to Deal 142–143
When Objects Talk 148–150
Wicked History of the World: History with the Nasty Bits Left In 17–19, 27, 169–170
Wilson, Charles 125
Wilson, Daniel H. 12
Windling, Terri 76
Wislon, Sara 120
Witch Child 131
witch doctor 18
Wong, Janice 56
Workers of the World Parade 20
The World According to Dog: Poems and Teen Voices 75
The World of the Spider 106–107
World Series 48
World War I 17
World War II 86, 149–150
A World with No Crime 48
Worlds Afire 70–71

The Worst-Case Scenario Survival Handbook: TRAVEL 144–146
Write Your Own Villainous Story 76
writing 8, 9, 12, 14–15, 18–19, 26, 32, 33, 44, 47, 56, 59, 76, 78–79, 88, 91, 97, 105, 110, 111, 112, 116, 117, 133, 152, 154, 156, 163
Written in Bone 19–20

Yan, Ma 31
Yang, Gene Luen 87
Young Pioneers Movement 20
Your Own Guerilla Art 65
Your Weird Town 8
YouTube 31

Z-Day Emergency Preparedness Plan 165
Zero-G: Life and Survival in Space 101–102
zodiac 159–160
zombie 161, 163–165
Zusak, Markus 157